LITERARY CULTURE IN TAIWAN

LITERARY CULTURE IN TAIWAN

■ ■ ■ ■ ■ ■ ■ ■ ■ ■ ■ ■ ■

Martial Law to Market Law

Sung-sheng Yvonne Chang

COLUMBIA UNIVERSITY PRESS　NEW YORK

Columbia University Press wishes to express its appreciation for assistance given by the Chiang Ching-kuo Foundation for International Scholarly Exchange and the University of Texas in the publication of this book.

COLUMBIA UNIVERSITY PRESS
Publishers Since 1893
NEW YORK   CHICHESTER, WEST SUSSEX

Copyright © 2004 Columbia University Press

Library of Congress Cataloging-in-Publication Data
Chang, Sung-sheng, 1951–
    Literary culture in Taiwan : martial law to market law / Sung-sheng Yvonne Chang.
        p.   cm.
    Includes bibliographical references and index.
    ISBN 0–231–13234–4 (cloth)
    1. Chinese literature—Taiwan—20th century—History and criticism.   I. Title.

PL3031.T3C4468 2004
895.1'509951249—dc22

2003068776

Columbia University Press books are printed on permanent and durable acid-free paper.

Printed in the United States of America

c 10 9 8 7 6 5 4 3 2 1
p 10 9 8 7 6 5 4 3 2 1

CONTENTS

This historical overview is for readers unfamiliar with Taiwan's modern era. Taiwan experts, go directly to the introduction.

Taiwan, an island 90 miles off the southern coast of mainland China, saw an influx of Han Chinese settlers from China's Fujian (Fukien) and Guangdong (Kuangtung) provinces in the 1600s, and was formally incorporated into the Qing Empire as a prefecture of Fujian province in 1684. In the second half of the nineteenth century, China suffered a series of losses to western and Japanese imperial aggression. After losing the first Sino-Japanese war in 1895, the Qing court ceded Taiwan to Japan, already modernized and newly powerful thanks to the Meiji Restoration. During 50 years of colonial rule, the Japanese exploited Taiwan's agricultural wealth, but also built a modern industrial infrastructure on the island and introduced modern institutions, including a new public education system. One far-reaching consequence of these changes was that when Taiwan was returned to China at the end of the Second World War, most educated Taiwanese spoke and wrote in Japanese.

The colonial period was mostly orderly, but tensions rose after Japan invaded China in 1937, and again when it expanded the war zone to the Pacific in 1941. Tens of thousands of young Taiwanese were drafted to support Japan's war efforts in Southeast Asia and China; many never returned. The banning of Chinese-language publications early in this period and the imposition of wartime mobilization programs, including the *Kominka* (Japanization or Imperialization) campaign, brought to the surface latent tension between the colonizers and the colonized.

The retrocession of Taiwan to the Nationalist-controlled Republic of China in 1945 came with its own difficulties. The Nationalists (Kuomintang, or KMT) used Taiwan's resources to support their fight against the Communists on the mainland, and failed miserably in their early attempts at governing the recovered territory. Discontent over rampant inflation, official corruption, and administrative incompetence erupted into spontaneous rioting that spread throughout the island in February 1947. The new government summoned soldiers from the mainland and brutally suppressed the riots, killing many thousands of Taiwanese, including a large number of the social elite. The "February 28 Incident," as it came to be known, has played a divisive role in Taiwan's society and politics ever since.

In 1949, the Nationalist regime, led by Generalissimo Chiang Kai-shek, lost its war with the Communists on the mainland—now declared the People's Republic of China (PRC)—and retreated to Taiwan, where it continued to reign in the name of the Republic of China. During the massive retreat of 1949, around two million people relocated from various parts of the Chinese mainland to Taiwan. These new arrivals became known as "mainlanders," as opposed to earlier settlers, who are often called "native Taiwanese." Conflict and cooperation between these two population groups continue to play a prominent role in the cultural configurations that this study explores.

The Nationalists' resettlement in Taiwan was consolidated when, following the outbreak of the Korean War, the United States decided to help defend and develop the island nation-state as an anti-Communist outpost in East Asia, initially by sending the Seventh Fleet into the Taiwan Strait. Meanwhile, the Nationalist government declared martial law and, on Chiang's orders, earnestly prepared to "launch a counterattack" and regain the mainland, a plan unlikely to succeed and not included in the U.S. Cold War agenda. The two Chinese regimes separated by a narrow strait achieved a de facto truce after an aborted attempt by the PRC to force Taiwan into submission by heavily bombarding two offshore islands, Jinmen (Quemoy) and Mazu (Ma-tsu), in 1958.

By suppressing civil rights and freedom of speech in the immediate post–1949 decades—an era known as the "White Terror"—the Nationalist regime maintained social stability while instituting successful economic and educational programs that led to accelerated growth, followed by remarkable prosperity. However, the sociocultural order sustained by authoritarian rule began to erode in the early 1970s, when Nixon visited China (1971) and Taiwan was ousted from the United Nations, events that undermined the Nationalist regime's claim to be the "sole legitimate Chinese government." When Chiang Ching-kuo (CCK), eldest son of Chiang Kai-shek, took over the reins of power after his father died in 1975, he faced grave challenges on both the domestic and the diplomatic fronts. Overall, Chiang Ching-kuo's era (the mid-1970s to the late 1980s) was more enlightened, a period of "soft-authoritarian" rule marked by serious efforts to "nativize" the ruling KMT regime by means of a peaceful transition of power from mostly mainlander administrators to more native Taiwanese. The leadership also made pragmatic adjustments to Taiwan's newly isolated position in the international community. This, and the impressive performance of capable KMT technocrats, helped make Taiwan a growing economic force on the world stage and a leader among East Asia's remarkable group of Newly Industrialized Countries (NICs).

Prosperity changed things. In the 1970s and 1980s Taiwan's new affluence, a rising middle class, and a less repressive, more open-minded ruling regime fostered political opposition, especially among native Taiwanese tired of the mainlander population's hegemony and eager for a more democratic society. The 1979 Kaohsiung Incident (or Meilidao Incident) was a turning point for political opposition. A clash in the southern city of Kaohsiung between political demonstrators at an International Human Rights Day rally and KMT troops sent to stop the demonstration resulted in the arrests of fifteen of Taiwan's most important opposition leaders, a group of writers and intellectuals organized around the *Meilidao* [Formosa] magazine. The well-publicized trial and sentencing of these political activists in military court caused a great stir, reminding people of the lack of real democracy in Taiwan under martial law.

The Kaohsiung Incident was followed by a decade-long struggle between the mainlander-controlled KMT and *"dangwai"* ("outside the party") political forces. The Nationalist government was forced to make significant concessions. In 1986, a homegrown political party, the Democratic Progressive Party (DPP), was founded in Taiwan. Then, in 1987, shortly before the death of Chiang Ching-kuo in January 1988, martial law was lifted after 38 years. Radical intellectual ferment, militant political protests, and grass-roots civilian demonstrations made the last years of the 1980s at once tumultuous and euphoric.

Post–martial law Taiwan turned out to be more disorderly and confrontational than most had perhaps anticipated. Native Taiwanese and mainlanders continued to face off over the epic, inevitable redistribution of political, economic, and cultural capital at the center of the rapidly changing society. The 1990s saw the rise of "money politics," increased corruption, and loss of discipline within the ruling KMT party. And electoral democracy was made difficult by ferocious partisanship, fueled by irreconcilable differences over the issue of *tongdu*—whether Taiwan should move toward reunification with China or independent statehood.

Despite some progress made during the 1992–93 Cross-Strait talks, on the whole the relationship between Taiwan and the PRC has deteriorated in the post–martial law period. Early in his first term, Lee Teng-hui, the first Taiwan-born President of the Republic of China (1988–2000), accelerated former President Chiang Ching-kuo's "Taiwanization" of the KMT, a process intended to bring the ruling party's membership and policies more in line with the aspirations of a majority native-Taiwanese public that would soon be choosing its leaders by direct election (Lee became Taiwan's first democratically elected president in 1996). This and Lee's "Taiwan first" initiative were preludes to a more explicitly separatist turn in Taiwan's public policy in the mid-1990s, which drove the PRC to some drastic countermeasures, including overtly threatening military maneuvers in the Taiwan Strait just before the first presidential election in 1996.

Lee's Taiwancentric policies were popular enough in principle, but also a source of considerable anxiety and controversy over the significant risk involved in overt challenges to the powerful PRC and its unpredictable leadership. Some segments of the society vociferously opposed the policy shift, and complicating factors, like the growing number of Taiwanese businessmen investing in mainland China, contributed to the already intense political strife on the island. In the 2000 presidential election, KMT supporters split their votes between an independent candidate and one selected by the party leadership, allowing DPP candidate Chen Shui-bian to win the election by a narrow margin. This ended the Nationalists' half-century rule of Taiwan, and along with it much of the unique climate and circumstances that shaped the distinctive literary culture examined in this book.

ACKNOWLEDGMENTS

The writing of this book was supported by the following grants: a Research Grant from the Chiang Ching-kuo Foundation for International Scholarly Exchange, 1996–1998; a Faculty Research Assignment at the University of Texas at Austin, fall 1997; and a Research Grant from the Pacific Cultural Foundation of the Republic of China, 1996–1997. The work has also received a University Cooperative Society Subvention Grant from the University of Texas at Austin and a publication grant from the Chiang Ching-kuo Foundation for International Scholarly Exchange.

Two subsections of chapter 1 are taken from "Representing Taiwan: Shifting Geopolitical Frameworks," a chapter in *Writing Taiwan: A New Literary History* (ed. David Der-wei Wang and Carlos Rojas, Duke University Press, forthcoming). Some materials in chapter 6 are also used in "*The Terrorizer* and the 'Great Divide' in Contemporary Taiwan's Cultural Development," to be included in *Island on the Edge: Taiwan New Cinema and After* (ed. Chris Berry and Feii Lu; under consideration by Hong Kong University Press).

LITERARY CULTURE IN TAIWAN

■■■■■■■■■■■■■■■■■

Introduction

With the monumental changes of the last fifteen years or so, Taiwan is making itself anew. The process commands serious scholarly efforts at remapping Taiwan's recent past, not least, its literary past. Though unquestionably a crucial component of local cultural production, for various reasons contemporary Taiwanese literature has been consistently neglected and frequently misrepresented by literary historians inside and outside Taiwan. One purpose of this study is to redress those problems. In addition, though, if an in-depth account of contemporary Taiwanese literature is important for Taiwan itself, it is also valuable for illuminating larger issues of cross-border literary phenomena in a globalized context. With this case study approach in mind, in my earlier work, *Modernism and the Nativist Resistance: Contemporary Chinese Fiction from Taiwan* (Durham: Duke University Press, 1993), I examined Taiwan's modernist literary movement in the 1960s and 1970s, situating it in the context of a powerful artistic current that ran through many parts of the nonwestern world in the mid-twentieth century. I initially set out on the current project to explore the intimate relationship between politically instituted cultural ideology and the mechanisms of literary production in Taiwan, as borne out by its mainstream literary output. Ongoing events, however, soon forced me to adjust my perspective to address a literary field already transformed by its race toward market-authorized autonomy. This would also require a more inclusive and nuanced theoretical framework. A trip or two to the drawing board later, I arrived at the critical approach that resulted in the present study, canvassing half a century, tracing the trajectory of Taiwan's post–1949 literature through complex and shifting political and market currents.

Literature in Taiwan today, having traveled a long way from simple political subordination, is now compelled to negotiate a path between residual high culture aspirations and the emergent reality of market domination in a relatively autonomous, increasingly professionalized cultural field. My new approach incorporates the important understanding that this has not happened just within Taiwan's unique historical environment but also in the context of a modernizing local economy, a globalizing world economy, and a postcolonial, Cold War, then post–Cold War world order. In this respect there are important affinities between Taiwan and other contemporary East Asian societies, including, but not limited to, China.

This contextual approach faces an immediate challenge: how to conceptualize in nonreductive terms the relationship between external determinants—i.e., political and economic forces—and various literary configurations they act upon in direct or mediated ways. This has been less than satisfactorily attempted in recent scholarship on modern Chinese literature from postcolonial, feminist, and other cultural studies perspectives. My goal here is not only to delineate the gradual but profound exchange of position between political and market forces in Taiwan's literary universe but also to explore the closely connected, complex history of the struggle for position among multiple literary movements responding to one another and to dramatic transformations in the political and social realms around them. A brief tour of the territory and how I try to understand it is conducted below, followed by an outline of the book.

NEW VANTAGE

No sooner had I started research for this project than momentous changes began occurring in Taiwan in a breathtaking, exasperating manner. Martial law had been lifted in 1987, and now the impact of that watershed event was suddenly arriving in regular tidal waves. The environment and modes of cultural production in Taiwan were changing so fundamentally that a new critical paradigm would be required to fully comprehend the patterns underlying them. Most significantly, the literary record from before 1987 would now appear in a different light.

The cultural sphere was thoroughly tossed by Taiwan's extraordinary political and economic transformations. Released from official censorship, it was immediately consumed by the political upheavals attending the introduction of electoral democracy, legalized opposition parties, and an increasingly lively civil society. Politics raged on three related fronts: an amazing power struggle between the governing Nationalist Party (KMT) and the fast-rising, opposition Democratic Progressive

Party (DPP); the aggravated identity politics of the divide between Taiwan's two major population groups, "native Taiwanese" and "mainlanders" (pre– and post–1949 settlers from mainland China, respectively); and a societywide debate about Taiwan's national and cultural identity, and how the question of "reunification" with China or independent statehood should be decided. Twists and turns in negotiations with the mainland, sporadic military threats in the Taiwan Strait, and rapidly growing business investments in China added complexity and pressure on all fronts. As Taiwan's politics changed, so did the terms of literary discourse. The value of certain cultural currencies went up at the expense of others, and individuals saw their cultural capital, and hence their positions in the literary field, significantly altered. Polemics of varying levels of sophistication zeroed in on a question of naming: "Taiwanese literature" or "Chinese literature in Taiwan."

Ironically, however, just as "Taiwanese literature" was elevated to serious symbolic status within the literary field, the significance of literature in everyday life was rapidly diminishing. Intellectual freedom, even in the cause of Taiwanese nationalism, was suddenly achieved, but accelerating economic liberalization brought competition from the full range of cultural products available in the global marketplace. This came as a shock. Modern as it regarded itself, Taiwan's literary community was nonetheless used to the respect accorded to intellectuals in Chinese tradition, and unprepared for the deflating effects of capitalist competition in a global market.

Serious literature lost ground on both sides of the Taiwan Strait in the 1990s. In post–Tian'anmen China, popular culture thrived in an increasingly depoliticized cultural market, a phenomenon that has received considerable scholarly attention.[1] Behind controversies revolving around Wang Shuo, Jia Pingwa's *Feidu* [Abandoned capital], Jin Yong's martial arts novels, and Wei Hui's *Shanghai baobei* [Shanghai baby] was a poignant recognition of literature's susceptibility to consumer-driven commodification.

In post–martial law Taiwan, one measure of literature's dwindling status was its dubious role in the progressive cultural trends—the feminist/sexual revolution, gay and lesbian rights campaigns, and critiques of the media and global capitalism—that flourished in the 1990s. Literary treatments of the progressive agenda were largely disposable. Many appropriated radical gestures to position themselves in the market, while few stood out as genuinely provocative.

The recent exponential growth of market forces in Chinese cultural fields can hardly be ignored, but the truth is that, at least in Taiwan, we have been overlooking the market dimension that existed before this. Previous studies have focused on a presumed binary opposition between the political and aesthetic dimensions of contemporary Taiwanese literature. Little attention has been paid to the additional tug that market forces have all along exerted, albeit more subtly in the early decades of the post–1949 era than in the most recent decade and a half. A major purpose of the present study, then, is to reexamine the whole of contemporary Taiwanese literary history in light of this added dimension, especially the transformation of the literary field from near complete political subjugation in the early 1950s to market domination in the 1990s.

Incorporating the tug of market forces pops our heretofore two-dimensional perspective into something more like three-dimensional reality, but we still need an account of just how these political, aesthetic, and market forces have actually played out on Taiwan's unique social and historical stage to render contemporary Taiwanese literature. We need the local history of Taiwan's literary movements and background on how individuals and groups within the literary field interacted with one another and with these broad forces of change over the decades.

A shift to the local is already apparent in recent U.S. literary scholarship on mainland China. Before the emergence first of "scar literature" and then of the modernistic "root-seeking school" in the 1980s, the best known contemporary Chinese writers, like Bai Xianyong and Yu Guangzhong, were almost all from Taiwan. The obvious reason was that during the third quarter of the twentieth century, literary production in China was so tightly constrained in an ideological straitjacket and so subservient to political purposes that it inevitably scored poorly on the aesthetic scale. The assumed dearth of "artistically accomplished" imaginative writings in socialist China, however, is currently being reassessed. As scholars search for new perspectives to better comprehend the role of literature in Mao's era, they are taking issue with the established criteria for judging literary excellence. What exactly constituted the mechanics of these odd (to western eyes) literary forms? To what extent did assumptions about the nature and value of literature rooted in Chinese culture prepare the way for vulgar political manipulation? Some China scholars are lately exploring the possibility of a different "aesthetics" that explains rather than accuses.[2] These attempts at accounting for "local experience," what actually governed literary production and reception on the ground in Communist China, promise a more nuanced understanding of a previously obscure period of mainland Chinese literature.

While contemporary Taiwanese literature has fared better than China's "dark ages" in the literary academy, it has also suffered from being analyzed chiefly in terms of cut-and-paste concepts suggested by aspects of Taiwan's experience that fit easily into familiar analytical categories. Issues pertaining to postcoloniality—identity construction, language battles, modernization strategies, and nationalism—have ruled the day. Important as they are, much finer attention to Taiwan's particular history is imperative. The gradual transition from regimented, military-style governance, via what some social scientists have dubbed the "soft-authoritarian" rule, to democratic state and free economy has so significantly shaped post–1949 Taiwan that postcoloniality cannot be properly understood without reference to it. In fact, as scholars inside and outside Taiwan have begun to note, in its first decades the KMT was itself a colonial ruler, so Taiwan's experience of colonialism and postcoloniality is uniquely layered. Within this local frame lies the real excitement in Taiwan's various and changing literary formations as they ride evolving identity discourses, reflect the growth and shifting ground of political movements and parties, and respond to increasingly powerful market forces. Here too are the ethno-linguistic struggles and generational differences within the literary community that reviewers of my previous book (c.f. Edward Gunn and Jeffrey Kinkley) wanted to hear more about. This, then, is the territory for the present study.

CONCEPTUAL FRAMEWORKS

A major focus here is interpositional competition in Taiwan's literary field, and what it reveals about the relative importance of political and market forces in the contemporary period. Faced with organizing a vast body of raw material for systematic analysis, I find the work of two European theorists, Pierre Bourdieu on the "field of cultural production" and Raymond Williams on hegemony and cultural formations, excellent tools. (Let me just take note here of a key difference in their terminology: "culture" is understood as "whole ways of life" in Williams's discussion of hegemony, whereas Bourdieu's "cultural field" refers more narrowly to the space of imaginative, creative activities, and is used interchangeably with "literary field.")

From Bourdieu, with certain modifications, I derive the notion of "aesthetic position," and apply it to four groups of key players in contemporary Taiwan's literary field: Mainstream (which can be roughly translated as *zhuliu*) literary agents ("literary agents" denotes people involved in the dissemination and consecration of literature as well as writers), Modernists (*xiandai pai*), Nativists (*xiangtu pai*), and Localists (*bentu pai*). These widely recognized literary formations emerged at different points in post–1949 Taiwan, rising and falling with momentous changes in the larger historical environment. When the literary agent occupies an aesthetic "position" in the literary field, he or she does not simply subscribe to a specific aesthetic standard but also is situated within a network of relationships with other agents in the same field. However, whereas Bourdieu stresses that correspondences between positions in the literary field and in society's general field of power are primarily governed by the former's laws of operation, the situation in Taiwan has been quite different, especially in the early part of the contemporary period. Under martial law, cultural institutions in Taiwan were firmly under government control and political legitimacy generally overshadowed other principles of consecration. Hence, developments within and outside the literary field were much more strongly related. This is where Raymond Williams's notion of a tripartite structure of dominant (hegemonic), alternative, and oppositional cultural formations is useful.

Dominant: the Mainstream. The Nationalist government's cultural policies in the immediate post–1949 years imposed strict restrictions on intellectual and artistic activities. Mainstream literary agents either tacitly acknowledged or unwittingly internalized these limits, contributing to the development of the martial law period's conservative, conformist, and neotraditionalist dominant culture. When this culture came under attack after the lifting of martial law, first- and second-generation mainlander writers, the majority of whom occupied the Mainstream position, were caught in an emotional quandary, while seeing the value of the symbolic capital they possessed abruptly diminish.

Alternative: the Modernists. The Modernist cultural and intellectual movement of the 1950s and 1960s, and the various radical trends of the 1980s and 1990s (subsumed under the rubric of "postmodernism"), were inspired by American liberal humanism and global progressive trends, respectively. The alternative cultural visions they introduced were initially fraught with center-threatening emancipatory potential. However, led by the country's intellectual elite, both formations were quickly assimilated by the establishment. This examination places greater emphasis on the Modernists because, having arisen to a prominent position early in the era, they have exerted more far-reaching influence on the literary field than the postmodernists.[3]

Oppositional: the Nativists and the Localists. In the 1970s and 1980s, ongoing capitalist modernization, diplomatic setbacks, and the gradual loosening of government control set the stage for serious challenges to the KMT-endorsed dominant culture—first from the socialist-minded Nativists, then from Localists favoring Taiwanese independence. Both the Nativists and the Localists were patently oppositional cultural formations. Leaders of the Nativist movement used literature as a means to voice criticism of the government's pro-West, pro-capitalist policies in an oblique manner. The lifting of martial law eventually allowed them to speak much more openly, but their leftist ideology and pro-China (PRC) stance have remained unpopular. The Localist position in the literary field was from the beginning a product of the Nationalist government's repression of Taiwan's local cultural heritage, particularly from the Japanese colonial period, and the social tension between native Taiwanese and mainlanders. A latent resistance formation early on, it gradually became more self-aware and openly counterhegemonic until it emerged as a powerful contender for the dominant position in the post–martial law cultural sphere, alongside Taiwanese nationalism in the political realm.

Almost from the start, and unlike on mainland China during most of the same period, politics did not entirely prevail in Taiwan's cultural field. Beginning early in the KMT's rule, market forces gradually undermined the control of political authorities, picking up speed in the mid-1970s. During the ten to fifteen years before the lifting of martial law, with the Mainstream position thriving, the power of literary agents to manage the distribution of capital and to determine what constituted "a truly cultural legitimacy" (Bourdieu's term—more on this later) visibly increased. Although the government maintained its grip on the cultural infrastructure, the market had already begun to facilitate what Bourdieu calls a "process of autonomization" of the literary field. The relationship of its aesthetic positions to external forces was increasingly mediated by the field's own operational laws. Gradually shedding their original ideological inscriptions, various positions interacted more frequently, resulting in fragmentation and intermixture of their former salient traits.

These transitions laid the foundation for what happened after the "Great Divide" (marked by the lifting of martial law), when electoral democracy and global capitalism combined to produce a much more professionalized cultural field in Taiwan. As the state withdrew from direct interference in cultural affairs, market forces and a new managerial cultural bureaucracy emerged as the dominant authorities. Striving to adjust to the new institutional environment and to grasp the new rules of the game, most literary agents developed a vocationalism that visibly affected their creative activities while blurring whatever residual influences the four literary formations from the previous era still exerted. For good or ill, having acquired a fairly high degree of autonomy, the literary field in Taiwan now bears greater resemblance to its counterparts in other advanced capitalist societies.

The closely intertwined stories of literature's involvement in the power struggles of Taiwan's larger social space, and the autonomization of the literary field under market influences, are the subject of this study. The next section broadly sketches the historical trajectories of the four literary formations—along with their corresponding aesthetic positions—as they have intersected with larger sociopolitical developments in Taiwan's contemporary period.

HISTORICAL TRAJECTORIES

Under authoritarian rule, the Mainstream position is by definition instituted and constrained by the ruling political regime. In the years immediately following its retreat to Taiwan in 1949, the Nationalist government exercised highly coercive cultural control, stipulating literature's role as subordinate to the purposes of political propaganda. In addition, cultural production as a whole carried the burden of the nation-building ideology that had dominated the mainland Chinese intellectual community in the preceding Republican era, before traveling to Taiwan with the Nationalists. The state conducted various literary mobilization programs, after models established during the Sino-Japanese war. At the same time, however, a revival in Taiwan of the *wentan* (literary arena) that had first taken shape in the urban environs of mainland China in the 1920s through the 1940s opened up spaces for relatively autonomous cultural production.

From the mid-1950s onward, the KMT's cultural program gradually moved from "rule" to "hegemony," from direct political coercion to an effective "interlocking of social, cultural, and political forces" (Williams, *Marxism* 108). The literary field responded with "*chunwenxue*" or "pure literature," which, by endorsing genteel, ostensibly apolitical genres, lent indirect support to the Nationalist hegemony. As most active writers of the period were mainlander émigrés, this support for the government and its primary agenda of preventing Communist insurgency was largely voluntary. In due course, moreover, the dominant culture's pressures and limits were internalized by writers and, through the mediation of a number of sanctioned aesthetic categories, a set of behavior patterns originally adopted out of necessity and political compromise were transformed into positive values. A conservative literary culture was formed.

The coming of age of a new generation of writers educated in the postwar period, however, brought new challenges to the conservatism of the 1950s, in the form of the Modernist and Nativist literary movements. As early as the late 1950s, various strands of avant-garde modernism began to capture the fancy of Taiwan's literary agents. A more serious assimilation of modernist aesthetics and ideology followed over the next two decades. In fact, the Modernist artistic formation was significantly underpinned by a westernization discourse favored by the KMT, and helped along by the prominent U.S. presence in postwar East Asia. It promoted cultural visions divergent from the Nationalist cultural hegemony, but without challenging the regime's political foundations. The same could not be said about the Nativist movement that erupted in the 1970s. With a series of diplomatic setbacks that culminated in the Republic of China's forced withdrawal from the United Nations in 1972, domestic restlessness began to grow. Largely composed of intellectuals from the same postwar generation, the Nativists directed their fire against the Modernists for their alleged complicity in advancing western cultural imperialism. While ostensibly attacking its cultural hegemony, the left-leaning Nativists unmistakably implicated the KMT's political rule as well. The Nativist literary movement thus should be regarded as the first oppositional cultural formation in contemporary Taiwan.

The structural positions of literary figures associated with various artistic stances shifted as events unraveled. The elitist, liberal-minded Modernists of the 1960s offered a critique of Mainstream writers who gained literary recognition in the 1950s, pointing to their immediate predecessors' political compromise and amateurism. Meanwhile, the Modernists' aesthetic obscurantism and arrogant iconoclastic gestures initially caused uneasiness and suspicion among the cultural bureaucrats of the Nationalist government. Later, when the heated Nativist debate broke out in 1977–78, however, the menace of a new Communist threat (from the Nativists) quickly led to a closer alliance between the Modernists and conservative, pro-government Mainstream writers.

The Modernist and Nativist movements were both rooted in the country's intellectual elite. These Third World intellectuals' liberal-versus-leftist ideological dispute was compounded by a disagreement over the methods of modernization and nation building, and frequently boiled down to the merits (or menace) of western assistance. By the 1980s, however, the growing importance of mass-mediated cultural consumption, accelerated internationalization and liberalization of Taiwan society, and the deeper saturation of western influence significantly eroded the foundation of this contention. As both the Modernist and the Nativist formations became increasingly marginalized, Mainstream literature reemerged with a vengeance.

Instrumental to the Mainstream's renewed success was the institution of *fukan*, or cultural supplements to newspapers, in particular the two major newspapers, *Lianhe bao* [The united daily news] and *Zhongguo shibao* [China times]. Through annual literary contests, the modernized, professional institution of *fukan* became both the major sponsor of production and the dominant agent of consecration. Effectively assimilating the literary innovations of the Modernists and the sociopolitical concerns of the Nativists, the new brand of Mainstream literature was also directly susceptible to market influences and of a predominantly "middle-class" character. A persistent subtext of this literature was complacent celebration of urban lifestyles and Taiwan's newly acquired affluence. While occasionally challenging a social or political taboo, these works were generally nonsubversive, catering to the taste of the country's growing middle class.[4]

Parallel to the rejuvenation of the Mainstream position in the 1980s was a new challenge emanating from the deep-seated tension between the island's two major population groups, "mainlanders" and "native Taiwanese." The Kaohsiung Incident[5] in 1979 rang in a decade of growth in organized political opposition forces, beginning with the "outside the party" (*dangwai*) alliance and followed by a landmark event, the founding of the Democratic Progressive Party in 1986. In the cultural field, the Localist movement began opposing "Taiwanese consciousness" to the government's sinocentric ideology. In fact, this position had always been present in the work of a marginalized group of native Taiwanese writers under the leadership of several veteran writers from the Japanese period. Reduced to near silence in the 1950s and 1960s by an unfavorable political climate, the Localists partnered with the Nativists in the 1970s to launch a frontal attack on the Nationalist cultural hegemony. The two groups, however, harbored very different agendas, and eventually parted ways in the early 1980s. The core Nativists endorsed Chinese nationalism, while the Localists became increasingly vocal in their advocacy of a Taiwanese cultural nationalism, tracing the formation of Taiwanese identity to the Japanese colonial period.

Right at this moment, mainland China emerged from its three decades of isolation. Its new international presence, combined with the Localists' efforts at "de-sinicization" (qu zhongguo hua), quickly dismantled the Nationalist political myth—the KMT regime's claim to be the sole legitimate "Chinese" government—removing an important foundation of the neotraditionalist, sinocentric dominant culture. While this did not immediately translate into a Localist coup in the cultural field, an increasing number of Mainstream literary agents shifted to a neo-Nativist stance, which might be characterized as studied ambivalence on all fronts.

The erosion of the Nationalist cultural orthodoxy proceeded apace, most dramatically as an effect of the robust growth of oppositional political forces, but ideological challenges were not confined to organized politics. Enjoying greater affluence and freedom of information, the society as a whole began questioning the conservative dominant culture. Taking advantage of the open climate, progressive intellectuals, many of them newly returned from abroad, successfully indigenized cultural trends from the West, especially gender politics. The result was an upsurge in radical cultural formations rallying under the (also imported) rubric of "postmodernism." Skillfully utilizing the recently liberalized and ferociously expanding media and aligned with global intellectual movements, these new "alternative" cultural formations emerged as prominent players on the post–martial law cultural scene, gaining support from the country's younger intellectuals and high visibility in the society at large. Although the impact of the radical trends on literary production itself was limited, their influence on the overall intellectual climate was prominently reflected in the newly institutionalized academic discipline of Taiwanese literary studies.

Before the lifting of martial law, the Localist formation was clearly oppositional, squarely against the one-party authoritarian rule of the mainlander-dominated Nationalist regime. As martial law receded into the past, however, the successful "Taiwanization" of the Nationalist party by President Lee Teng-hui and the continuing growth of the DPP helped the Localists to rapidly expand.[6] Pressure from mainland China also increased in the mid-1990s, and a thoroughgoing reconstitution of Taiwan's dominant culture was under way.

As the Localist formation was transformed from a struggling vanguard into an important constituting element of the new dominant culture, its impact was enormous. As Bourdieu argues, the central dynamic of any literary field is in the struggle among agents occupying different positions for the power to define and monopolize legitimate literary discourse. Taiwan's cultural field was energized in the 1990s by a fierce struggle for Mainstream status between the emerging Localist and the residual Nationalist-endorsed cultural formations. The DPP's victory in the 2000 presidential election has compounded and complicated the struggle in the cultural field, and that is where I have had to leave it in this volume, a brief outline of which follows.

This book is arranged in three parts. The first part deals with broad issues. Given the dramatic recent changes in Taiwanese literary studies, chapter 1 first offers a survey of the state of the field. It then lays out a theoretical framework, paying special attention to Peter Hohendahl's notion of the "institution" of literature and certain key concepts of Bourdieu's theory. Chapter 2 begins with a review of three pieces of critical work on earlier periods when modern Chinese and Taiwanese literature were extensively affected by market forces, a fact largely neglected in previous scholarship. The chapter concludes with a case study of the 1950s anti-Communist novel, *Xuanfeng* [Whirlwind], which demonstrates the complex interplay of political and cultural legitimacy principles in Taiwan's literary field in the immediate post–1949 years.

Part 2 focuses on the development and interaction of the Mainstream, Modernist, and Localist literary formations in the early period. Chapter 3 discusses the distinctive traits of Mainstream culture under the authoritarian Nationalist regime. Noting the presence of some significant legacies from mainland China, the chapter traces the revival of the "literary arena" and the reincarnation of "pure literature" through the work of a key figure, editor-writer Lin Haiyin. Chapter 4 deals with the rise of an incipient Modernist formation that veered away from political subjugation and combated mediocrity. Two literary figures from the liberal intellectual elite, Xia Ji'an (T. A. Hsia) and Yu Guangzhong, are treated as representatives. This is followed by a discussion of how literary modernism influenced Mainstream literature in the 1960s and 1970s, as exemplified by the aestheticization of the "China" trope by three leading essayists, Wang Dingjun, Yu Guangzhong, and Zhang Xiaofeng. Chapter 5 examines the origin and evolution of "local consciousness" among native Taiwanese writers, using the experience of Wu Zhuoliu, Zhong Zhaozheng, and Ye Shitao as illustration.

The first two chapters of part 3 deal with the crucial transformation of Mainstream literature between the mid-1970s and the mid-1980s. Chapter 6 first tracks the rise of the two major newspaper *fukan, Renjian fukan* and *Lianfu*, to leadership positions in the cultural sphere, then introduces *fukan*-based "middle-class" fiction, addressing the evolving genre hierarchy and the potential of the baby-boom generation of Mainstream artists to transcend conservative political ideology, as evidenced in their works on the tabooed subject of political imprisonment. The thesis of the next chapter (7) is that, influenced by the Modernist and Nativist literary formations and increasing transnational cultural flows, the *fukan* literary culture was fraught with high culture aspirations. This considerably complicated the genre hierarchy, and writers of the baby-boom generation struggled with the constraints of the *fukan* literary culture in different, sometimes diametrically opposite ways. Two distinctive trends treated at length are the aesthetic transformation of the initially stigmatized "boudoir literature" of female writers and the emergence of a "neo-Nativist" subposition hospitable to western high cultural trends and plagued by thorny issues surrounding the notion of "China" as a new cultural Other. Finally, the last chapter introduces new developments in the post–martial law period. Following brief overviews of the new transformations of the Localist discourse, the radical intellectual trends going under the postmodern label, and the specialization and professionalization of the literary field, the chapter concludes with an analysis of a well-publicized media event, the Selection of Taiwanese Literary Classics, held in the last year of the twentieth century. Involving a broad range of literary agents and readers, this highly controversial event demonstrated the residual influences of the four aesthetic positions formed in earlier decades, while also witnessing a drastically transformed—and still transforming—literary field in the new era.

PART I

■ ■ ■ ■ ■ ■

CHAPTER I

Academic Contexts and Conceptual Frameworks

This chapter is divided into two parts. The first part surveys the current state of "Taiwanese literary studies," beginning with an introduction to the frames of reference that have colored the study of Taiwan and Taiwanese literature from outside, followed by a brief account of recent developments within Taiwan as scholars there increasingly take the lead in articulating their own cultural heritage.

Outside, various critical paradigms have governed the broader field of "Taiwan studies" over the last few decades. Particularly in the United States, the value of "Taiwan" as an object of scholarly inquiry tends to vary with its usefulness in illuminating aspects of the study of "China." The dramatic transformations of the post–martial law environment have resulted in a surge of Taiwanese literary studies at home, where its significance extends beyond the academy. Literary studies has become an important battleground on which larger forces within the society are contending.

The second part of the chapter proceeds with some key ideas employed in this study. First is a justification of the "epochal approach," followed by a discussion of the "institution of literature" concept. I argue that certain dominant aesthetic categories, established soon after 1949 through government sanctions, have substantially shaped the modes in which literature is perceived and appreciated in contemporary Taiwan, and may be considered "hegemonic." The remainder of the chapter treats several key concepts derived from Pierre Bourdieu's theory of the field of cultural production, and how I modify them for this study to accommodate the historically specific circumstances of modern Chinese societies, contemporary Taiwan in particular. The notion of "artistic position" is especially important. Other theoretical concepts introduced in this section include: the cultural field's process of "autonomization" in the early phase of capitalist development; structural "homology" between different "fields"; the mediation of "habitus" between society and art; and contending "principles of hierarchization."

ACADEMIC CONTEXTS

Shortly before Taiwan's 1996 presidential election, mainland China conducted a week of "missile tests" in the Taiwan Strait. The purpose of this military show, as everyone knew, was to deter the reelection of President Lee Teng-hui, whom mainland leaders blamed for the growing separatist tendency in Taiwan. While this blatant gesture of intimidation eventually backfired—Mr. Lee won by a landslide—people on the island were sufficiently harassed. The stock market plunged precipitously, some panic-stricken citizens rushed to buy gold, and others exchanged New Taiwanese dollars for U.S. currency. Reports of this crisis in the United States, as could have been expected, largely focused on its geopolitical implications in the new, post–Cold War world order. As revealed in the headline on the cover of *Newsweek*—CHINA: FRIEND OR FOE?—the threat against Taiwan was essentially considered a "China question." This episode aptly illustrates the equivocal position of Taiwan studies in the American academy. Taiwan does not often attract interest for its own sake; a formidable entity, "China," looms in the background of most scholarly attention.

Old Analytical Models: Taiwan Studies in the United States

A look at the analytical models that have dominated research on Taiwan in the United States until quite recently makes evident its subordinate status. The prevalent attitude toward Taiwan in the early postwar years regarded it as "the other China." Echoing the Cold War formulation of "Red China versus Free China," this approach was fixated on the rivalry between liberal democracy and communism.

Residues of this binary mode of thinking remain in the more recent writings of some first-rate China specialists. Lucien Pye, for example, in Jonathan Unger's 1996 collection *Chinese Nationalism*, faults China's political authorities for stigmatizing populations in China's coastal regions, Taiwan, and Hong Kong who have successfully "modernized" themselves. The late John King Fairbank betrayed a similar preoccupation with the ideological split that divided China's May Fourth intellectuals into liberal and radical camps, then grew into civil war and revolution. In the decades after the Korean War, Fairbank argued, the U.S.-backed stability of Taiwan provided the liberal wing of Chinese reformers, who fled China with the Nationalists, an opportunity to bring to fruition their gradualist reform program (268). Ultimately, these scholars sought to answer the hypothetical question: What would have happened to China without the Communist Revolution? The research value of Taiwan in studies fashioned with this implicit goal in mind rested squarely on the proposition that the island had traveled "the road not taken" by China.

A second research model treated Taiwan as "surrogate China," a compromise adopted in response to practical realities. Shut out by the bamboo curtain, an entire generation of western anthropologists, including such eminent scholars as William Skinner and Arthur Wolf, conducted fieldwork in Taiwan as a substitute for "China proper."[1] Since the anthropologists focused on markers that distinguish the Chinese people as a "we group," cultural sediments that took a long time to build up, the civilizational frame tended to be inclusive. Taiwan was seen as a "part" from which one could infer conclusions about the "whole," probably even with greater authenticity, away from the Communists' extensive interference in people's lives.

A third model might be called "the case study model," commonly adopted by social scientists. With their discipline's predominantly modernist orientation, they regarded Taiwan as either one among many political entities on the rapidly transforming globe or a developmental success story worthy of attention for its economic and political "miracles." Taiwan's relationship with China was not immediately relevant; its research value resided in its status either as a newly industrialized economy or as a former Leninist state that had managed to make a peaceful transition to electoral democracy.[2]

If in the case study model the "China question" was thankfully suspended, there was another, more problematic type of suspension frequent in studies specifically of Taiwanese literature. In a practice that I call "bracketing," scholars unconsciously or half-consciously evaded or deferred attention to some crucial aspect(s) of the research subject. Students of Taiwanese literature treated Taiwan simply as "part of China," without fully addressing the historical record. A majority of English-language anthologies and studies of modern Chinese literature have resorted to juxtaposing works from China and Taiwan without any serious attempt at historical contextualization. This practice is increasingly inappropriate as scholars begin to trace the history of modern Taiwanese literature back to the Japanese colonial period and as greater attention is given to Japanese-language literature written by Taiwanese in the 1930s and 1940s.[3]

"Bracketing" deserves particular attention because it occurs not only as a direct result of the political constraints and ideological hang-ups frequently identified by postcolonialist critics but also as a matter of habit or customary practice in academia, through which scholars acquiesce to implicit institutional demands. Rather than individuals' professional integrity, what is at issue are the mechanisms that produce distorted scholarly practices, including the near-entire neglect of Taiwanese literature written in Japanese. The high visibility of research questions stated in East-versus-West terms, for instance, helped divert attention from crucial aspects of modern Chinese and Taiwanese literary history.

The Impact of Changing Political Circumstances

Ultimately, these academic habits reflected the KMT's Cold War–sanctioned pose as a government in exile, the "Republic of China" on Taiwan. Until the early 1970s, when the ROC lost its seat in the United Nations, along with diplomatic recognition by major members of the international community, the Nationalist regime claimed that it was the "sole legitimate government of all China."[4] This unrealistic claim, supported from without in the early years of the Cold War, at once depended upon and helped to sustain the hegemony of sinocentric (China-centered) historical and cultural narratives within Taiwan itself. The ideological core of the KMT's cultural policies, sinocentrism functioned as a principal constant of literary imagination for more than one generation of writers and artists after 1949. When reversals in Taiwan's international status began to erode this narrative and to boost Taiwanese nationalism, therefore, the impact on literature—and cultural production in general—was enormous.

As the Localist trend accelerated in the 1980s, alternative historical discourses began to emerge. A popular Localist discourse asserted a hybrid "Taiwanese ethnicity" that included not only the heritages of the (majority) Han settlers from mainland China and of the island's (minority) original residents, the *yuanzhumin* (of Polynesian descent), but also Taiwan's inheritances from Dutch, Spanish, and Japanese colonizers. Migration, maritime trade, and repeated colonization had forged a unique "Taiwanese character." As Taiwan entered the post–martial law era, elements of this discourse made successful inroads into the public belief system. That the country's new establishment was actively appropriating the Localist discourse was evident in remarks made by President Lee Teng-hui during the 1996 presidential debate. Lee asserted that "Taiwan is a settler's state, situated at the meeting point of oceanic and continental civilizations," and that its population is characterized by a unique dynamism and adventurous spirit. Later, during a reelection speech to the press, Lee underscored the cultural openness of present-day Taiwan by alternating among Mandarin, Taiwanese, and English. Evidently, the vision of Taiwan as a polyglot, multiethnic state steeped in its own history, rather than the authentic heir to the Yellow Emperor and the "great Chinese civilization of five thousand years," had already risen to the status of an alternative national narrative.

Although these developments necessarily have exerted some influence on Taiwan studies in the United States, the U.S. academy is also responding to changes in its own environment. Once dominant analytical models are to varying degrees rendered obsolete by historical events, as well as new intellectual trends. With the Cold War over, Taiwan as "the other China" has lost much of its research appeal. The world is now eagerly witnessing how postsocialist China handles its own capitalist experiment, and as the country opens up, a substitute is no longer needed for empirical research. The 1990s saw a sharp decline in anthropologists who specialize in Taiwan, and a corresponding rise in China specialists.[5] Notably, too, some younger anthropologists have explicitly rejected the old sinocentric premises that allowed Taiwan to be taken as an undiluted specimen of Chinese folk culture. By contrast, the "modernist" approach of social scientists fares better in the post–Cold War milieu, yet, adhering to the "modern nation-state" as its primary point of departure, it tends to fall short on points related to globalization, undeniably a significant force in contemporary Taiwan.

The invalidation of older research models in Taiwan studies contrasts with a general rise in interest due to the higher visibility Taiwan has enjoyed over the last decade. More courses are being offered and more conferences held. Moreover, much of the focus is on new questions, such as extraterritoriality and the notion of "cultural citizenship," or how societies—in this case, societies in the "Greater China" sphere, including various Chinese diasporas—separated by national boundaries but connected by culture relate to one another in a globalized world.[6] Tawian's existence, its global presence, and its undeniable fraternity in the reproduction of Chinese culture challenge both the boundaries of the mainland's political claim and essentialist notions of Chineseness. Thus, a critical research issue is how different

frames of reference—ethnicity, cultural heritage, and political sovereignty—
are pitted against one another. This is particularly obvious in the increasingly frequent perspectives on Taiwan submitted by scholars of mainland
Chinese origin working in the United States and elsewhere.[7]

The need to negotiate competing referential frames was so compelling
in the 1990s that questions of history and identity sometimes overshadowed other disciplinary priorities. As the repressed political unconscious
returned, the practice of bracketing was denounced with a vengeance. The
complacent professionalism that once dominated academic circles was replaced by contentious claims built upon explicit or implicit agendas. Not
until more recent years did new critical models begin to take shape—a
positive sign for the elevation of Taiwan studies' disciplinary status in the
American academy.

Meanwhile, within Taiwan, once the officially sanctioned sinocentric
frame of reference was rendered problematic, the self-other relationship
became a multiple-choice question, thanks to the island's complex historical legacy. One could align with the Chinese community at large (the
huaren shijie, roughly an equivalent of the popular English label "Greater
China," initially used by scholars in response to particular phenomena of
economic globalization) and take the West as "Other," adopting an
ethno-linguistic and civilizational frame. One could also cling to the Cold
War anticommunist fellowship and regard mainland China as the Other—
albeit in the new global milieu this mindset is increasingly manifest in
terms of economic competition rather than ideological hostility. Or, one
might try to reconnect ties to Japan, the former colonizer—ties already revamped through business partnerships and pan-Asia pop culture in recent
decades—acknowledging the positive legacy of modernization during the
colonial period. In fact, the recent surge of public, not just scholarly interest in the study of Taiwanese literature within Taiwan fully demonstrates that the politics of referential frames in a scholarly discipline may
indeed have significant repercussions in larger arenas.

Recent Growth of Taiwanese Literary Studies Within Taiwan[8]

The lifting of martial law in 1987 transformed Taiwan almost overnight
into an open society consciously adapting to liberal democracy. The cultural sphere was likewise restructured. Localism, after enjoying robust
growth for more than a decade, now effected a general overhaul of the
public perception of Taiwanese cultural products. At the same time, aided

by the newly liberated print and electronic media and energized by younger scholars returning from abroad, indigenized versions of imported intellectual programs like postmodernism and cultural studies had a profound impact on cultural production and literary scholarship.

During the martial law period, modern Chinese and Taiwanese literatures were heavily censored areas of knowledge. They were not considered legitimate subjects of scholarly inquiry, and for the most part did not appear in school curricula. Most Chinese new literature from the May Fourth movement was banned until the mid 1980s, and contemporary literature from the mainland was also inaccessible. The Nationalist regime's prolonged censorship of May Fourth literature was rooted in a phobia left over from its civil war experience, when leftist intellectuals used literature as a powerful ideological tool. At the same time, many works of modern Taiwanese literature from the colonial period were written in Japanese and not translated into Chinese until the 1990s.

Scholars, meanwhile, shunned the very words "Taiwanese literature," not just to avoid allegations of separatism but also because the idea was considered heretical to the sinocentric order. With a few prominent exceptions (notably, Lin Ruiming's study of Lai He, the pioneer of Taiwanese new literature), from the mid-1970s through the early 1990s it was researchers outside Taiwan, primarily in the English-speaking world and Japan, who led serious scholarship on modern and contemporary Taiwanese literature. Often, these researchers were expatriate scholars. This anomalous situation has rapidly reversed itself in the post–martial law period. The most dramatic change of all, though, came several months after the new DPP-led government took office, when it issued an official document encouraging institutions of higher education to establish Taiwanese literature departments.[9]

For a while after the lifting of martial law, ideological strife between academics aligned with either ascendant Taiwanese nationalism or wounded sinocentrism sapped the energy of the new field. Lately, however, the discipline has become much more professional, and the increased availability of public resources is affording large-scale, foundation-building research projects, as well as the translation of Japanese-language literature by prominent Taiwanese writers. Prestigious academic institutions have launched large-scale projects to collect research materials, in addition to sponsoring multiple conferences and symposia on literature from both the Japanese and postwar periods. At the same time, the fresh face, society-wide implications, and high visibility of Taiwanese literary studies has led many of the country's brightest scholars to switch their specialization from other national literatures to that of Taiwan, many with the expressed ambition of producing a new Taiwanese literary historiography. All signs point to a new era in Taiwanese literary scholarship. Before proceeding, however, it will be useful to pause for a moment and reflect upon the current status of two nonacademic precursors to Taiwanese literary studies that developed during the martial law period, critical traditions that will be further discussed in later chapters.

One important tradition of literary criticism developed in association with a powerful agent of literary production and distribution, the *fukan*, or literary supplements to newspapers. Between the mid-1970s and late 1980s in particular, *fukan* actively appropriated and assimilated Modernist, Nativist, and Localist ideas and offered a major forum for book reviews, literary criticism, and other commentaries on literature. *Fukan* publishers have remained active in the post–martial law literary field, sponsoring a series of scholarly symposia and the Selection of Taiwanese Literary Classics in 1999, but the authority of *fukan*-based criticism is being challenged on two fronts. The lingering ideological imprints of its roots in the martial law era make *fukan* a vulnerable target now, and the introduction of Taiwanese literary studies as an academic discipline is also exerting pressure. Previously, scholar-critics interested in contemporary Taiwanese literature had no choice but to write for the *fukan* and *fukan*-affiliated presses. Making necessary compromises, these critics became accustomed to the institution and prospered in the interstices between journalism and academia. Now that it is possible to treat Taiwanese literature according to the more rigorous standards of scholarly research, a new division of labor is developing as scholarly critics move away from *fukan*.

A second tradition of literary criticism comes from a handful of Localist-minded writer-critics and scholars who advocated Taiwanese cultural nationalism even before the Localist movement proper gained broad public attention in the mid-1980s. Motivated by a belief that literature represents the community's spiritual heritage, and touting a longstanding "realist" tradition that regards literature as a vehicle powered by the "real lives of the people," critics like Ye Shitao, Zhang Liangze, Lin Ruiming, Peng Ruijin, and Li Qiao engaged in research and criticism of native literature, including works from the Japanese period. Their small band was strengthened briefly by an association with the Nativist literary movement in the 1970s, but eventually split off again to organize their own literary camps (e.g., the *Yanfen didai wenyiying* [Salt belt literary workshop]) and short-lived journals (e.g., *Taiwan xinwenhua* [New Taiwanese culture] and *Wenxuejie* [Literary world]) in the late 1970s and early 1980s in southern Taiwan.

By and large, before the mid-1980s this group lacked symbolic capital and had little access to public resources. This has changed dramatically since the mid-1990s. Ironically, however, now that "Taiwanese literature" is gaining legitimacy in the public sphere, many who formerly held reservations about the term are also claiming it for their own, and redefining it in very different ways. Feeling undermined, the Localists have tried to re-center debate on the "China question," asking: Is Taiwanese literature "national literature"? Do works written by Taiwanese writers during the colonial period count as Chinese, Taiwanese, or Japanese? Can one consider the mainlanders in Taiwan, those who settled here since 1949, local writers, given the fact that some of them insist on considering themselves "Chinese writers"? These same disgruntled Localists also instigated a public protest against the Selection of Taiwanese Literary Classics, a seminal event that will be much discussed in the closing chapter of this book.

The Impact of Transnational Cultural Trends

While the politics of historical and ethnic referential frames remains a core issue within the Taiwanese literary studies community in Taiwan, there is another set of issues contained in the exchange between intellectual and cultural trends imported from the West and local scholarship, issues common to nonwestern scholarship in a postcolonial world.

The terms "exile" and "dependency" suitably convey the plight of Taiwanese literary scholarship. As we have seen, Taiwanese literary studies was effectively a discipline "in exile" for decades before returning to Taiwan's own academy in the 1990s. Now, besides the challenges of Taiwan's extraordinary domestic politics, it faces the additional challenges of its return from exile, namely the politics of an academy overshadowed by imported critical methodologies and scholars trained abroad, mostly in the United States.

Taiwan's academic community always had competent scholars. Literary specialists returned from regimented training in U.S. graduate programs—especially comparative literature programs—have in particular been an elite group, and many have switched to Taiwanese literary studies from other concentrations over the last decade. These scholars are inclined to work with imported theories, aligning more closely with scholars outside of Taiwan than with those trained at home in the strong empirical tradition of Taiwan's Chinese and history departments.

Chinese literary studies in the United States has also changed.[10] It has gradually shifted away from New Criticism's "close reading" and the liberal humanist approach endorsed by pioneers like C. T. Hsia and Joseph Lau, responding to changes in literary studies generally over the last two decades. Between the late 1970s and the mid-1980s, in particular, comparative literature scholars championing theory developed an openly confrontational relationship with the more historically and empirically based sinologist tradition in literary studies. Unsurprisingly, a similar "theory boom" occurred among comparative literature experts in Taiwan's foreign language and literature departments around the mid-1980s, making intellectual facility with cutting-edge theories a prestige capital in the academic community.[11]

Since the late 1980s, what Arjun Appadurai calls the "transnational cultural flow" has increasingly synchronized the critical approaches of western and Asian literary scholars. Right at the end of the 1980s, an activist group of returned scholars began to launch radical critiques of the state's ideological apparatus, critiques that sprouted new social movements and gender discourses, pushing a radical turn in the country's liberal-dominated intellectual sphere. A decade later, the activist agenda of the returnees has apparently been adopted by locally trained scholars, although they are still more inclined to employ conventional empirical research methods in their pursuit of the common goal: a critical reassessment of Taiwanese literary traditions. In the meantime, implicit ties between intellectual traditions and historical impulses, the longstanding tension between native and imported systems of knowledge, and the value of intellectual pedigree have gone beyond the enclaves of academia, dividing antagonistic groups in the society at large as well.

The "referential frames" fielded in western theoretical discourses—feminist, postmodern, postcolonial, and queer, each challenging older frames implicit in the dominant discourses of patriarchy, Enlightenment rationality, Eurocentrism, and heterosexuality—have been strategically adopted by Taiwanese literary scholars, who adapt and apply these alternative theoretical frameworks to issues prominent in post–martial law Taiwan, inevitably tied to the contestation of sinocentric cultural hegemony, the growing passion for Taiwanese nationalism, and the redistribution of resources among different ethno-linguistic identity groups.[12] The result is a unique cultural landscape, at once pedantically progressive and deeply political. Following are some current examples.

Several scholars have vowed to write a "women's literary history" for Taiwan, and four highly publicized anthologies were published between mid-2000 and mid-2001 alone (Li, Yuanzhen; Mei, Jialing; Qiu, Guifen; Fan, Mingru and Baochai Jiang). The value of these projects goes beyond simply honoring the highly visible presence of women writers in contemporary Taiwan literary production to include the strategic use of women's perspectives to engage in progressive dialogues with the dominant voices in the field. (Qiu Guifen, for instance, takes issue with the unexamined patriarchal assumptions in Localist historiography.) Chen Fangming's yet-to-be-completed *History of Taiwanese Literature*, encompassing both the modern (Japanese) and contemporary (postwar) periods and ostensibly employing a postcolonial perspective, has attracted much attention for its stated intention to construe a "Taiwanese national literature." Liao Binghui's discussion of "alternative modernity," highlighting the fundamentally hybrid nature of Taiwanese culture and identity by situating it within a global as well as pan-Asian context, engages even more closely with rapidly evolving theoretical discourses on nonwestern cultures.[13] As part of his formulation of "repressed modernity," David Der-wei Wang (Wang Dewei) sees a reincarnation of late Qing fiction's thematic paradigms in contemporary Taiwanese literature, employing a historical frame that valorizes a pan-Chinese cultural-linguistic community, the "*huaren shijie*," extending beyond the confines of Taiwan's local history and geography (*Fin-de-siècle* ch. 6).[14] In the meantime, old and new versions of leftist ideology remain potent and viable among particular intellectual groups in Taiwan. Veteran Nativist critic Chen Yingzhen still equates modernism with western cultural imperialism, reductively treating developments in Taiwan's literary sphere as indices of the century-long imperialist/capitalist aggression suffered by the "oppressed people" of Taiwan and other Third World countries.[15] Scholars of the postmodern and cultural studies schools, on the other hand, are alerting us to subtler forms of invasion threatened by global capitalism, especially transnational cultural products that undermine local identity and the viability of "local literature."

Local intellectuals' application of globally traveling cultural theories to social conflicts at home makes the abstract formulations relevant to the individual's experienced life-world. Coupled with the force of Taiwan's competing nationalisms and differing interpretations of what it means to be Taiwanese, theoretically informed research is producing a qualitative leap in Taiwanese literary studies. In a field that is experiencing a sudden boom, however, remaining methodologically self-reflective can be challenging. For instance, as scholars pursue insights generated by currently valorized categories of analysis—gender, ethnicity, history and memory, the modernist project of nation-building, etc.—the situatedness of individual texts within the multiple, complex, interlocking networks of sociological forces surrounding the process of cultural production is often left unconsidered. As a result, critical issues pertaining to the representational status of individual texts have rarely been raised by the theory-focused scholars reading them. The problem is aggravated by the fact that rigorous historical work on contemporary Taiwanese literature has been scanty. The contextual approach adopted here is intended partly to address these problems; its basic terms are sketched below.

For its temporal frame, the study adopts an epochal approach, departing from Taiwan's mainstream Localists, whose emphasis on the understudied colonial legacy has an obvious ulterior motive: the assertion of a "Taiwanese subjectivity." The inauguration of a new epoch is often accompanied by drastic changes in the government's cultural policies, the dominant ideology, and relations between the state and the market. These changes directly affect the structure of the field of literary production and generate a different literary culture. Hence, my emphasis on historical continuity between post–1949 Taiwan and Republican-era (1911–1949) mainland China—as opposed to colonial Taiwan—does not necessarily imply an endorsement of sinocentric ideology. Rather, it is based on the fact that after settling in Taiwan in 1949 the Nationalist regime reproduced many of the cultural institutions it had previously established in mainland China during its Republican-era tenure. At the same time, thematic and other lineages between the literature of contemporary Taiwan and that of pre–1949 mainland Chinese literature must be examined with extra caution. A key argument this study makes is that institutional changes in Taiwan since 1949 have given rise to a distinctive literary culture, transforming the meaning of textual features ostensibly similar to those found in the Republican era on the mainland.

Ethnically, this study admittedly still uses "China" as its main reference point, appearing to share much with the "Greater China" referential frame. However, my approach differs from some politicized versions of the latter on a few fundamental points. Most important, I try to refrain from sinocentric culturalist assumptions, and instead strive for perspectives based on more systematic analyses of cultural developments in the early phase of capitalist modernization, à la Hohendahl and Bourdieu. Such analyses allow for macro-level comparisons between literary developments in Taiwan and those in other modern societies, particularly societies that have gone through the modernization process under authoritarian regimes. Comparative perspectives are also potentially useful against the Chinese and Taiwanese exceptionalism that is increasingly popular in the field.

Conceptual Frameworks

Particular periods in literary history are associated with specific defining features. British literature of the Victorian period is constrained by the imperatives of decorum, while European literature produced between the two world wars is characterized by a transgressive energy unleashed by aesthetic high modernism. Since contemporary literature from Taiwan cannot be said to have carved an international image for itself yet, for years I have been gathering opinions on it from readers in mainland China, Hong Kong, and other contemporary Chinese societies. Anecdotally, while informed readers in Hong Kong give considerable weight to the achievements of Taiwan's Modernist generation, mainland intellectuals tend to favor such mainstream literary products as lyrical prose and popular romances. To be sure, such impressions are largely explained by patterns of cultural flow among the three Chinese societies. Hong Kong has enjoyed close cultural interaction with Taiwan. Some core members of Taiwan's Modernist group in the 1960s, including Dai Tian and Ye Weilian (Wai-lim Yip), were in fact "overseas Chinese" from Hong Kong who attended college in Taiwan. Stories by the leading Modernist Bai Xianyong appeared in middle-school textbooks in Hong Kong. Even after Modernism's heyday, some very fine Hong Kong writers of modernist and postmodernist bent— Xi Xi, Xinqishi, Huang Biyun, and Dong Qizhang are among the best known names—were consecrated by Taiwan's aggressive *fukan*, and enjoyed high renown among their Taiwanese readership. In contrast, after Taiwan and mainland China resumed cultural exchanges in the post–Mao era, writers of popular romances such as Qiongyao and Sanmao were the first to be introduced and gain popularity on the mainland. Traditionalist prose writers followed.[16] Even among the more serious writers, those who display a traditionalist tendency, such as Bai Xianyong, Yu Guangzhong, Zhang Xiaofeng, and Wang Dingjun, are likely to fare better in the mainland market than writers known for modernistic experimentation, such as Wang Wenxing, Li Yongping, and Wang Zhenhe.

Such historical factors, however, do not account for the impression of Taiwanese literary culture held by Wang Meng, an eminent PRC writer and former Vice Minister of Culture. During a 1998 visit to Rice University in Houston, when queried about the enthusiastic reception Shanghai-based essayist Yu Qiuyu had received in Taiwan, Wang suggested that Yu's "sweet-sour, moderately bitter, and pedantic (or bookish)" style catered well to the taste of Taiwanese readers.[17] The three adjectives in Wang's off-the-cuff remark accurately captured the aesthetic sensibility of Taiwanese readers raised on the lyrical, sentimentalist, nonsubversive strand of Chinese new literature that was sanctioned in Taiwan in the early post–1949 years and contributed significantly to shaping contemporary Taiwan's distinctive literary culture.

In fact, a central argument of this study is that such images projected by Taiwan's officially sanctioned mainstream literature during the martial law period identify a "hegemonic category"—defined by Peter Bürger, as cited by Peter Hohendahl, as something that "determines the outlook of subjects who participate in literature" (*Building* 31)—that dominated literary production and reception for the better part of the contemporary epoch, the residues of which were still readily discernable in the early post–martial law years, when the sudden popularity of Yu Qiuyu took many by surprise. Wang's unflattering comment on Yu Qiuyu's work can be inferred to implicate contemporary PRC readers as well, since Yu was also quite popular in mainland China. Indeed, Wang added that the genteel, lighthearted disposition of Taiwanese writers does not befit their mainland counterparts, who are charged with the serious mission of representing the brutal realities of a history "covered with blood stains."

Somewhat unexpectedly, an echo of Wang's inward-pointing criticism is found in remarks made by another important, but very different mainland literary figure, Wang Shuo, the brilliantly cynical, hugely successful bad boy of PRC literature, television, and film. In 1999, Wang published some negative comments on the writing of Jin Yong, the erudite Hong Kong writer and businessman whose martial arts novels rank among the most popular ever read by modern Chinese readers ("Wo kan"). The challenge to someone of Jin's stature and visibility stirred up a controversy that spread in Chinese newspapers, in magazines, and on the Internet.[18] Wang responded, declaring that his criticism was actually motivated by a sense of frustration: "I was one of the makers of contemporary Chinese culture, especially the new culture of Beijing, which included literature, film, and music. But today, everyone, including my daughter's generation, has lost his/her head over the culture of Hong Kong and Taiwan. I do not understand why things have declined so rapidly" (Dai, Tian 44).[19]

Here Wang Shuo of course primarily refers to products of mass culture from Hong Kong and Taiwan, as his earlier essay juxtaposes Qiong Yao, Jackie Chan, and pop music superstars with Jin Yong. But what strikes me as revealing is that the two Wangs, whatever their differences elsewhere, apparently share some fundamental assumptions about what constitute worthy literary projects for Chinese writers. The "popular" tastes of the Chinese reading public run against the idealist vision cherished by the modern Chinese intellectual class. The prevalence of elitism in literary discourse becomes even more conspicuous when evoked by unlikely candidates—Wang Shuo himself is considered "popular" by most critics and his membership in the intellectual class by no means unequivocal.

My efforts to point out these contradictions are geared toward explaining why so little scholarly energy has been invested in examining the corpus of contemporary Taiwan's mainstream literary products, which have arguably bestowed upon the epoch's literary culture its defining features. The same elitist attitude that the two Wangs subscribe to also dominated scholarship on Taiwanese literature until very recently. Taiwan's Modernists and Nativists have long been recognized as respectable research subjects. Even products of the essentially market-oriented Taiwanese literary culture since the 1980s have often been scrutinized for progressive messages, although what is "progressive" is construed differently than in earlier periods, in accord with currently valorized theoretical discourses.

I am not attempting to redefine "literature" as something other than a form of elite culture or to challenge the established hierarchy of cultural products in modern Chinese societies. Rather, by reexamining certain assumptions, I am calling attention to a prevailing tendency in Chinese literary scholarship to relegate an unduly large portion of mainstream literature to secondary status, and to point out that the tendency is ideologically induced. A great advantage of the contextual approach adopted in this study is that it systematically examines the basic conditions "under which writing and reading occur" (Hohendahl 34), requiring the inclusion of literary practices heretofore regarded as conservative or reactionary and therefore summarily dismissed. It is only through investigating these mainstream literary activities that we can understand some of the basic processes that give shape to a particular literary culture. In this study, these include the formation and transformation of dominant aesthetic categories, changes in

the institutional environment of literary production, and the effects of external historical, political, and economic factors. These choices are directed by a conception of literature as an institution, a perspective that is elab-
orated in the following section.

Literature as an Institution, and Mainstream Literature in Contemporary Taiwan

In his book *Building a National Literature: The Case of Germany 1830–
1870*, Peter Hohendahl explains what an adequate theory of the institution of literature ought to be concerned with:

> First . . . [it] is directly concerned neither with the analysis of texts nor
> with their genesis and dissemination, but rather with the conditions
> under which writing and reading occur. . . . Moreover, one would ex-
> pect a theory of the institution to deal systematically with the basic con-
> ditions. When we speak of conventions and norms, we are concerned
> not with individual traits but with a system. Third, one would expect the
> specific character of the institution in relation to other cultural social in-
> stitutions . . . to be clarified. Finally one would expect historical speci-
> ficity to be taken into consideration, for example, the differences be-
> tween various historical epochs and social formations, and the evolution
> of the institution of literature itself. (34)

Conventional scholarship that focuses on authors, artistic schools, and
formal or thematic qualities of literary texts still predominates in modern
Chinese literary study, but the institutional approach has made inroads,
most notably in Leo Lee's works on print media of the late Qing and early
Republican eras and the *wentan* (literary arena) in the 1920s and 1930s,
Perry Link's study of the popular fiction of the "mandarin duck and butterfly" school in the 1910s, and Edward Gunn's book on wartime literature in Shanghai and Beijing under Japanese occupation. These studies
touch upon the development of two modern institutions in urban China,
newspapers and the publishing industry, and their close relationship with
the production and consumption of literature. They also shed light on literary development in post–1949 Taiwan, inasmuch as Taiwan's inheritance from the Republican era included the Nationalist regime's cultural
bureaucracy, the mainland coastal cities' media and publishing industries,
and the liberal-humanist strand of the May Fourth intellectual tradition.

Taiwan's unresolved political status since 1949 has deeply affected "Taiwanese literature." Even regarded as a branch of "literature written in the Chinese language" (*huawen wenxue*), it is very distinctive. Taiwan has clearly developed its own institutions of literature in both the modern and the contemporary periods.[20]

Although the Taiwanese new literary movement that began in the 1920s was initially inspired by the May Fourth movement on the mainland, within a decade it embarked on a separate journey. With the banning of Chinese language publications at the outbreak of the Sino-Japanese war in 1937 and the maturation of a generation of Taiwanese educated within the colonial system and versed in Japanese, a colonial literary institution was further consolidated. A major part was contributed by young Taiwanese elites who had studied and formed ties in Japan. However, the retrocession of Taiwan to the Republic of China in 1945 completely reversed this course, as the Nationalist Chinese government immediately launched various "resinicization" programs, including a ban on Japanese. After losing the civil war in 1949, the Nationalist regime would retreat to Taiwan altogether, and Taiwan and the mainland would again diverge. It is undoubtedly true that, sharing cultural roots in imperial China and then in China's Republican era, the literatures of these two societies exhibited significant affinities. However, from 1949 to the early 1980s, the policies and mechanisms of cultural control in Taiwan and the PRC were guided by diametrically opposed ideological doctrines, and there was virtually no communication between them, so that by the end of that time their respective literary cultures reflected more differences than similarities.

The basic conditions for literary production and consumption in Taiwan gradually changed over the second half of the twentieth century from state-engineered cultural hegemony to market-oriented media domination. To examine this course of development in its full complexity, I find Hohendahl's understanding of the institution of literature as including both abstract and concrete dimensions most useful. The abstract dimension describes dominant conceptions of literature, or general ideas of its function in society held by a specific class or social group, and norms and conventions that regulate the production and consumption of texts. The concrete dimension indicates "the concrete, material organizations that constitute the apparatus transmitting [the conceptions, norms, and conventions] to society" (*Building* 29). I first take a brief look at the abstract dimension of Taiwan's contemporary literary institution.

Specific aesthetic categories and officially sanctioned modes of literary expression were developed right after 1949 and gradually achieved something like hegemony. To the extent that this process was part of the mainlander-dominated government's program of ideological indoctrination carried out in schools, the media, and the cultural bureaucracy, it was inevitable that mainstream literature adhered to a core spirit of China-centeredness, or sinocentrism. Inevitably, the sanctioned aesthetic categories also shaped the artistic outlook of native Taiwanese writers and readers who went through the rigidly controlled education system. At the same time, the Nationalist regime's policies constituted mainlanders as a uniform ethno-linguistic-ideological group with greater cultural and social capital and easier access to state-controlled resources, giving them an advantageous position in Taiwan's mainstream literary production for most of the martial law period.

In the 1960s and 1970s, the alternative Modernist and oppositional Nativist cultural formations took issue with the Nationalist regime and its ideology. Their (respective) liberal-humanist and leftist-humanitarian aesthetic ideologies exerted considerable influence on mainstream literature, including its sinocentric imagination. From the mid-1970s forward economic development steered mainstream literature toward the country's middle class, without immediately undermining the KMT-instituted culture, which remained an important part of the emerging literary field sponsored by commercial media. More drastic changes came after the lifting of martial law, when a reconstitution of the country's dominant culture began in earnest. As the oppositional Democratic Progressive Party gained force, localism, underpinned by Taiwanese nationalism, quickly became a prominent motif in the mainstream literature of the 1990s. In the meantime, advancing capitalist development emerged as a formidable force reshaping the conventions and norms of mainstream aesthetic categories.

The development of aesthetic categories and literary ideology described above was necessarily mirrored by corresponding changes in the more concrete, organizational dimension of contemporary Taiwan's literary institution. In the early years of the epoch, the KMT resorted to military force and coercive cultural policies to consolidate its rule. Harsh censorship, party-owned magazines, state-sponsored writers' associations, workshops, prizes, and various mobilization programs (notably "cultural sanitization" campaigns, "combat literature," and "anti-Communist literature") dominated literary production in the 1950s. With increased political stability and economic growth, however, the government loosened its cultural control, and by the late 1950s, Taiwan's liberal-inclined intellectual elite began to assume leadership roles. Between the late 1950s and the mid-1970s, elitist coterie journals, published by independent intellectual groups (the liberal Modernists and the socialist-inclined Nativists) or affiliated with academia, were key players in literary production.

As general levels of education and affluence continued to increase, market forces began to modernize and professionalize the media and the publishing industry. Beginning in the mid-1970s, *fukan* rapidly grew into the dominant institution of literary production and consecration. *Fukan*-sponsored annual literary contests became the major channel for new writers to enter the profession and gain membership in the expansive network of writers, critics, editors, and publishers deployed around these newspaper supplements. As part of the commercial mass media, *fukan* still came under close government supervision, even while they were increasingly subject to the demands of the market. This put them in an ambiguous position over the decade or so preceding the lifting of martial law in 1987. Extremely resourceful and politically seasoned *fukan* editors managed to tactfully manipulate the social fomentation for greater civil liberties, using it to bargain for their own independence from the state. They also made skillful use of the hegemonic cultural values inculcated by the Nationalist government's indoctrination efforts to garner greater readership and profits.

After the lifting of martial law, direct political interference was largely removed and the market quickly emerged as the leading force in literary production. Following a short depression in the literary market in the early 1990s, the importance of *fukan*-sponsored annual prizes steadily declined, while medium-sized and more specialized publishing houses grew in importance. With adaptation to market logic now the only way to survive, literary agents began to take greater notice of "popular culture," and to varying degrees relinquished their old high culture aspirations. In both abstract and concrete terms, then, a new literary institution is gradually taking shape in Taiwan.

The Field of Cultural Production Under State-Sanctioned Cultural Hegemony

While the notion of literature as institution helps to define the scope of inquiry for this study, it does not in itself offer sufficient terms of analysis.

This is where I find Pierre Bourdieu's discussion of the "field" of cultural production helpful.

For Bourdieu, any social formation is structured as a hierarchically organized series of fields—the economic field, the educational field, the political field, the cultural field, etc. Each is defined as a structured space with its own internal laws of functioning and relations of force "independent" of those of other fields. Each is relatively autonomous, but structurally homologous with the others (*The Field* 6). The great advantage of Bourdieu's theory, then, is that it takes pains to theoretically generalize the literary field's own laws of functioning and relations of force, while keeping in view its interaction with the society's general field of power, especially political and economic power.

I have found the following concepts from Bourdieu's theory of the field of cultural production most useful in contextual study of literary development in contemporary Taiwan.

ARTISTIC POSITIONS

The first important concept I borrow from Bourdieu is his notion of "position."

> The science of the literary field is a form of *analysis situs* which establishes that each position—e.g. the one which corresponds to a genre such as the novel or, within this, to a sub-category such as the 'society novel' [*roman mondain*] or the 'popular novel'—is subjectively defined by the system of distinctive properties by which it can be situated relative to other positions; that every position, even the dominant one, depends for its very existence, and for the determinations it imposes on its occupants, on the other positions constituting the field; and the structure of the field, i.e. of the space of position, is nothing other than the structure of the distribution of the capital of specific properties which governs success in the field and the winning of the external or specific profit (such as literary prestige) which are at stake in the field. (*The Field* 30)

Here Bourdieu associates "position" with a literary genre or subgenre, but the implications of the term are clearly broader than what is usually meant by "genre." We can see this in Bourdieu's discussion of the structural relations between symbolist poetry, the bourgeois theater, and social novels in the literary field in France during the second half of the nineteenth century

(46–67). He treats these genres not in conventional terms of aesthetic qualities, but rather in terms of their position within the field as determined by such factors as the social class of and the economic and educational capital possessed by the producers and consumers of each genre/position.

Following Bourdieu's idea, I use a slightly modified concept, "artistic position," and apply it to the four major artistic formations found in the literary field of contemporary Taiwan: the KMT-endorsed, sinocentric Mainstream; the liberal-minded Modernist literary movement; the socialist-inclined Nativist movement; and the Localist trend affiliated with Taiwanese nationalism. These "artistic positions" interact and intersect over a period of several decades. Each position springs from interlocking social, political, and cultural forces that impose specific determinations on its occupants and shape particular aesthetic categories through which they perceive and appreciate literature.

My choice to use "artistic position" in this specifically qualified sense is motivated by several obvious advantages. Above all, it frees me from the major deficiency of the conventional periodization, which divides Taiwan's contemporary literary history into periods dominated by the Modernists, the Nativists, and urban literature. It is easy to show that even after the heyday of a particular literary movement or artistic formation, its aesthetics and ideology continue to affect the literary field, and it still constitutes a position within the "system of distinctive properties." Cultural agents still can and still do hold, or partially hold, Modernist or Nativist positions in the post–martial law period, deriving the benefits and suffering the liabilities therefrom. Another advantage of specifying the four major artistic positions is that it facilitates the task of tracing their trajectories and interactions across several decades.

Conceptualizing the transformation of a politically instituted Mainstream artistic position—which carries a particular set of "hegemonic" aesthetic presuppositions—during the course of Taiwan's liberalization and commercialization especially benefits from this analytical scheme. Not normally considered a literary movement *per se*, the "Mainstream position" in my view is a specific, state-sanctioned position in the literary field that corresponded to a particular socio-ideological position within the KMT-instituted dominant culture and, more important, was supported by the state apparatus throughout the martial law period. Its privileged position was guaranteed as long as the KMT-instituted culture remained dominant, despite increasing challenges from alternative and oppositional cultural formations. Thus, it was only in the 1990s, when the "Taiwanized" KMT under Lee Teng-hui began surreptitiously supporting Localism, that the formerly state-sanctioned Mainstream position was seriously undermined.

It is particularly challenging to chart the more recent development of the KMT-endorsed Mainstream because of the ongoing reconstitution of the dominant culture. The most obvious change has been a dramatic reversal of roles between Taiwan's two major population groups, but the culture is complicated further by the advance of pluralistic democracy and liberal economies. To clarify this situation, Raymond Williams's scheme of hegemonic, alternative, and oppositional cultural formations is useful, and not just with regard to the recent tribulations of the Mainstream position. Williams makes a point of saying that his theory of hegemony goes beyond "culture" understood as "intellectual life" and the "arts," to mean "whole ways of life" (*Marxism* 17, 108).[21] This makes the theory especially helpful for examining forces and events in Bourdieu's "general field of power" and relating them to particular artistic positions in the "relatively independent" subfield of literature. In part 2 and part 3, I do just this, considering each position in the literary field in terms of Williams's scheme applied to Taiwan's general field of power.

Returning to the particular point about the Mainstream, one of the complications it presents in the post–martial law era is semantic. The "Mainstream" position is so named because of its essential identification with the authoritarian state's sinocentric doctrine and martial law cultural policies, through which it attempted to inculcate sinocentrism as the defining feature of Taiwan's cultural identity. The state's long-term intention was not simply to impose its ideology but to naturalize it as a hegemonic cultural self-identification. This worked to an extent, but in the post–martial law period sinocentric identification has gradually lost the cultural high ground, and Mainstream literature has suffered in the open market. Hence the semantic problem: competing now on its own merits, minus the prop of political intervention, Mainstream (capital M) literature is no longer in the mainstream (small M) of the literary market. Chapter 8 offers an analysis of a major literary event that occurred in 1999, the selection by committee of "Taiwanese Literary Classics," as a swan song for the Mainstream position in contemporary Taiwan. In the meantime, keep in mind that the artistic position identified in this study as the "Mainstream" is currently struggling with its own identity, having been expelled from its accustomed place in the literary and cultural arena.

HOMOLOGOUS FIELDS AND "HABITUS"

Closely related to the idea of artistic positions in the literary field is Bourdieu's conception of the relationship between different fields, especially between the field of cultural production and the general field of power. Bourdieu describes this as "structural homology." Following this notion, I make an important assumption: that opposition between the Mainstream and Localist positions in the literary field corresponded to opposition between mainlanders and native Taiwanese in the society as a whole. However, it is necessary to state up front certain qualifications to this homologous relationship, in connection with another key concept from Bourdieu, "habitus" or the "socially constituted system of cognitive and motivating structures" (*Outline* 76) of individual agents, which mediates between their position in the class structure of the larger society and their position in the cultural field.

> The structures constitutive of a particular type of environment (e.g. the material conditions of existence characteristic of a class condition) produce *habitus,* systems of durable, transposable *dispositions*, structured structures predisposed to function as structuring structures, that is, as principles of the generation and structuring of practices and representations which can be objectively "regulated" and "regular" without in any way being the product of obedience to rules, objectively adapted to their goals without presupposing a conscious aiming at ends or an express mastery of the operations necessary to attain them and, being all this, collectively orchestrated without being the product of the orchestrating action of a conductor. (*Outline* 72)[22]

In "habitus," artistic practices and perceptions are seen to have their basic roots in the society's class structure. Here I expand Bourdieu's "social class" to incorporate the politically constructed and ethnically based hybrid "political" classes in post–1949 Taiwan, and argue that applying the concept of habitus to the relationship between opposition in the society's general field of power and opposition in the cultural field must be done with extra care.

On the one hand, the historically formed and politically reinforced opposition between the two predominant population groups in early post–1949 Taiwan's social structure necessarily affected individual artists' habitus, formed in the process of socialization. That opposition could not but function as a crucial differentiating factor in the field of cultural production. On the other hand, between the state's cultural in-doctrination efforts and the forces of modernization, new "material con-ditions of existence" emerged in the next few decades that inevitably pro-duced new types of habitus, most obviously among Taiwan's younger generations. Moreover, as an unrecognized Chinese government in exile, the KMT regime was increasingly forced to localize its power base and thus effected a gradual reversal of roles between the broadly defined "po-litical classes." The opposition within the cultural field was therefore in-creasingly played out in crude ideological struggles between competing political institutions.

Such struggles, manifested in the contending discourses of sinocentrism and Taiwanese nationalism, have underpinned changing relations between the Mainstream and the Localist positions in Taiwan's contemporary lit-erary field, especially over the last two decades. As a matter of fact, cor-responding relationships existed in regard to all four artistic positions, al-beit sometimes in a more oblique fashion. For instance, there was significant overlap between agents occupying Mainstream and Modernist positions in the early phase of the Modernist movement, largely due to the fact that mainlander émigrés who followed the Nationalist government to Taiwan dominated the literary field immediately after 1949. And antipa-thy between the Modernist and Nativist positions did not hinge solely on struggles in domestic politics but also on the intellectual class's ideologi-cal wrangling over such issues as the East-West confrontation, cultural im-perialism, and the Nationalist regime's postwar diplomacy.

RELATIVE AUTONOMY OF THE LITERARY FIELD AND
THE PROCESS OF AUTONOMIZATION

The development of the cultural field in post–1949 Taiwan appears to co-incide with Bourdieu's process of "autonomization," by which he means the field's progress toward greater ability to establish its own terms of aes-thetic worth and artistic legitimacy, away from external interference. This occurs as the commodity market increasingly dominates cultural produc-tion. However, the situation in modern and contemporary Chinese soci-eties is different from nineteenth-century France and Germany, where the process was correlated with the rise of the middle class. The political fac-tor featured much more prominently in Chinese literary development. The fact that capitalism reappeared in the third quarter of the twentieth cen-tury in Communist China necessarily sent its literary field on a complete-ly different historical trajectory. Likewise, in contemporary Taiwan and in post–Mao China, the presence of authoritarian states pursuing economic development according to a loosely defined "East Asian" model affected the progress of the cultural field toward relative autonomy.

In the opening passage of an essay called "The Market of Symbolic Goods," Bourdieu describes the long period of development that the cultural field in France had gone through by the mid-nineteenth century:

> Dominated by external sources of legitimacy throughout the middle ages, part of the Renaissance and, in the case of French court life, throughout the classical age, intellectual and artistic life has progressively freed itself from aristocratic and ecclesiastical tutelage as well as from its aesthetic and ethical demands. (*The Field* 112)

Judging from standards proposed in the same essay, the literary field in Chinese societies across most of the twentieth century was still largely dominated by "external" sources of legitimacy, albeit not aristocratic or ecclesiastical. Chinese cultural agents still spent most of their energy coping with aesthetic and ethical demands coming from the state and various ideological factions in the intellectual class. The modern Chinese and Taiwanese cultural fields in fact started moving toward relative autonomy early in the twentieth century, with the development of a commodity market in the urban areas, although it was circumscribed by "semicolonial" (mainland China) or colonial (Taiwan) sociopolitical orders. However, war and revolution, a succession of political regimes, and radically shifting economic policies repeatedly disrupted the process. This explains the recurring themes found in the literary fields of different epochs. The several short-lived Modernist trends—in Republican-era China (late 1920s through 1940s), in colonial Taiwan during the second half of the 1930s and postwar Taiwan during the 1960s and 1970s, and in post–Mao China (primarily in the mid-1980s)—make excellent cases in point. Direct and indirect lineages extend between epochs in complex patterns. This is why studies of the literary field in any particular period of modern Chinese or Taiwanese history cannot be confined to a single time frame, and research findings always carry implications beyond the immediate historical context.

Viewed from a broader historical perspective, progress toward relatively autonomous literary fields in modern Chinese societies has been disjunctive and frequently interrupted. Conditions conducive to rapid development existed in several historical periods—in mainland China in the 1920s and 1930s, in Taiwan in the 1930s and again from the mid-1970s on, and in mainland China again since the 1980s. During these periods of modernization in the capitalist mode there was a growing "public of potential consumers, of increasing social diversity" (*The Field* 112). Urbanization and the expansion of primary education turned new classes of people, especially women, into consumers of culture (113). The resulting diversification and multiplication of cultural producers, merchants, and agencies of consecration tended to support a standard of "truly cultural legitimacy," as against the "political legitimacy" principle that dominated modern Chinese literary history. In Bourdieu's terms, the literary field possessed greater autonomy at these times, when it was more able to "define its own criteria for the production and evaluation of its products" (115), "impose its own norms and sanctions on the whole set of producers" (40), and, above all, "*reinterpret* external demands in terms of its own logic" (55) (italics mine).

PRINCIPLES OF LEGITIMACY ("HETERONOMOUS" AND
"AUTONOMOUS" PRINCIPLES OF HIERARCHIZATION)

Bourdieu argues that the central dynamic of the cultural field is constant competition, among various "positions" and between two opposing legitimacy principles, the "heteronomous" and "autonomous" principles of hierarchization. The heteronomous principle locates value in a realm external to the work itself and to the literary field. In discussing it, Bourdieu obviously puts much weight on economic forces; the best known example is the thesis presented in his famous article, "The Field of Cultural Production, or: The Economic World Reversed" (*The Field* 29–73). By contrast, as argued in the previous section, until recently the most prominent heteronomous principle of hierarchization in the modern Chinese literary field was political efficacy. Therefore, much of this study is devoted to the competition between "political legitimacy" and "cultural legitimacy" in the contemporary Taiwanese literary field as it moves toward greater autonomy. Within this context, "cultural legitimacy" is notably different from the "pure art" concept that Bourdieu stresses, and tends to be a hybrid produced by market authorization and resistance to explicit political demands.

The autonomous principle of hierarchization locates the value of the literary product in the work itself. Bourdieu says that the most autonomous principles of differentiation in any sphere of activity are those "which most completely express the specificity of a determinate type of practice" (117). This suggests emphasis on form rather than function, mode of expression rather than objects of representation, language and style rather than theme and content. It follows that this set of terms naturally becomes the "privileged subject of debate among producers (or their interpreters)" (117).

In Taiwan, western-influenced Modernists forcefully pushed for artistic autonomy. Something of the sort also happened in China when the literary field was overtaken by an avant-garde movement in the late 1980s. Still, Bourdieu's autonomous principle of hierarchization, the art-for-art's-sake principle so central to the development of western cultural fields, has never been fully realized in the literary field of any modern Chinese society. One likely explanation is the conditions under which the market has developed in those societies. Bourdieu makes a connection between the emergence of the pure theory of art and the development of the commodity market: the more the market develops, the more writers and artists feel compelled to proclaim that works of art are irreducible to "simple article(s) of merchandise" (113–114).

> The emergence of the work of art as a commodity, and the appearance of a distinct category of producers of symbolic goods specifically destined for the market, to some extent prepared the ground for a pure theory of art, that is, of art as art. It did so by dissociating art-as-commodity from art-as-pure-signification, produced according to a purely symbolic intent for purely symbolic appropriation, that is, for disinterested delectation, irreducible to simple material possession. (114)

He also suggests that the ascendance of this "autonomous principle of hierarchization" in the literary field is likely to be manifested in internal debates and polemics, which contribute to the construction of the myth of "pure form."

Such was obviously not the case in modern Chinese societies until a relatively late date—with the Taiwanese Modernists in the 1960s and the PRC avant-gardists in the late 1980s—and even then, it typically met with strong and immediate resistance. During periods when cultural production was closely controlled by a totalitarian or hard authoritarian government—the first three decades of the PRC, and Taiwan during the early 1950s—there was little room for debating artistic matters *per se*. Even during periods when the cultural field had more room to move, literary debates usually centered on ideological issues, driven by political struggles in the society at large. In retrospect, even the best known advocates of less politically driven literature in pre–1949 China, including the Association for Literary Creation and the Crescent Moon Society, were motivated more by liberal-humanist ideals than by the concept of artistic autonomy.

As noted, to a certain extent, the concept of artistic autonomy and advocacy for "disinterested" aesthetic principles did briefly surface during different western-influenced Modernist literary movements—not just in Taiwan after 1949 and China after Mao, but also in the 1930s and 1940s in Republican China and colonial Taiwan—yet, as I tried to demonstrate in *Modernism and the Nativist Resistance*, it was primarily dissatisfaction with politically instituted culture that drove all these movements. In other words, prior to the 1990s, a greater need to resist political pressure, rather than the pressures of commercialization, probably accounts for the unimpressive development of the pure form of Bourdieu's autonomous principle of hierarchization and the lack of efforts to dissociate art as commodity from art as pure signification. This historical circumstance has made the market and its "mass readership" virtuous by comparison. Many literary agents in different Chinese societies probably share the view expressed by Zhang Ailing (Eileen Chang), one of the most popular icons in the literary arena of "Greater China." Against the background of Shanghai's commercializing media culture in the 1940s, Zhang remarked that if a writer has no choice but to subject him- or herself to the rule of some master, it is of course preferable to be enslaved by a collective and "abstract" one, like the mass readership ("Tongyan" 98).

To sum up, while the overriding dominance of political factors in Chinese cultural fields is hardly a new idea, in this book I revisit it using this new analytical scheme, which gives a central place to "political class" and "political capital." A final point that deserves further elaboration is the distinction between "official" and "nonofficial" political factors in the cultural field. Subscription to a nationalist-moralist intellectual discourse has motivated some intellectuals to actively support the state, even as it has driven others to oppose politically prescribed discourses. At the same time, cultural controls imposed by the state and intellectual discourses stressing literature's political utility have fed into and reacted against each other. To the extent that both privilege "political legitimacy," they are at odds with the growing tendency to affirm "truly cultural legitimacy" in the field of literary production. The next chapter takes up the interaction of official and nonofficial political factors with forces coming from the commodity market.

CHAPTER 2

Political and Market Factors in the Literary Field

Students of Chinese literature are well aware that politics plays an over-riding role in modern Chinese literary history. In fact, some of the land-mark scholarly works on modern Chinese literature are by social scientists writing primarily about the Communist state's mechanisms of cultural control. Merle Goldmann's *Chinese Literary Dissent* (1967) is an example *par excellence*. However, as many observers have noted since C. T. Hsia's famous remark on Chinese writers' perpetual "obsession with China" opened the door to this insight, in China political control over culture is not simply an imposition of the state's will—a traditional self-regulatory impulse and a relatively new (century-old) sense of responsibility to China's modernization project also contribute. The literary vocation in modern Chinese societies is inextricably linked to both the traditional-ist Chinese worldview—the Confucian idea of the gentry's social respon-sibility—and the all-absorbing modernist project of nation building. Left- and right-wing intellectual discourses of the prewar period agreed on one point—the intellectual class's obligation to the "common people" or the "masses," and to the nationalist project that would constitute them as a modern state society.

In recent years, however, the market factor has emerged as a prominent focus of attention in mainland China, challenging the values of the political and social elite. Many literary scholars sense the need to reconsider the issue. Chen Pingyuan, for instance, uses a play on words to convey the case, distinguishing between "*hua dazhong*" (to transform the mass) and "*dazhong hua*" (to become popular, or be transformed by the mass) (318). More and more Chinese intellectuals have resigned themselves to the reali-ty of a culturally stratified modern society and a new division of labor that changes their own role.[1] They stress the importance of professionalism, and of giving up the traditional role of the Confucian scholar-official as advisor to the ruling regime. Even so, it has proved difficult for Chinese intellectuals to completely forgo their other traditional mission: morally enlightening the people. As the Chinese cultural field progresses toward greater autonomy under capitalist development, professionalization of the scholarly vocation is inevitable, but the educated elite's deep immersion in the traditional moralist discourse makes the process disenchanting. It is nonetheless productive, in that it forces literary scholars to reexamine the whole modern period, giving more serious consideration to the effects of the market on literary production and consumption.

In Taiwan, the development of a relatively autonomous cultural field began decades earlier than in the PRC, but, partly because it has been gradual, the market factor has not been a prominent focus of scholarly attention. This chapter maps out some contextual frames that bring the market into sharper relief. The first section focuses on the immediate post–1949 years, when the state's intervention was most pronounced but coexisted with market forces in an interesting way. A vivacious *wentan* (literary arena) emerged against the backdrop of high-handed political control, in many ways carrying forward two opposing models of the cultural field established in prerevolutionary China. As we will see in chapters 6 and 7, contemporary Taiwan's literary field has been deeply influenced by the *wentan* that developed in prerevolutionary China's urban areas. Here, however, I would like to focus on the political factor in the early years, when the Nationalist government's top-down literary mobilization programs recycled policies and practices it had established in China during the Sino-Japanese war.

The second section draws some generalizations about the effects of what I call the "nonofficial" political factor, recasting some previous scholarly work in new terms. I hope to highlight the structural affinities between literary fields in Chinese societies of different periods, against which their dissimilarities may be more fruitfully explored. The persistence of the nationalist-moralist discourse, always at odds with the literary field's progress toward autonomy, speaks to Chinese intellectuals' abiding ambivalence toward modernity, and scholarly views on the subject are hardly less conflicted. The nonofficial political discourse also significantly contributes to the blurring of the genre hierarchy, as intellectual critics routinely overlegitimize works with middle-class formal attributes, products of a burgeoning market.

The last part of the chapter continues and expands previously presented arguments with a case study. Despite its literary merits and ostensible support of the KMT political agenda, the highly regarded anti-Communist novel *Xuanfeng* [Whirlwind] (completed in 1952) initially had difficulties in reaching the market. A brief look at the novel's publication history reveals multiple factors whose intricate interplay shaped the particular literary culture under consideration.

BETWEEN THE STATE AND THE MARKET: REVIVAL OF THE *WENTAN* (LITERARY ARENA) IN POST–1949 TAIWAN

In his introduction to the literary anthology *Roses and Thorns*, Perry Link describes how a new cultural "control system" was established in the first decade of the People's Republic of China.[2] A material apparatus was set up, including the establishment of writers' associations at every administrative level, national to local. With the literary profession contained within this institutional extension of the state, the party line was enforced largely through the use of "negative examples"—unacceptable cultural products singled out and subjected to relentless campaigns against their ideological shortcomings, often followed by harsh punishment of their producers. This and similar mechanisms were quite effective at delimiting the "permissible scope" of creative expression, establishing habits of self-censorship, and, ultimately, transferring literary agents' power to define and monopolize legitimate literary discourses to political authorities. While this system existed in its purest form only during the Cultural Revolution, it is clear that China's field of cultural production operated with very little autonomy throughout the Mao era.

Revival of the *Wentan* (Literary Arena)

By comparison, in Taiwan's immediate post–1949 years the political authorities' endeavors to control legitimate literary discourse were carried out by trusted cultural agents and mediated through the governing laws of a semiautonomous cultural field. To be sure, political power permeated the field of literary production, with all cultural institutions (schools, the publishing industry, and the media) under close supervision of the party-state, as were most spheres of civilian activity. However, as the country moved steadily toward a more complete market economy, the field of cultural production remained quasi-autonomous.

The cultural field in Taiwan after 1949 derived from historically specific conditions. An important one was the Nationalist government's compulsory language policy, which meant that non-Mandarin speaking native Taiwanese had very little chance of success in the literary field. Trusted mainlander writers thus dominated. At the same time, predisposed to compliance as they were, these literary agents also had a vested interest in fending off excessive political interference. They explored their limited autonomy, trying to carve out a creative space relatively free from external demands. In due course, however, their tactics of camouflage were themselves incorporated into the functioning rules of the literary field.

A few examples will demonstrate that a semiautonomous cultural field did exist, and that the impact of political forces in the general field of power was mediated by the field's operational laws. For instance, contrary to the common impression, several winners of the prestigious annual prizes awarded by the *Zhonghua wenyi jiangjin weiyuanhui* [Chinese literature and the arts awards committee] between 1951 and 1956 were native Taiwanese, including Liao Qingxiu, Zhong Lihe, and Li Rongchun.[3] The awards, however, did not secure a safe place for these writers in the literary field. Liao remained a lesser-known writer on the margins for several decades. Zhong's obviously superior talent for realistic fiction earned recognition only posthumously, thanks to Lin Haiyin's gallant use of borrowed funds to publish Zhong's works a year after his death from tuberculosis and poverty. Li fared even worse. Encouraged by the award, he devoted all his waking hours to creative writing, except for the manual work he did to maintain a basic livelihood. However, lacking the right kinds of cultural and linguistic capital and with no ties to the mainlander-controlled *wentan*, his lifelong endeavor proved futile.[4] Clearly, even in the immediate post–1949 years political authorization alone did not guarantee membership in the *wentan*; it had its own laws, separate from external political constraints, and literary success depended on adherence to both sets of rules.

A more positive contribution of this doubly constrained system was its development of ostensibly apolitical genres and aesthetic practices that proved popular and in the long run pushed the literary culture toward greater autonomy. Collectively labeled *chunwenxue*, or "pure literature," these innovations were vested with subtle notes of political legitimacy. Some, for instance, parlayed an underlying sinocentric motif.

As the market and the mass media rapidly developed in the 1970s and 1980s, the autonomous aspect of the *wentan* thrived. Arguably, the emerging urban-centered publishing industry and thriving *fukan* carried forward legacies from the prewar and wartime urban centers of mainland

China, including those under Japanese occupation, where literary activities were insulated from the drastic transformations taking place elsewhere, largely continuing in prewar commercial mode. The powerful fascination with Shanghai in Taiwan's literary field of the 1980s bears witness to this lineage.

In its early phase, however, the *wentan* undoubtedly faced considerable constraints. The word "*wentan*" connotes an image of refined culture, of "modern Chinese literati," men and women with elegant tastes, celebrity status, and allegedly great talent engaged in lively activities.[5] The image matches Bourdieu's claim that "what attracts and fascinates in the occupation of artist is not so much the art itself as the artist's lifestyle, the artist's life" (*The Field* 66). Despite its glamour, the *wentan* that mainlander literary agents revived in Taiwan after 1949 necessarily exhibited traits resulting from its rebirth from the ashes of the civil war. It thus differed significantly from the Shanghai *wentan* of the 1920s and 1930s, vividly portrayed in Leo Lee's book, *The Romantic Generation of Modern Chinese Writers*.

Jianying hua wentan [Reminiscences of the *wentan* through clippings of images], a 1984 memoir of the recently deceased editor-writer Lin Haiyin, a central figure in the reemerging *wentan* in Taiwan, nicely conveys the distinctive features of this particular instance of the literary field. Entries in *Reminscences* make it evident that *wentan* of the 1950s was sustained primarily by KMT-sponsored cultural programs, as well as magazines and *fukan* closely supervised by the state. The political imprints, however, were pasted over and effectively diffused by a genteel, affective, ostensibly apolitical ambience, which is the defining trait of *chunwenxue*. Undoubtedly, Lin's generation of literary agents engaged in a struggle that typifies intellectual life under an authoritarian regime. To understand the nature and necessity of their promotion of a subjective and sentimental creative style within a polite and harmonious literary community, one has to delve a little further into the institutional environment of literary production in the 1950s.

The War Model and Its Legacies

It may be hard to imagine from today's vantage how closely the literary environment in 1950s Taiwan resembled that of wartime China, but the "collectivist paradigm" of literary production established during the Sino-Japanese war (1937–1945) in both the Communist- and Nationalist-controlled regions did in fact carry over to Taiwan, lasting well beyond

1949. In his article "The Battlefield of Cultural Production: Chinese Literary Mobilization During the War Years," Charles A. Laughlin argues that the conditions of literary production were fundamentally changed by the Sino-Japanese war, rendering former aesthetic criteria and modes of production untenable and accelerating their replacement by the collectivist mode of production. Previous literary scholarship has largely stressed—and rightly so—the negative effects of war on Chinese new literature, and how it stunted the development of artistic trends like modernism in the latter part of the Republican era. The shift of perspective in Laughlin's article is refreshing because it suggests how paradigms of cultural production developed during the war exerted far-reaching influences on literary institutions in both the PRC and Taiwan after 1949.

With the shift to a collectivist mode, some formerly dominant urban centers of the publishing industry were debilitated, if not entirely demolished. Answering the special requirements of the war, new practices were established, including regimentation of literary activities by military authorities, close contact between writers and their new most frequent subjects, soldiers on the front line, and voluntary participation in literary mobilization programs. These wartime practices, Laughlin argues, laid the foundation for the literary system of the future PRC.

For my purposes, the second part of Laughlin's article, where he contrasts the fortunes of two collective writers' groups, is most interesting. "The Writers' Front-Line Interviews Corps," a right-wing group, originated in the Nationalist-controlled hinterland. "The Northwest Front-Line Service Corps," led by the famous left-wing writer Ding Ling, set up shop in Yan'an, the Communists' wartime base. Laughlin points out that notions central to left-wing literary thinking, such as collective artistic creation and the potential of "bourgeois" writers to assume the consciousness of the laboring masses, were in a curious way realized in wartime (85–86). Making a distinction between the conceptual and material aspects of the literary institution, he suggests that the material conditions of literary production in wartime facilitated the (partial) achievement of conceptual formulations prevalent among left-leaning Chinese writers and intellectuals before the war. These ideals had remained unrealizable as long as literary production was dominated by the urban, market-oriented publishing industry.[6]

It is important to stress that the traditionalist, sino-liberal ideals of the right-wing writers, while less ideologically vigorous, were also significantly affected by the "Chinese experience of war and the military nature of the social space in which the literary campaigns were carried out," albeit in a more negative fashion, as wartime demands for unconditional patriotism necessarily compromised their liberal principles (100). In short, the war and its interruption of the market-oriented mode of literary production effected a comprehensive transformation of the Chinese literary institution. The collectivist mode of production and the centralization of cultural control within the Party and the military were then carried over in both the PRC and Taiwan after 1949 for different lengths of time.

In actual practice, the wartime collectivist paradigm was configured differently in post–1949 Taiwan. Taiwanese scholar Zheng Mingli's 1994 historical overview of contemporary Taiwan's cultural policy, "Dangdai Taiwan wenyi zhengce de fazhan, yingxiang yu jiantao" [An examination of the development and influence of cultural policy in contemporary Taiwan], identifies three strands of policy in the early years: that of the party (KMT), led by Zhang Daofan;[7] of the military, led by General Wang Sheng, Chiang Ching-kuo's right-hand man;[8] and of President Chiang Kai-shek himself. These last are gleaned from Chiang's 1953 "Minsheng zhuyi yu le liang pian bushu" [Supplements to the chapters on education and entertainment in the principle on people's livelihood] and his annual state addresses on New Year's Day. Obviously, while Chiang Kai-shek's traditionalism and spiritual leadership set the tenor for Taiwan's cultural and literary discourses, in terms of institutional control over literary production, the party and the military generally held sway.

To get at the central spirit of the party's cultural policies, Zheng cites an essay written by Zhang Daofan in 1942, "Women suo xuyao de wenyi zhengce" [The cultural policies we need], arguing that it may be taken as the KMT's official response to Mao Zedong's famous Yan'an Talks on Literature and Art. Claiming ideological adherence to Sun Yat-sen's "Three Principles of the People," Zhang's essay served as the blueprint for official cultural policy in early post–1949 Taiwan, when Zhang served as head of the *Zhongguo wenyi xiehui* [Chinese writers' and artists' association], the most powerful organization of government cultural control.

Zheng makes the point that, insofar as both understood literature to be subservient to politics, Zhang's thinking was not very different from Mao's. Zhang, for instance, said: "Since the Resistance War, literature is no longer for language games and frivolous content for the leisure class. Rather, it has assumed the positive mission of 'awakening the people, organizing the people,' serving society, the Resistance War effort, and national construction" (14). Zheng argues that Zhang's doctrine was a hodgepodge of socialist ideals, poorly integrated with the KMT's reliance on capitalists. This view is corroborated by Laughlin's discussion of the Chongqing (Chungking)-based Writers' Front-Line Interviews Corps, whose mobilization campaign was aborted, Laughlin suggests, essentially because it lacked ideological strength.

Arguably, it was this ideological weakness that caused the Nationalist cultural policy to quickly degenerate into sinocentric rhetoric and neotraditionalist moralism. For instance, to combat the Communist espousal of class hatred, the KMT's right-wing ideologues extolled the Confucian idea of the innate goodness of human nature, *renxing*, which became sentimental rhetoric in the hands of cultural bureaucrats. The passive strategy of encouraging intellectuals to shy away from subjects that touched on hardcore socioeconomic issues, making discussions of "class" taboo, eventually backfired, especially in the counterhegemonic Nativist Literary Movement of the 1970s. In the meantime, those more susceptible to the KMT's ideological indoctrination developed conservative views, which became pervasive among cultural agents occupying the Mainstream position.

The war model of the literary institution changed over time. In the 1950s, when the Nationalist government anticipated imminent war with the Communists, mobilization was the impetus behind the most influential literary organization, the Chinese Writers' and Artists' Association, for which the *Wenxie* [The all-China resistance association of writers and artists] established in 1938 during the resistance war was a prototype. As the menace of war gradually dissipated in the ensuing decades, active mobilization faded as the principal objective of cultural policy. Still, the organizational framework remained in place to facilitate such missions as maintaining control over the ideological content of cultural products, pacifying and coopting potential opponents in the literary circle (nonconforming native Taiwanese writers, for instance), and indoctrinating school-age youth.[9] So important elements of the war model persisted, including the government's emphasis on a positive spirit of "cultural assent," something Laughlin also finds in the PRC's literary supervision, encouraging active support of officially sanctioned modes of literary expression, mutual supervision, and self-censorship (101).

It is difficult to draw a clear line between the ruling Nationalist party's and the military's involvement in cultural affairs, but it is widely believed that an intense power struggle between the party and the military at critical points determined the direction of the government's cultural policy.[10] What is certain is that the paramilitary organization of cultural activities during the Sino-Japanese and civil wars equipped the military with both experience and an organizational structure for regimenting cultural affairs. Furthermore, the high percentage of military writers active in Taiwan's literary field is often cited as evidence of the success at least of the "military literary campaign" (*junzhong wenyi yundong*), a particularly aggressive initiative attributed to Chiang Ching-kuo's protégé, Wang Sheng, leader of the Political Warfare Division faction of the military.[11]

Behind the success of the military literary campaign, however, were specific historical conditions. The two consecutive wars had caused massive dislocations of population, and a large number of young and adolescent men and women from traditional gentry families, seeking educational opportunities unavailable in their war-trodden, enemy-occupied hometowns, left home to attend government-sponsored, militarily structured middle schools.[12] A portion of these *liuwang xuesheng*, or dislocated students, eventually joined the military and retreated to Taiwan with the Nationalists in 1949. These young, relatively better-educated military personnel, largely of upper-class family backgrounds, constituted a unique subculture of people living in Taiwan's *juancun*, or housing compounds for military dependents. That a majority of the writers from the baby-boom generation who rose to fame in the 1980s were second-generation mainlanders brought up in *juancun* is explained partly by this heritage and partly by their superior connections in the literary field of the moment, in which the first-generation military writers were still influential.

It is important to add that, contrary to what might be expected, the military exhibited an "enlightened"—in a qualified sense—and above all pragmatic leadership style in cultural affairs, and this was its greatest attraction to young writers in the military ranks. Tolerance of western influences was part of this quasi-liberal gesture, and also explains the active role played by military writers in the modernist poetry movement of the late 1950s and early 1960s. An interesting mixture of loyalty and patriotism on the one hand, and stylistic avant-gardism and creative free play on the other, gave these writers an edge in the competition for both political and cultural legitimacy. At a higher level of policy making, the role of General Wang Sheng was critical. As Zheng notes in her article, even in 1978 when Wang was trying to put a stop to the politically disruptive Nativist debate, his speech was underlined by an almost ideology-free pragmatism. Wang stressed national security as the bottom line of cultural policy. The result, a policy that combined outward pragmatism with strong control behind the scenes, was characteristic of the soft-authoritarian governance of the Chiang Ching-kuo era (roughly from the early 1970s to late

1980s), a period of vigorous growth in politically conservative, market-oriented, middlebrow literature.[13]

To sum up, beginning in the late 1950s and throughout the 1960s and 1970s, the collectivist model of literary production dominated, but was challenged by elitist coterie journals first advocating Modernism, then Nativism. The challenges quickly evolved into a militant oppositional force, the Nativist cultural formation, in the mid-1970s, a real threat to the KMT-instituted cultural hegemony. It may be argued that the party's success in regaining control of the literary sphere in the aftermath of the Nativist debate owed much to Yaxian, a Modernist poet from the military ranks in his younger days, who assumed editorship of the *fukan* section of *Lianhe bao* [The united daily news] in 1977 and emerged as a literary media guru in the 1980s. In fact, in the latter part of the martial law period, with the relaxation of explicit political censorship, growing social affluence, and increased media independence, the civilian model from prewar mainland urban centers came to dominate cultural production in Taiwan. As *fukan* and the affiliated literary publishing industry successfully appropriated KMT-endorsed official culture for profit in an increasingly commercialized environment, they benefited from some of the mobilization strategies and organizational schemes of the early post–1949 period. Likewise, state agencies in charge of distributing public resources to cultural agents in the more specialized, differentiated, and professionalized cultural environment of post–martial law Taiwan—such as the *Wenjianhui* [Council of cultural affairs] at the national level and the *Wenhua zhongxin* [Cultural centers] at the local level—inevitably inherited some of the earlier period's ideas about the value and functions of literature and the arts. Most of the remaining chapters in this book are devoted to characterizing literary development in contemporary Taiwan as a process of incrementally dismantling the collectivist cultural institution, with slow progress toward a (re-)entrenchment of the civilian model dictated by the developing market and freer society.

THE NONOFFICIAL STRAND OF THE POLITICAL FACTOR: NATIONALIST-MORALIST DISCOURSE ON LITERATURE

Peter Bürger's notion of the literary "institution" directs attention to discourses that shape that institution, and in the present case to the distinctive discourse that has prevailed in modern Chinese cultural fields, including Taiwan's. It is effectively a political discourse but is not imposed as a matter of policy; rather, it constitutes what I call the "nonofficial political factor." Bürger refers to "general ideas about the function of art or literature," and the existence of a "hegemonic category" that "determines the outlook of subjects who participate in literature" (cited in Hohendahl's *Building a National Literature* 31). As an example of such a category, he cites artistic autonomy, prevalent in Europe since the late eighteenth century, which implies "that art has been freed from the realities of social life; a realm has been created for it in which purposive, rational thinking is not applicable" (30–31).

The "hegemonic category" in modern Chinese societies seems to be precisely the opposite. The literary discourse in modern China has generally freighted the literary vocation with heavy social functions like moral edification, political utility, and enhancing the well-being of the community. More specifically, for the last century or so it has been a nationalist-moralist discourse in aid of national strengthening and social reform aimed at modernization. As is frequently observed, the belief in literature's social efficacy has both boosted the position and increased the stakes of Chinese intellectuals' participation in literary activities. At the same time, the nationalist-moralist rhetoric is easily appropriated by authoritarian Chinese governments, whose cultural policies, ironically, are always geared at keeping the intellectual class under effective control.

Even as direct political control gave way to market forces in the literary field, the nationalist-moralist discourse persisted. In Taiwan, it animated the highly politicized Nativist and the Localist movements. Despite its populist appeal, this discourse behind both movements' idealism about literature is fundamentally at odds with the reality of literary production and consumption in contemporary Taiwan. The political legitimacy principle privileged in nationalist-moralist discourses on literature and art, whether of liberal or socialist-leaning movements, has constantly clashed with the more "truly cultural" legitimacy principle that underlies competition in Taiwan's increasingly autonomous literary field.

Three important scholars of modern Chinese and Taiwanese literature, Leo Lee, Shi Shu, and Chen Sihe, have spoken particularly well to the persistence of the nationalist-moralist discourse in modern Chinese literary culture at different moments. A review of their work below also highlights the tension at these different moments between the still hegemonic nationalist-moralist discourse and evolving conditions conducive to a more autonomous literary field.

Literary Imagination and Modern *Wentan* of the Republican Era

The first two chapters of Leo Ou-fan Lee's 1973 *Romantic Generation of Modern Chinese Writers* reveal a latent tension between the didactic intellectual discourse on literature and the market-oriented reality of cultural production in the 1920s and 1930s. Lee cites a letter typical of what literary magazine editors received from young people yearning to pursue a literary career:

> I want to do something beneficial to human society. So I have chosen literature. I intend to use literature to plead against the darkness of society and the sufferings of mankind, to convey my own thoughts and feelings, to portray the brightness of future. (37)

Commenting on this naïve but sincere expression of youthful passion, Lee suggests that although the notion of literature as a medium "beneficial to human society" is universal, in early modern China it was more particularly nationalistic, following conceptions of vocational obligation promoted by Liang Qichao and Lu Xun. May Fourth men of letters regarded themselves as "social reformers and spokesmen for the national conscience . . . consistent with the prevalent ethos of nationalism in the May Fourth era" (37).

Beneath the apparent consistency, however, is a definite incongruity between the young man's sense of mission and the reality of the *wentan* that attracted him to it ("what attracts and fascinates in the occupation of artist is not so much the art itself as the artist's lifestyle, the artist's life" [Bourdieu, *The Field* 66]). Lee portrays a fashion-driven *wentan*, immersed in occidental exoticism parading as political progressiveness and modern open-mindedness, but really largely playing to the market. Two sets of disparate historical forces were at work: those behind the young protégé's sense of mission and those behind the formation of a modern urban "literary arena" in the major Chinese cities of the 1920s and 1930s. On the one hand, the traumatic encounter with the West necessitated cultural rejuvenation as a means of social reform and national strengthening. This lent a halo of progressiveness to "modern men of letters," while recalling the traditional hegemonic discourse that regarded the primary function of literature as the enhancement of the material and spiritual well-being of the community. On the other hand, market forces were the main impetus behind the establishment of modern literary institutions, the publishing industry, and its increasingly apolitical, nonideological agencies of consecration. This latter set of market-driven forces constituted the principal dynamics and shaped the general outlook of the cultural field.[14]

Lee's chapter may be the first scholarly work that points to a modern literary field in prewar China that had achieved a substantial degree of autonomy, making it capable of imposing its own norms that appropriated and undermined the hegemonic discourse on literature. Particularly noteworthy is the paradoxical way the didactic nationalist-moralist discourse and the hedonistic international/occidental elements (dandyism, bohemian lifestyle, pseudo avant-gardism, etc.) were conjoined in constituting the contemporary literary imagination—both were integral parts of the cultural field in prewar, modernizing China.

"Colonial Modernity" and Taiwanese Literature of the Japanese Period

The discordance between intellectual literary discourses and actual practices also featured in the history of Taiwanese new literature, beginning in the mid-1920s. Taiwan's colonial status and the special type of modernization it underwent may have even widened the gulf. This is a central issue in Shi Shu's 1997 essay, "Shou yu ti" [Head and body], which focuses on the rise of a modernistic, "decadent" literature in Taiwan in the mid-1930s.

Shi argues that this literature's "decadence" was rooted in the temporal and spatial reorientation instituted by a "colonial modernity" that effectively transformed urban Taiwanese writers' cognitive mapping. The Japanese colonial government introduced Greenwich Mean Time in 1896; this was one way it began to regulate people's lives as it modernized Taiwan's industry, education system, and government bureaucracy. While Shi argues that it took a long time for the different temporal frame to sink in, the spatial transformation of cities in Taiwan appeared to exert immediate effects on writers' consciousness. The colonizers used traditional Japanese principles of space management to completely redesign and reconstruct the capital city of Taipei. The city and its surrounding mountains and rivers were thus laced with an elaborate structure of symbols conveying the imperial grace and exalted power of the Japanese empire.[15] All these became material manifestations of modernity:

Taiwanese writers and characters in their fiction who received a Japanese colonial education in the early 1930s and who lived in the new cityscape of Taipei—a central stage for the Taiwanese New Literary Movement—had grown up together with the Japanese colonial reign and lost their own history. In addition to the omniscient but elusive imperial majesty, what directly provided them with a new spatial imaginary were street scenes with a distinctively modern flavor, made of neon lights, automobiles, display windows of stores, as well as fancy places to loiter, like the asphalt-paved avenues, the open spaces of the traffic circles, the bazaars, the cafés, the movie theaters. Of course, included among these were all those transplanted fineries: the Japanese pleasure-house, the kabuki, the flute performances, the haiku, the cherry blossoms, and so on; they exuded a beauty that belonged to nowhere but Japan, the colonial motherland. (208–209)

By the mid-1930s, Japanese-flavored cityscapes assumed a new significance in Taiwanese fiction. At this time, many Taiwanese writers were either studying in or had recently returned from Japan. The modernized urban space in Taiwan evoked nostalgia for Japanese metropolises like Tokyo, which had become their "second home." Senses of loss and yearning became important sources for imagination and style that produced a literature of "romantic, bourgeois decadence."[16]

Beginning somewhat before this outflow of romantic "modernist" literature, and compounded by its colonial status, Taiwan had spawned reformist and nationalistic intellectual discourses in the 1920s strikingly similar to those in mainland China. Initially through such intermediaries as Lai He and Zhang Wojun, Taiwanese intellectuals were introduced to the literary concepts and writings of the May Fourth movement. During the 1930s, ties to the mainland movement loosened, but left-versus-right ideological strife in Japan continued to fuel politicized intellectual discourses on literature. Thus, when "decadent" modernist works appeared on Taiwan's literary scene in the mid-1930s, both left- and right-wing intellectuals sternly voiced their disapproval. They accused the modernist writers of indulgence, and of forfeiting the goal of Taiwanese new literature, which was "to enlighten the people and to achieve social reform."

The significant contribution of Shi's article, then, is that its attention to literary developments fired by Japan-looking nostalgia and responses to the colonial-modern cityscapes of Taiwan in the 1930s complicates Taiwanese literary history. It adds to the familiar tension between a persistent nationalist-moralist discourse and market forces notes about Japanese cultural influence and other colonial legacies.

Traditional Literati and Modern Chinese Popular Literature in the Urban Setting

Finally, a 1995 essay by the PRC scholar Chen Sihe calls attention to another important phenomenon: political and cultural terms of legitimacy may have actually fed into each other and become conflated in the consecration of modern Chinese literature. Chen wrote a series of essays in the early to mid-1990s exploring the problem of modern Chinese intellectuals' self-positioning. He proposes three basic orientations: orientation toward the political center ("consciousness of the court and temple," or *miaotang yishi*), emulation of western Enlightenment traditions ("public square consciousness," or *guangchang yishi*), and the more recently evolved professionalism ("consiousness of one's own position," or *gangwei yishi*).

Particularly relevant to this discussion is the second section of Chen's article "Minjian he xiandai dushi wenhua" [The "folk" and modern urban culture] (280–285), which deals with the intricate—both competitive and mutually implicating—relationship between the Enlightenment-minded public intellectuals of the May Fourth generation and the producers of China's popular (modern, urban) culture in the early part of the twentieth century. In essence, Chen suggests that modern Chinese urban popular fiction—referring primarily to the Mandarin Duck and Butterfly School fiction produced between the 1910s and the 1920s—was a byproduct of a drastic restructuring of the cultural field in the early twentieth century by members of the politically and morally conservative educated elite of the previous era. First defeated in the imperial reform of the late Qing dynasty, they found themselves excluded from the May Fourth new culture movement, which was dominated by knowledge systems imported from the West and brokered mainly by intellectuals returned from abroad. However, under a succession of reactionary Republican governments, this group came to assume control of various means of modern urban cultural production, including newspapers, magazines, photography, and film studios, and became modern China's first generation of urban cultural producers (281–282). While Enlightenment-minded May Fourth "new intellectuals" dedicated their literature to criticizing both the dominant and the dominated classes in the society, these conservative gentry-class artists adhered to residual worldviews and constantly sought to play up thematic features that embodied common desires shared by the state and the public. The popular, middlebrow literature they produced often imitated and parodied the progressive new literature, which acquired high culture status in the May Fourth movement. Throughout the 1920s and 1930s, these two intellectual groups constantly struggled over the urban cultural space, courting the same readership. While the nationalist-moralist discourse lived on in the work of both, aided by more powerful distributing agencies in the publishing industry and the mass media, the conservative group's more traditionalist, entertainment-oriented rendition enjoyed a substantial advantage in the market.

Chen cites the serialization and commercial promotion of Ba Jin's novel *Jiliu* [Rapid torrents] in the newspaper *Shibao* [Times] in the 1930s as a rare exception, an instance of popular success of May Fourth literature (285). Viewed from a different angle, however, to the extent that the family romance featured in Ba Jin's novels came closer to sentimental melodrama than most other May Fourth writings, it is possible to attribute their simultaneous appeal to high- and middlebrow readers to a happy convergence between the nationalist-moralist impulse and popular taste. Rather than treating it as an exception, we might consider this new formula's appearance in various urban art forms (fiction, drama, and film) that flourished in the 1920s and 1930s as a replacement of the earlier, more traditionalist popular genre, the Mandarin Duck and Butterfly School. The "historical romance" novels—by such writers as Xu Xu, Xu Su, and Wang Lan—that became immensely popular in Taiwan and Hong Kong after 1949, as well as a good number of Mainstream literary products in 1950s Taiwan, undoubtedly inherited this extremely viable formula.

Chen's work thus highlights—not necessarily intentionally—such important phenomena as the historical and social factors behind the production and distribution of modern Chinese urban culture at its early stage, the gray area between the high and popular cultures as the market expanded in the 1930s and 1940s, and the perennially intriguing role played by the nationalist-moralist discourse, with its high-voltage legitimating power for art forms everywhere in the genre hierarchy.

Recapitulations

The literary field in modern Chinese societies is typically conditioned by the convergence and interpenetration of the politically legitimate (authorized by either the state or the nationalist-moralist intellectual discourse) with the culturally legitimate (authorized by the market, at least in a transitional sense), and characterized by the constant assimilation and popularization (vulgarization) of legitimate culture by the market-oriented institutions that dominate the production, consecration, and dissemination of literary products.

The genesis of modern Chinese literature, or "new literature," was deeply embedded in political struggles in the general field of power and driven forward by prominent reformist intellectuals like Liang Qichao and Lu Xun. Their May Fourth disciples, by literally "taking over" and transforming magazines, the *fukan* of major newspapers, and publishing companies that originally produced popular literary works—*Xiaoshuo yuebao* [Monthly fiction], *Xuedeng* [Lamps of learning], and *Shangwu yinshuguan* [The commercial press] were well-known examples—elevated new literature to prominence. The cultural field at the time was hierarchically constituted, with commercially viable works such as the best-selling popular fiction of the Saturday School (or the Mandarin Duck and Butterfly School) at its lower end.

As all modern forms of high culture in modern Chinese societies tended to be imported from the West, traditionally educated men of letters caught in the transition found their cultural capital suddenly devalued. Western-influenced literary genres gradually replaced, or pushed to the periphery, traditional forms. This re-valuation had other notable effects. As shown in Chen Sihe's discussion, early in the twentieth century descendants of former traditional gentry families became producers and agents of the popular literature that emerged in China's commercialized urban markets. To a lesser extent, this phenomenon was repeated in post–1949 Taiwan. For instance, writers of the former gentry like Gao Yang and Nan Gongbo, extremely erudite in traditional Chinese learning, wrote historical novels employing certain generic and narrative conventions from premodern vernacular fiction, aiming them at the popular, less respected end of the established genre hierarchy. Unambiguously market-oriented, works like these still won attention from the more traditional sector of the scholarly community. For the most part, however, the interpretive frames applied to modern Chinese literary products tend to be derived from newly valorized, imported conceptions of high culture.

With a few exceptions, academic critics are contemptuously dismissive of market forces in literary production. As a result, the gray area between high and popular culture, the hybridity in genres, and the "middle-class" tastes that dominate the literary market in a transitional stage of capitalist development are seldom properly addressed. Even in the work of such highly respected scholars as those previously cited, despite their discerning observations on the contradictory factors in literary production, the primary concerns are still high culture issues (e.g., Leo Lee's reference to the May Fourth nationalist ethos, Shi Shu's attention to a modernistic aesthetic sensibility, and Chen Sihe's affirmation of the redeeming virtue of "folk" literature). By and large, the privileging of high cultural terms in modern Chinese literary scholarship has resulted in neglect of such matters as the shifts in genre hierarchy and literature's reciprocal relationship with the reading public. For instance, the "popular" aspects of some May Fourth literature are rarely a focus of critical deliberation for their own sake. Meanwhile, and more notably, we see the "overlegitimization" of the mundane, entertaining bourgeois literature cast in native or imported high culture categories.[17] It was not until the 1990s, after the market had become such an undeniable force in the cultural life of Chinese societies on both sides of the Taiwan Strait, that the analytical category of "popular culture" acquired a certain degree of legitimacy of its own, resulting in some revisionary perspectives in literary scholarship.

However, the market did not suddenly appear out of the "Great Divide" that heralded the post–Mao and post–martial law periods in mainland China and Taiwan, respectively. During the modern period—whether in prerevolutionary China or colonial Taiwan—the market was already an important complicating factor, playing host to coexistence and clash, competition and compromise between the opposing principles of political and cultural legitimacy in cultural production. As discussed, direct state intervention and a nationalist-moralist intellectual discourse complemented each other in imposing a controlling principle of political legitimacy on modern Chinese literary fields. Bourdieu calls this a "heteronomous principle of hierarchization" because it confers value according to standards derived from a sphere of activity external to the literary field—society's general field of power.

In modern China, during periods when the state's control over cultural production was strongest, the nationalist-moralist discourse could be turned to the state's advantage, but it could also be utilized by political challengers or social reformers to promote counterhegemonic activities. In periods of less state intervention and robust growth of an autonomous cultural field, the nationalist-moralist discourse could be even more ambivalent, more heavily mediated by the field's own operational laws. This kind of complexity reigned in Taiwan in the early part of the post–1949 era, when cultural agents were caught in extremely fluid and ambiguous conditions fostered by the interaction of political and market factors, and when respected academic critics—especially expatriate scholars in the western academy—held exceptional authority in literary consecration. Below is the publication history of an "anti-Communist" novel, Jiang Gui's *Whirlwind*, to illustrate the confusion. This perplexingly high-profile case from contemporary Taiwanese literary history demonstrates well the interaction of various forces that supported the contending legitimacy principles at work in the modern Chinese literary field, and how that interaction was manifested in shifting genre hierarchies.

COMPETING LEGITIMACY PRINCIPLES IN THE LITERARY MARKET: A CASE STUDY

Absolute control over literary production by the state lasted only a few years in Taiwan after 1949, and was followed by a prolonged period of competition between political and cultural legitimacy principles, beginning as early as the mid-1950s. Sometime around 1956, cultural agents occupying the Mainstream position, while ultimately adhering to the principle of political legitimacy, began actively experimenting with new aesthetic forms, and succeeded for the most part in establishing the norms and conventions (explored further in chapters 3 and 4) that have prevailed ever since in Taiwan's Mainstream literature.

Taiwan's precarious circumstances immediately after 1949 ensured support of the Nationalist regime by the majority of the country's mainlander intellectuals. Meanwhile, the wartime collectivist mode of literary production established the institutions of governmental control. However, inherent tensions existed in the objective conditions under which literary writing and reading occurred. The choice of a capitalist economy made market forces indispensable, and cultural producers had to honor commercial imperatives, even as they strove for political correctness, in order to survive in the quasi-autonomous field. The interaction of political and cultural legitimacy principles, however, was never direct and predictable. Among complexities surrounding the publication of *Whirlwind* was the disparity between the ways political authorities and intellectuals (academic critics) conceived of "anti-Communist" literature.[18] A superficial understanding of the government's political aims could obscure the broader intent of the dominant culture that it promoted, which exceeded the ostensible objective of resisting communism. Furthermore, scholar-critics and ordinary readers might disagree strongly about an individual work's cultural value. Hence, *Whirlwind*, a work of seeming political *and* cultural worth, was ironically snubbed by important segments of the literary field. This apparent paradox begs consideration of ulterior factors, such as the reading public's image of specific genres, the transitional nature of the literary market, and other issues involving reception and the functioning laws of the literary field.

Generally rated among the best "anti-Communist novels" from the early post–1949 decades,[19] *Whirlwind* nonetheless had an unusually rough start, being rejected by many magazines and publishers. The failure of its contemporaries to recognize this well-written, highly entertaining novel that is also sincerely anti-Communist remains a mystery to many in the literary community even to this date.

Jiang Gui was a former colonel in the Nationalist army and evidently began writing *Whirlwind* in response to the government's "anti-Communist literature" campaign in the early 1950s. The story revolves around a host of villains and victims, with virtually no hero. It is at once a story about the pathetic decline of several landowning gentry families in a northern Chinese province, modeled on the author's own clan relatives in real life, and a fictional account of the Communist peasant revolution in a regional context. The latter provides the master plot, around which a string of lively episodes are arranged. Two misguided former members of the local gentry get involved in the Communist uprising in their hometown, witness bloody struggles among revolutionaries, bandits, Japanese, and warlord armies, and finally find themselves ludicrous victims in a world overtaken by madness.

To his great surprise, when Jiang submitted the manuscript to magazines upon its completion in 1952, it was rejected by all. Bewildered and frustrated, he finally raised the money for a private edition of 500 copies in 1957. Copies circulated among the author's friends and KMT dignitaries gathered high praise. In the end, prefaced by a handwritten letter from Dr. Hu Shi,[20] the novel was published in 1959 by Minghua Publishing Co., a company with close connections to the United States Information Service (USIS). However, sales were unimpressive, and the publisher itself folded several years later.

Whirlwind's surprising failure has typically been interpreted in the following way. That the novel does not make a clear distinction between the corrupt Nationalist/warlord army and local bandits/Communists has been seen as a major political liability that could not be easily offset by the limited political capital Jiang himself possessed. Still, the offense was vague enough and not unpardonable, which explains the usefulness of endorsements from such prominent figures as Hu Shi and Jiang Menglin in finally getting the work published. Meanwhile, the commercial failure of this highly entertaining book has sometimes been attributed to oversaturation of the market by propagandist works in the few years separating its initial composition and final availability to the public—the author's original intention to appeal to anti-Communist sentiment simply backfired. In any case, the circumstances of the novel's publication offer a wealth of materials that promise to enhance our understanding of the literary culture of the 1950s.

First, it is clear that *Whirlwind*'s unusual journey to publication is not just about political control but also about the emerging bourgeois literary market, in which ideological content was by no means the most pertinent factor—the novel's genre characteristics were at least as important. As Perry Link points out in his introduction to *Roses and Thorns*, the primary task faced by creative writers in an environment permeated by political power is to make correct judgments about the constantly shifting "permissible scope" of subjects and thematic complexity tolerated by the authorities. Jiang Gui's misjudgment of the Nationalists' "permissible scope" may be regarded simply as inadvertent. What merits greater attention, in my opinion, is Jiang's inability to judge correctly contemporary readers' genre preferences.

Divergent Views of Consecrating Agents: "Old Fiction" Versus "New Fiction"

Most likely out of concern about his novel's marketability, for the 1957 private edition Jiang Gui tried to repackage it with a title in classical Chinese, *Jin Taowu zhuan* [A new biography of evildoers], and traditional-style chapter titles and subheadings (typically consisting of a rhymed couplet in classical Chinese summing up the content of the chapter), following the convention of vernacular fiction of the imperial period (Ying, *Jiang Gui* 243–244). Later, probably suspecting that the traditional-style embellishments might have actually turned away certain readers, he retracted these changes and restored the new literature-like title, "Whirlwind." Judging from Hu Shi's letter (printed as the preface to the novel's 1959 edition), Jiang seemed to have mentioned his difficulty deciding which image was more appropriate in a previous letter to Hu. Hu dismissed Jiang's concerns, reassuring him that his *baihua* (modern Chinese vernacular, or literally "plain speech") style was impeccable, and implying that this alone was sufficient warrant of the novel's worth for contemporary readers.

As Yu Guangzhong, Taiwan's preeminent poet-essayist, has rightly pointed out, Hu's opinion represents a layman's view that regards lucid and fluent narrative language as a criterion for literary excellence (*Wangxiang* 129). As a leader of the May Fourth language revolution championing writing in the vernacular, Hu understandably overrates the importance of the linguistic medium. While written in perfectly good modern Chinese, *Whirlwind* nonetheless does not exude the right flavor of "new fiction." Its indebtedness to traditional vernacular fiction (*jiu xiaoshuo*— "old-style fiction") is immediately recognizable: in the novel's episodic, plot-oriented structure; mode of characterization; and, most important, its residual worldview that readers intuitively associated with China's feudal past. As a matter of fact, C. T. Hsia, who played a crucial role in the novel's consecration by calling it "one of the greatest works of modern Chinese fiction," deemed Jiang's successful exploration of resources of the native tradition particularly noteworthy (523).[21]

Whether classing it with "new" or "old" fiction, both Hu and Hsia acknowledged *Whirlwind*'s cultural legitimacy. More important, both critics, well known for their anti-Communist feelings, seemed to place an even higher value on the novel's ability to capture the dark reality of the Communist insurgence on mainland China, a realism largely absent in officially approved anti-Communist literature. In a letter to this author in the late 1980s, C. T. Hsia still complained that Jiang's marginality in Taiwan's literary circle "was not his own fault," strongly implying that this lack of recognition had something to do with political interference.

Conditions of Reception in the Literary Market

Taiwan's reading public in the 1950s apparently held quite a different opinion about literature in general, and about *Whirlwind* in particular, than these elite reviewers. Jiang's uncertainty about the popular audience was justified. The mixed readership targeted by books like *Whirlwind* was composed of mainlander émigrés, Taiwanese gentry (older members of the gentry class, educated in traditional *shufang*, or tutorial classes for children, before they were abolished around 1920, were well-versed in classical Chinese), and students, who made up the bulk of the literate population at the time. Despite the unknown reading market of the first decade after Taiwan's retrocession—when a percentage of educated native Taiwanese were more fluent in Japanese than in Mandarin—it is safe to assert that for the educated class, mainlanders and Taiwanese alike, *Whirlwind*'s "old fiction" image evoked immediate association with outdated, feudalist worldviews. This undoubtedly hurt its reception. A remark by Ye Shitao, a leading Taiwanese critic brought up in the Japanese period and broadly read in world literature through translation, provides a good example. Pointedly identifying *Whirlwind* with the crude verges of traditional fiction, Ye observes that the novel is essentially a modern rendition of the *"caizi jiaren* (talents meet beauties)" stories, a popular traditional literary type with strong feudalistic implications, and not at all on a par with intellectually conceived "anti-Communist literature" *(Yige* 23). The assumption that "old-style fiction" occupies a low position in the genre hierarchy betrays influences from the nationalist-moralist literary discourse, dominant since the new culture movement in both mainland China and Taiwan in the 1920s, that stigmatizes traditional cultural products for their feudalistic roots. In other words, in justifying his taste judgment, Ye has resorted to a legitimacy principle that can be traced to the same nonofficial political discourse discussed in previous sections.

Further compounding such ideologically informed cultural legitimacy was another important factor, the emerging bourgeois literary market, with its own distinctive taste preferences. To this market, Jiang's writing in *Whirlwind* smacked of vulgar entertainment, often indulging in the salacious details of earthy subjects like whoring, and his dubious personal reputation didn't help matters.[22] The standard praise for *Whirlwind* is that it exposes the decadence of the morally corrupted gentry class, but in doing so it seems to have tarred itself with the same brush. In the judgment of Wang Dingjun—writer, retired editor, and cultural bureaucrat—the book's low-culture image could very well be what initially deterred editor-bureaucrats looking for more unequivocally "wholesome" model pieces of "anti-Communist literature." Indeed, in the 1950s the Nationalists pursued an energetic "cultural sanitization" campaign aimed at "cleansing" literature and the arts of "black" (criminal) and "yellow" (pornographic), as well as "red" (Communist) elements. The lack of enthusiasm for *Whirlwind* among both editors and readers in the 1950s, despite its engaging narrative and entertainment potential, was therefore symptomatic of the emergence of a new set of hegemonic aesthetic categories and evaluative criteria overdetermined by various factors in the society at large. The stark contrast between the reception of *Whirlwind* and that of *Lianyi biaomei* [My cousin Lianyi], another anti-Communist novel of the 1950s that earned not only the prestigious prize given by the Chinese Literature and the Arts Awards Committee but also enduring literary fame for its author, Pan Renmu, helps to illustrate the point.

My Cousin belongs to the genre of urban middlebrow fiction of pre-revolution Shanghai, a mature (print) media culture sustained by middle-class readers to which Mainstream literature in Taiwan is heavily indebted. What made *My Cousin* more attractive to critics and readers in 1950s Taiwan was, arguably, its "modern" image. This is conveyed in its narrative strategies: a focus on the heroine's personality, psychology, and motives, and interludes of sentimental romance. The two novels are set apart primarily by their genre attributes. Both are plot-oriented, richly entertaining "popular" fiction, but they are from different aesthetic time zones. While *Whirlwind*'s vernacular depiction renders human vulnerability into grotesqueries, *Cousin*'s polite approach always shields readers from what is truly disturbing. *Whirlwind* lost out, then, on two accounts: its anti-Communism was diluted by realistic ambiguity and it failed to account for changing tastes. Besides correct ideology, inoffensiveness of form had also become a requirement.

The new era was busy finding its own favorite forms of literature, and the government eagerly helped works like *My Cousin* achieve canonical status to fill a vacuum created by the absence of genuine high culture. That Pan Renmu was likened to Zhang Ailing, who was so successful with Chinese critics and readers everywhere, made perfect sense. Both women enjoyed an ideal position between high and popular culture in the genre hierarchy.

Deeper Political Undercurrents

I have argued that the market-driven cultural standard that stigmatized *Whirlwind* for its unsavory "old fiction" qualities included elements traceable to the new culture movement, a nonofficial political discourse prevalent in modern Chinese societies. Here I would like to stress the fact that this standard of cultural legitimacy, largely driven by middle-class tastes, also had roots in the Nationalist-endorsed official culture. While prison and censorship were the most notorious forms of cultural control, the limits and constraints indirectly imposed by cultural policy makers and tacitly supported by writers and artists played much more significant roles in shaping the general cultural outlook. Ultimately, *Whirlwind* compels a focus on the issue of officially approved expressive modes and aesthetic choices, which has not been given much attention recently in Taiwan's overheated political climate. For instance, disputes over the value of 1950s literature often revolve around a category of works by mainlander writers collectively labeled "*fangong huaixiang*" (anti-Communist nostalgia) literature, and generally boil down to questions about the comparative cultural capital of different groups in the population. Whose historical memories and trauma (or whose "*beiqing* [sadness]," to use the popular catchall phrase) should be privileged in literary representation—mainlanders', recalling their displacement by two major wars, or Taiwan natives', recalling their grievances from being twice colonized? Should recognition of one require rejection of the other? Politically motivated discussions like this obscure the real complexity of contemporary literary evolution. The fate of *Whirlwind* suggests something a great deal more intricate than mere political divisiveness: choosing the wrong literary mode to address one's own history can be equally problematic. Borrowing a metaphor from Bourdieu, the largest bank offering loans of cultural capital (literary prestige) to individual writers at the time was the government-sponsored system of cultural organizations like the Chinese Literature and the Arts Awards Committee. The bank's policies inevitably affected the nature of the projects individual artists chose to pursue. That Jiang Gui's work did not get him a loan directs us to the fine print of the bank's "anti-Communist" promotion in the 1950s. The government was not interested in sophisticated political fiction; serious considerations of ideology promote open debate, something the authoritarian government was keen to avoid. It is imperative that propagandistic literature be maximally readable and ideologically unambiguous. In Taiwan, the ideal type at the time was middlebrow romance, touched up with uncomplicated loathing for Communism. *Fukan* and literary magazines were filled with popular stories of the sort, especially personal reminiscences and lyrical sentimentalism. *Whirlwind*'s macabre presentational style, harking back to the dark, satirical mode of traditional vernacular fiction, did not fit the model.

Behind the scenes, there was some ambivalence among the government's cultural policy makers. Opinions were initially divided between hardcore anti-Communist ideologues and others who favored using literature and art as a diversion, a means of steering people away from subversive political activities. In an interview, Wang Dingjun recalled that on a certain day in the 1950s the China Broadcasting Company, where he was employed, was ordered to shop for popular songs to replace the military-style propaganda that had dominated their broadcasts. This incident, as Wang saw it, marked a turning point in cultural policy from strident to more moderate methods of control, while succumbing to the market's demand for entertainment.[23]

To conclude, despite their different points of reference, the three scholarly works cited in the second section of this chapter all deal with periods when, as in Taiwan shortly after 1949, robust growth of a relatively autonomous literary field was propelled by rapid capitalist economic development. In contemporary Taiwan, moreover, the shadow of the authoritarian ruling regime and the persistent presence of a nationalist-moralist discourse on literature created a distinctively mixed literary field with features both resembling and departing from those of the previous periods. First, the requirement of political legitimacy not only limited cultural expression but also engendered specific forms of conformist, complicitous popular culture, endowed with a special kind of legitimacy that made them competitive within the politically subjugated, quasi-autonomous field of cultural production. Second, urban popular culture also tried to claim the cultural high ground defined and endorsed by progressive public intellectuals. Whether they criticized or collaborated with the state, these intellectuals provided models that were subject not only to appropriation and parody but also to adulteration and popular conversion, generating a recurring pattern in which the intellectually legitimated culture, still under the sway of the nationalist-moralist discourse, was assimilated by the embryonic bourgeois culture, resulting in a typically hybrid literary product.

Whirlwind's early journey to publication further highlights some of the key arguments put forward in this study. The political factor, while unquestionably omnipresent in contemporary Taiwan's literary field, assumed various, sometimes veiled forms and affected the terms of cultural legitimacy, often in indirect, highly equivocal ways. Factors within the literary field, including middle-class taste preferences and the various predispositions of consecrating agents, supported competing legitimacy principles that inevitably mediated the impact of the government's official efforts. The clash of discrepant legitimacy principles also greatly complicated the genre hierarchy, a point to be developed further in chapter 7.

PART 2

CHAPTER 3

Soft-Authoritarian Rule and the Mainstream Position

A scene from President Chiang Kai-shek's funeral in 1975 is featured in a PBS television documentary on the history of contemporary Taiwan, *Tug of War*, first broadcast in November 1998. Crowds of civilian mourners form long lines on the desolate-looking streets of Taipei, many weeping on their knees and some climbing up construction fences to pay their last respects. The scene lasts for approximately one and a half minutes, but the narrator, who has focused on the political and diplomatic implications of this momentous event, makes virtually no comment to account for what the screen is showing—throngs of people obviously consumed by grief.[1] The narrator's underplay of the intense emotional drama silently unfolding at this moment betrays the filmmakers' general lack of interest in the complex cultural dimension of their subject. In particular, they attribute no significance to the fact that the Nationalist regime had successfully indoctrinated the majority of Taiwan's population and enjoyed considerable popular support, which only began to wane in the late 1970s, sometime after Chiang's death.

Typical of journalistic representations of contemporary Taiwan in the 1990s, the documentary weighted its coverage heavily toward the development of oppositional political formations and the Localist cultural awakening from the state's sinocentric historical narrative. The Nativist literary movement in the 1970s arguably marked the beginning of this process, and one scene in the film uses lines from a Nativist short story, Wang Tuo's *Jinshui shen* [Aunt Jinshui], to drive home this point. The use of a literary product to demonstrate the presence of popular resistance against a repressive political regime is of course extremely common. What is left out in this one-dimensional representation is the anxiety and uncertainty, the strenuous relearning and readapting that many writers, politicians, and ordinary citizens must undertake when officially sanctioned, dominant cultural discourses are challenged and pronounced illegitimate. The shift from sinocentric to Localist cultural frames between the 1970s and 1990s, both cause and effect of the disintegration of the Nationalists' authoritarian rule, was precisely such a process of reconstituting the dominant culture in Taiwan. It was at once liberating and disconcerting, while also generating tremendous energy and dynamism in the cultural sphere.

In response to drastic political changes, people in contemporary East Asian societies have time and again been required to renounce cultural values sanctioned by authoritarian governments and to varying degrees internalized by the majority of the publicly educated population over the course of the previous political epoch. Post–Mao China is the most dramatic case of wholesale value exchange—the experience of the Red Guard generation is an example *par excellence*—but similar reconstitution processes in places like South Korea and Taiwan also certainly warrant the growing scholarly interest in topics related to public memories of historical trauma.

A closely related issue is predominantly text-oriented literary studies' neglect of works by writers occupying the Mainstream position in literary fields of societies under authoritarian rule: postwar South Korea and Taiwan, Singapore, and post–Mao China. The power of authoritarian governments depends heavily on effective cultural control, yet the requirements of modernization dictate that cultural fields accommodate both the intellectual class's desire for freedom of expression and the mass audience's tastes. The system of cultural control is thus filled with provisionary devices, strategies of expediency, and a great deal of obligatory rhetoric, which together define the paradoxical nature of the Mainstream literary position. Each individual case, of course, is affected by historically specific factors. This chapter addresses the case in Taiwan by taking a closer look at the cultural control mechanisms through which the Nationalist government dominated Mainstream values until the "grand awakening."

"Positive" Cultural Control and Mainlander-Dominated Cultural Production

In his 1992 article, "Cultural Policy in Postwar Taiwan," Edwin A. Winckler coined a term to characterize the cultural policies enforced by Taiwan's Nationalist government: "The basic Nationalist line, in all genres, has been 'Sunist realism'—not just preventing heterodox statements, but promoting orthodox ones that stress the upbeat side of Taiwan's development." Cultural officials, moreover, constantly tried to "provide healthy alternatives to what they regard as unhealthy leisure activities" (36). This positive, forward-looking spirit constituted an important part of contemporary Taiwan's dominant culture, and its far-reaching influence on the collective psyche fits Raymond Williams's description of "hegemony":

> Hegemony is then not only the articulate upper level of "ideology," nor are its forms of control only those ordinarily seen as "manipulation" or "indoctrination." It is a whole body of practices and expectations, over the whole of living: our senses and assignments of energy, our shaping perceptions of ourselves and our world. (110)

A good illustration of the sustained ideological influence of the Nationalist-instituted dominant culture is the 1994 Taipei mayoral election. One of the contending parties, the China New Party, composed mainly of second-generation mainlander politicians who had split off from the Nationalist Party in opposition to President Lee Teng-hui's "Taiwanization" line, resorted heavily to its healthy, conservative, "middle-class" image in rallying the crowd. One much publicized claim was that New Party supporters politely cleaned up after each of their campaign rallies, and none of them wore sandals or chewed betel nuts during parades—a statement reminiscent of the New Life campaign launched by the Nationalists in the 1930s. The image of modern civility helped the New Party to reach urban middle-class voters and to differentiate itself from the grass-roots, lower-class supporters of the Democratic Progressive Party. People's internalized values from the conservative dominant culture of the martial law period thus have continued to play a significant role in later political struggles.

The inculcation of positive, moralist values, however, could not have been achieved without an effective control system, including a structure of enforcement agencies. The martial law–era KMT regime used both bluntly coercive measures and more subtle techniques to forge its cultural hegemony, but it is mainly the latter that have had a sustained effect on the society. Unlike the Communists' substantial reliance on "negative examples" to regulate the cultural field in Mao's China, the control system in Taiwan relied heavily on what Winckler calls "establishment cronyism." He includes this among other factors that conditioned literary production in Taiwan's martial law period:

As regards state, market and networks, for most of the postwar era, Taiwan had the worst of all three—political censorship, economic commercialism and establishment cronyism. The state was tough with its interventions and tight with its money. . . . Personal networks made objective reviewing and dispassionate discourse difficult, not to mention their use for surveillance and manipulation. (41)

Winckler puts his finger on a singularly important mechanism of cultural control in Taiwan after 1949, the placement of politically trustworthy agents at all levels of the cultural bureaucracy and educational system. This practice goes to the core of the "ethnic" or "provincial identity" (*shengji*) problem that plagued Nationalist rule in Taiwan for decades.

In the early post–1949 years, mainlander émigrés were the government's trusted allies; through them, it was able to effectively impose guidelines on and set parameters for media representations, school curricula, and all kinds of cultural activities and discourses. In the field of literary production, a large majority of publishers, editors of *fukan* in newspapers and literary magazines, and cultural bureaucrats were mainlanders. Competition was made much easier for mainlanders by the drastic policy that declared Mandarin the official language and banned Japanese, virtually excluding most established Taiwanese writers educated in the colonial period. This meant that political force played a significant role in delimiting the literary field for the early part of the post–1949 era, giving mainlanders a decisive advantage over native Taiwanese.

Needless to say, the mainlander-dominated literary field in the 1950s and 1960s was itself subject to a high degree of political constraint. Fortunately, however, over time the Nationalists' cultural policy gradually shifted from "coercion" to "hegemony," from heavy censorship and frequent incarceration of cultural agents to tactful engineering of broad-based voluntary support. Thus, a viable new dominant culture eventually developed, with several distinctive features. It was first and foremost conformist, not only because of direct political controls but also because agents with personal stakes in the culture industry were prone to develop coping mechanisms, to actively internalize the limits and constraints built into the field. It was also characteristically moralist, and in a society whose population had survived prolonged turmoil and war, the government's promotion of a moralist, uplifting, positive cultural outlook performed a much-needed function of collective healing. The moralist element, moreover, allowed those who served in "surveillance and manipulation" roles to rationalize their collaborative behavior. A benign patron-client relationship was consciously cultivated among the government, mainlanders, and native Taiwanese cultural producers (writers, artists, publishers, etc.). To pursue common goals, the right-wing government and the liberal intellectual community (mostly mainlanders in the early years) espoused a conservative culturalism that elevated traditional Chinese heritage and western classics. The affirmation of a "high culture" agenda, besides offering rich cultural resources, also functioned to divert attention from the poor circumstances in Taiwan prior to its economic takeoff in the 1960s and 1970s.

This study argues that this matrix of core values eventually played a determinant role in shaping contemporary Taiwan's literary culture and, for the sake of convenience, subsumes them under the term "sinocentrism." A rough equivalent, *da zhongguo yishi*, later became a catchword for the Localist critiques of the Nationalists' authoritarian and discriminative cultural practices. The official endorsement of sinocentric values directly affected what kinds of cultural capital were valued in the literary field, and its products were affected in turn. The recent displacement of this exceptionally potent cultural ideology will be discussed later. First we need to consider the historical circumstances that motivated the official sanctioning of sinocentric values, as well as the mechanisms through which sinocentric culture affected the literary field.

POLITICAL MOTIVES BEHIND THE SANCTIONING OF LITERARY MODES

In an authoritarian state, political objectives are often directly translated into the practice of literary production and consumption through strict regulatory controls. As we have seen, in early post–1949 Taiwan, mainlanders dominated the field of cultural production and coincidentally served as the government's tools of surveillance and manipulation. The mainlander monopoly inevitably affected the privileged modes of literary expression, as cultural agents' collective "habitus" naturally shaped legitimate literary discourse and evaluative criteria.[2] Writings in the approved literary modes gained access to the market and greater opportunity for recognition and prestige. The result was obvious inequity between those who possessed the right kinds of cultural capital—competence in Mandarin, familiarity with particular stylistic and generic conventions, and, above all, thematic resources in the right kinds of personal life experience—and those who did not.

It is relatively easy to discern the negative limits on cultural expression imposed by the ruling regime. Everyone was aware of the forbidden zones during Taiwan's forty-year-long martial law period. Public discussions of Marxism, Communism, or any brand of left-wing ideology were strictly prohibited, and even the most oblique criticism of the government and national leaders could incur severe punishment. Less apparent but equally important were covert forms of control and manipulation, like the sanctioning of particular literary modes. Such sanctions are established through tacit recognition among the producers of literature of which modes of expression might receive awards and which might be risky. Over time, hegemonic aesthetic categories are formed within these boundaries. The categories, affecting language, style, and thematic and generic conventions, have a profound impact not only on the creative side but also on the ways that people appreciate and assign value to literary products.

That the values endorsed by mainlander cultural agents tended to be sinocentric, focused on both the experientially recollected and the discursively constructed "China," may not be at all surprising. This tendency was strongly reinforced by specific political objectives the Nationalist regime sought to achieve in the aftermath of its mass retreat in 1949, motives important to our understanding of stylistic and thematic patterns in Taiwan's contemporary literature.

For the Nationalist regime, the number one political task immediately after 1949 was preparation for war. Following the outbreak of the Korean War, the United States began to assist in Taiwan's defense, including sending the Seventh Fleet to patrol the Taiwan Strait, helping the island to narrowly avert a threatened attack from the Chinese Communists. The Nationalists, however, still faced the prospect of Communist military assaults, while continuing to nurture their own hopes of regaining the mainland. Party leaders painfully realized that they had lost to the Communists not only on the battlefield but also on the ideological front. They were therefore very much on guard against a possible Communist insurgency and placed a high priority on thought control and ideological policing of Taiwanese and mainlanders alike.

Most previous studies of Taiwanese literature in this period emphasize the explicit manifestations of this political objective, especially the use of literature for propaganda in the anti-Communist and "Combat Literature" campaigns. It is true that literary publications were inundated with works that condemned the evil doings of the Communists while eulogizing the heroism of the Nationalist soldiers. However, the amount of overtly political, formulaic literature sharply decreased as soon as the Cold War standoff became a reality and the government's war preparations slowed down, becoming perfunctory by the mid- to late 1950s.

By contrast, broader and more long-term effects on literary production and reception resulted from the Nationalist regime's effort to achieve two other political goals. First, the government felt it incumbent on itself to "re-sinicize" the "descendants of the Yellow Emperor" in Taiwan who had lived under Japanese colonial rule for half a century. This meant that the social effects of a relatively successful Japanization program had to be reversed.[3] What is more, when the Nationalists retreated to Taiwan in 1949, mainlander refugees found themselves outnumbered by native Taiwanese by about three to one. It became a practical necessity for the Nationalist government to safeguard its minority rule by asserting its cultural superiority. The intense hatred of the Japanese invaders harbored by mainlanders, who had suffered tremendously in the eight-year resistance war, was quite different from the native population's ambivalent feelings toward their former colonizers, who had made a considerable contribution to modernizing Taiwan. Pejorative terms like *nuhua* (to transform into slaves), used in the government's official language to categorically condemn the Japanese colonial influence, stigmatized an integral part of the local cultural heritage and inevitably fostered discontent among the former colonial subjects (Huang, Yingzhe, *Zhanhou* Sec. 3).

The second political goal was in a sense imposed on the Nationalists by the Cold War world order. The Nationalist-ruled Republic of China remained a member of the United Nations Security Council until its forced resignation in 1972. To maintain its status in the international community as the sole legitimate representative of all China, the Nationalist regime resorted to valorizing a traditional Chinese cultural heritage, and stressed its own importance to preserving this heritage at a time when the Chinese Communists threatened to destroy it.

These political realities were behind the Nationalist government's strong backing of the monopoly position of mainlander cultural producers, which also privileged certain themes and subjects. The most obvious example is the delimitation of historical and geographical references in literary and artistic representations. While depictions of the Japanese period were restricted and virtually nonexistent, certain periods of the Republican era on the Chinese mainland became favorite, heavily romanticized subjects. Most works, not just patriotic tales revolving around the resistance and the civil war, were set in mainland China. These included lyrical reminiscences of gentry-class family life (Lin Haiyin, Pan Renmu, Qijun), imaginary reconstructions of folk legends and rural life (Sima Zhongyuan, Zhu Xining, Duan Caihua), and middlebrow novels of historical romance (Wang Lan, Yang Nianci, Pan Renmu, Fan Lu). References to the Communist Revolution and left-leaning intellectuals, obviously present in the real historical background, were either conspicuously absent or presented in censor-proof formulas.

Political manipulation of the public memory of the recent past and selective valorization of cultural traditions that serve to legitimize the ruling regime are of course common features in many postwar societies, East and West. In Taiwan these tactics were usually most obvious in the mass media, since they were under the strictest government surveillance. Large areas of historical experience—life in colonial Taiwan, for instance—were conspicuously absent from the space of cultural representation. Language was similarly controlled, with Japanese entirely out of the picture, and only a small quota of Taiwanese-language programs allowed on prime-time television. Thematically, TV drama series set in the early Republican era (*minchu ju*) and during the resistance war enjoyed disproportionately high popularity for nearly two decades. In contrast, it was not until the early 1990s, with popular TV drama series like *Ai* [Love] and *Taiwan shuihu zhuan* [Tribulations of the Taiwanese], that references to the ordeals and sacrifices of many Taiwanese soldiers, enlisted by the Japanese colonizer to fight in the Southeast Asian front of the Pacific War, became acceptable in popular culture.[4]

THE RISE OF THE *CHUNWENXUE* AESTHETIC CATEGORIES

The previous section focused on the impact of external determinants in delimiting the space of literary production. The government's political objectives charted forbidden zones and encouraged writing that fit into specific approved modes. Moreover, the authorities' reliance on a network of mainlander cultural agents for control resulted in the establishment of a prevailing sinocentric frame of reference. However, whereas the sanctioned literary modes were by definition imbued with a degree of political legitimacy, that alone was insufficient to "win the game" in a literary field that was to some extent still governed by its own laws. In "Principles for a Sociology of Cultural Works," Bourdieu says:

External determinants—for example, the effect of economic crises, technical transformations or political revolutions—which the Marxists invoke can only have an effect through resulting transformations in the structure of the field. The field exerts an effect of *refraction* (much like a prism) and it is only when one knows its specific laws of operation (its "refraction coefficient," i.e. its *degree of autonomy*) that one can understand what is happening in the struggles between poets, between the partisans of social art and the defenders of art for art's sake, or, in a broader sense, in the relationships among genres, between the novel and the theatre, for example, when one passes from a conservative monarchy to a progressive republic. (*The Field* 181–182)

Clearly, the 1949 Nationalist retreat resulted in a major transformation in the structure of the cultural field in Taiwan, superimposing a new logic, largely through government-trusted mainlander agents. But in order to understand exactly what happened within the literary field, what the objective relationships between different aesthetic positions were, and what strategies the government-trusted agents employed, one must examine the "specific laws of operation" of this social microcosm. Two significant phenomena of the early post–1949 era, the rise of the *chunwenxue* aesthetic and the establishment of *fukan* as the dominant publishing outlet, seem to have arisen precisely through refraction of specific political circumstances. Their entrenchment in turn shaped the specific laws of operation that governed competitive relationships among literary agents and among genres for decades to come.

Initially, the concept of *chunwenxue*, or "pure literature," was employed by Mainstream literary agents in their struggle for cultural legitimacy in a quasi-autonomous field of literary production. Despite the fact that the term had been used long before 1949, it acquired a new significance in contemporary Taiwan. The subjugation of literature to political control did not necessarily mean that political capital was directly translatable into cultural capital. Writers could utilize their political assets only to a point, after which they still had to earn recognition according to rules dictated by the cultural field itself. What is more, they were also anxious to defend the limited degree of autonomy still afforded to cultural production, so that what they did might become meaningful in a properly "cultural" sense. It was in these circumstances, then, that *chunwenxue* flourished in post–1949 Taiwan. As a means to fend off the government's efforts to enlist "cultural workers" in political programs, even while they were still willing to lend their service on certain occasions, these writers publicly rejected the formula that privileged the political utility of literature, championing *chunwenxue* in its place.

According to the personal recollection of Mr. Wang Dingjun, writer and veteran cultural bureaucrat, the government made a conscious, rather abrupt decision to switch from hardcore anti-Communist literary mobilization to encouragement of less strident literary products sometime around the mid-1950s. Apparently cultural officials at the highest ranks, seeing the ineffectiveness and inevitable market failure of propagandist cultural products with predictable content, orchestrated the establishment of this new Mainstream position.[5] Among other strategies, this more moderate program of cultural mobilization extolled *renxing* ("human nature" or "human-ness") in literature and art as an antidote to Communist literature that set out to "reform" human nature. Critical commentaries and creative practices that soon appeared suggest that Mainstream cultural agents largely bought into this official discourse. Years later, in the heat of the Nativist debate, Mainstream writer Peng Ge was still waving the "human nature" banner in his well-known rebuttal to the Nativists: "Butan renxing, he you wenxue?" [Without human nature, how can we have literature?] (*Butan* 3–24).

Within the cultural field itself, the general climate in the mid-1950s was favorable to this liberal-sounding reformulation of literature. It was well known, after all, that Mao's Yan'an Talks had emphasized literature's subservience to politics; why should one follow the example of one's enemy? The liberal-dominated intellectual magazine, *Ziyou Zhongguo* [Free China review], offered a forum for a group of writers to assert their right not to write propaganda.[6] In fact, though, *chunwenxue* was less about principle than about camouflage for writers who wished to be excused from the government's political mobilization. Resistance to overt political interference, not a sincere belief in art for art's sake, was the motivation behind *chunwenxue*. Loyal to the Nationalist government, these writers disliked being told what to do, but otherwise continued to adhere to moralist ideas about the proper uses of literature for depicting human nature, enhancing humanity, and building the national culture. Some even continued to express anti-Communist sentiment in their work, albeit of their own free will.

Genres that flourished under the *chunwenxue* banner included traditionalist prose (or belletristic writing, after the fashion of the traditional literati), familiar essays of various sorts, and women's writings focusing on domestic, personal subjects in the *fukan* of newspapers.[7] Lyrical, expressive modes were favored over descriptive, realistic modes. Even western-style "new fiction" and "new poetry" tended to be nontendentious and personal, avoiding potentially subversive elements. In this way, Mainstream writers resisted the government's more egregious political demands, procuring a space of relative autonomy for literary expression while complying with the guiding spirit of its cultural policies, producing a "conformist literature" cast in the subjective mode. Its prevalence may be attributed to the fact that a significant number of writers who supported the allegedly apolitical, genteel forms of *chunwenxue* played dual roles as writers and literary bureaucrats, straddling the political and cultural fields.[8]

Behind the entrenchment of *chunwenxue* as a viable aesthetic position was another politically initiated phenomenon, the conspicuously successful government program that encouraged creative writing, not necessarily political, in the military. Military writers like Zhu Xining, Sima Zhongyuan, and Duan Caihua were among the most productive fiction authors in the 1950s and 1960s, and one of the three major poetry societies, Chuangshiji [The epoch], consisted largely of military personnel, including such important names as Yaxian and Luo Fu.[9] As important participants in the cultural field, these writers boosted the KMT government's cultural hegemony throughout the martial law period. During the 1970s, when the Nativist literary debate broke out, they constituted an important pro-government faction, and some played "hit man" for the government, publishing furious attacks on the Nativist position.

Even after political interference let up, *chunwenxue* absorbed elements of subsequent trends and remained popular with writers and consumers. In the 1970s and 1980s, when Mainstream literature faced challenges from the Nativist movement and the increasing commercialization of the field, the term *chunwenxue* assumed a defensive connotation and remained the cornerstone of the Mainstream position. The situation didn't change until the literary field underwent the more drastic transformation of the post–martial law period.

FUKAN AND GOVERNMENT-ENDORSED MAINSTREAM LITERATURE

If *chunwenxue* was the aesthetic core of the Mainstream position under martial law, then the material institution that housed the inception, growth, and transformation of the Mainstream was undoubtedly the *fukan* of Taiwan's major newspapers. Here I examine the relationship between *fukan* and the Mainstream literary position in the early years of the contemporary era. Chapter 6 is devoted to the even greater role *fukan* played following Taiwan's economic upswing in the mid-1970s.

Fukan as a Hybrid Cultural Institution

Contrary to what is commonly believed in Taiwan, *fukan* are not uniquely Chinese. In *The Institution of Criticism*, Peter Hohendahl notes that cultural supplements to daily newspapers, *feuilleton*, became well established in France and Germany in the mid- to late nineteenth century (1850s to 1870s) (16). He associates *feuilleton* with the appearance of a lesser form of literary criticism in the public sphere, generally regarded by academic critics as trivial, subjective, and lacking in rigor. The practitioners of *feuilleton* criticism "concentrated on contemporary literary life. They reviewed the latest novels of popular authors; they reported on the theater, and informed the public of cultural life in general" (16). The close relationship between this form of popular literary discourse and the market was unmistakable: after the founding of the Second Empire, profit-driven publishers dominated the press, and *feuilleton* adapted to "the taste of a mass audience that consisted of heterogeneous social groups" (16). While the *fukan* in Chinese newspapers obviously displayed similar characteristics and were also primarily a product of mass media growth in a market-oriented economy, the unusually prominent role they played in Taiwan's literary field suggests additional circumstances unique to the case.[10]

Because important positions in cultural institutions were largely held by mainlanders, the *fukan* in post–1949 Taiwan naturally inherited their general institutional character more from prerevolution China than colonial Taiwan. However, in terms of content, *fukan* pages were products of hybrid historical impulses. As supplements to daily newspapers, *fukan* functioned primarily as leisure reading; they commonly included riddles, jokes, recipes, and travel notes, in addition to social gossip and publication news. More important, *fukan* came to provide a space for amateur writers to share intimate personal feelings and unorthodox forms of knowledge in a more or less casual manner with a sympathetic readership. For twentieth-century Chinese intellectuals caught in a prolonged transition from tradition to modernity, *fukan* were a unique outlet for residual cultural sentiments, where remnants of norms and conventions from China's longstanding literati tradition were still valorized. This last feature is particularly noteworthy for its spillover effect: as *fukan* also promoted creative writing, especially in the modern style, the interaction between its traditionalist and western-influenced modern tendencies created an interesting literary mix.

In mainland China, during the new culture movement in the 1920s and 1930s, *fukan* published the "new literature." They also served as a forum for discussion of cultural issues and as vehicle for disseminating "new knowledge" to the public. Scholars usually trace the origin of these progressive functions to the four major *fukan* in the Republican era—*Xuedeng* [Lamp of knowledge] of the *Shishi xinbao* [New current affairs] and *Juewu* [Awakening] of the *Minguo ribao* [Republican daily news] in Shanghai, and the *fukan* of *Chenbao* [The morning news] and *Jingbao* [The capital news] in Beijing—all under the direction of May Fourth intellectuals (Qin). Serious-minded *fukan* editors in post–1949 Taiwan consciously upheld this social enlightenment tradition. Less consciously acknowledged, however, was that in this very capacity as a powerful mass educator and sponsor of literary writing, *fukan* in post–1949 Taiwan inevitably served as an important "ideological state apparatus" for the authoritarian Nationalist regime. Among the first missions assigned to them after 1949 was public language education. *Fukan* were used not only to teach Mandarin to native Taiwanese educated under the Japanese colonial system but also to provide literary education to young mainlander soldiers who followed the Nationalist government to Taiwan after the civil war. Lin Haiyin, chief editor of the *United Daily News fukan* (hereafter *Lianfu*) between 1953 and 1962, and widely regarded as the person most responsible for bringing about the revival of "literary *fukan*" in post–1949 Taiwan, once half jokingly remarked that she was chosen for the job because she spoke Mandarin with an impeccable Beijing accent. A brief look at Lin's career sheds significant light on the relationship between *fukan* and the authoritarian government in Taiwan.

Lin Haiyin and the "Literary *Fukan*"

Several of Lin's personal assets proved valuable when she was appointed editor of *Lianfu* shortly after the Nationalists' retreat to the island. A Taiwan native, Lin was brought up in Beijing, where she received professional training in journalism. Her pedigree and linguistic ability were undoubtedly useful, but her ethnic origin was equally valuable: it was to the advantage of the Nationalists as minority rulers to include sympathetic native Taiwanese in their cultural bureaucracy. Being female was also a plus, since cultural policies conceived within a harsh political reality might be softened somewhat by a feminine façade of gentleness and benevolence, which partly explains the high percentage of women editors at the time. In addition, Lin possessed a dynamic personality, resourcefulness, and disarming forthrightness, enabling her to establish extensive networks of cultural agents and to mediate between them and the government.[11] Since the 1990s, Localist critics have showered praise on Lin for her patronage of such native Taiwanese writers as Zhong Lihe, Huang Chunming, Qideng Sheng, Zheng Qingwen, and Lin Huaimin at a time when native Taiwanese suffered considerable discrimination. However, while Lin undoubtedly served as a liaison between the government and native Taiwanese writers, ultimately her importance as a promulgator of Mainstream literary values far outweighs her contribution to the Localist cause.

By the mid- to late 1950s, several state-run literary associations and magazines folded and, with the rise of independent artists, literary organizations, and journals, cultural production appeared to be opening up.[12] In particular, writers associated with two independent periodicals, *Free China Review* and *Wenxue zazhi* [Literary review], began to call for greater creative freedom, setting the stage for the Modernist literary movement. Most Mainstream literary agents—Lin Haiyin among them— chimed in. Lin herself contributed to the prestigious *Literary Review*, even declaring that a revision by its editor, Xia Ji'an (T. A. Hsia, 1916–65), "rescued" one of her short stories ("Xiaoshuojia" 22–23). A fine writer herself, Lin was a conscientious editor and generously mentored aspiring novice writers who submitted their works to *fukan*, quite a few of whom later had distinguished literary careers. This relationship, however, must not obscure the fact that within the structure of the literary field, the role played by *fukan* editors like Lin was essentially different from that played by liberal academics like Xia Ji'an and Yu Guangzhong, who straddled the Mainstream and Modernist positions. The latter tended to insist on artistic autonomy, grounded in literary concepts imported from the West, despite their political support of the government. In contrast, Lin and her peers had to be more responsive to demands from the political authorities and were more susceptible to the sinocentric dominant culture. This was the case because different standards were applied to academia and the media when it came to tolerance of dissent. Selecting and editing submitted manuscripts, Lin was in a privileged position to disseminate her own artistic views, but she was also actively engaged in shaping and nurturing a viable Mainstream aesthetic position within the confines of official ideology. An archetypal Mainstream cultural agent, Lin is frequently associated with advocacy of *chunwenxue*: she even used it as the title of a journal she co-founded in 1967. Her case makes it evident that Mainstream writers' advocacy of *chunwenxue* served simultaneously as a buffer against the government's political imposition and as testimony to their integrity as independent cultural agents.

Fukan Editors: Pillars of Politically Sanctioned Cultural Orthodoxy

There are two main features of the Nationalist government's management of Mainstream literature in the early days of the post–1949 era. The first was concern with decency and propriety in the country's cultural products, and *fukan*, as one of the most closely supervised media, were expected to set positive examples. In addition to explicitly propagandistic literary mobilization programs, the government endeavored in other ways to create an orthodox image for Mainstream literature that embodied state-sanctioned cultural values. This was clearly the objective of the *wenhua qingjie yundong*, or Cultural Sanitation Campaign, in 1954, aimed at weeding out the pornography, tabloid exposés, and "hoodlum" literature that were said to have inundated the market. While consistent with the Nationalist government's emphasis on a "positive" outlook, the campaign also revealed the miserable condition of the literary field at the time. The absence of elite native Taiwanese writers, a direct consequence of earlier harsh repressive measures taken against suspected Taiwanese dissenters, including the February 28 massacre in 1947, clearly contributed to the problem.

The second feature of the government's management of Mainstream literature was rooted in the fundamental need in any historical epoch to establish an orthodox genealogy that legitimizes contemporary practices, literary and otherwise. In the Nationalists' ideological battle with the Communists, a crucial task was to reinvent and redefine the May Fourth tradition, the acknowledged seedbed of all modern Chinese literature, in order to wrest it from the Communist version of literature that foregrounded its revolutionary aspect.

From the point of view of the majority mainlander writers, this was a conspicuous vacuum in the literary field. While most of them had come up in the new literature tradition, the leftist element of that tradition made it impossible for the Nationalists to endorse it wholesale. Consequently, the

Nationalists adopted a highly selective stance toward the legacy of the May Fourth movement. Its *chunwenxue,* "purely cultural" dimension and accomplishments, including its use of vernacular language, were selected for emphasis, while its antitraditional and populist, revolutionary aspects were condemned as "blind spots" that had aided the rise of Communism in China. Though relatively few in number, liberal intellectuals who had established reputations in the Republican era before going to Taiwan with the Nationalists, like Hu Shi and Liang Shiqiu, became literary gurus in Taiwan's post–1949 cultural world. Moreover, the selective honoring of romantic, traditionalist writers from before 1949, like Xu Zhimo and Zhu Ziqing, whose works were included in middle-school textbooks, helped to foster subjective, lyrically sentimental artistic visions

In her capacity as editor of a highly regarded literary *fukan*, Lin Haiyin did not just help to consolidate this selected May Fourth tradition and to integrate it into Taiwan's Mainstream literary production but also added her own, more realistically oriented stylistic preference. Avoiding subversive themes like "class" and "revolution," Lin focused on the humanist spirit of May Fourth and its lucid, easy-to-understand prose. In this manner, mainlander writers of Lin's generation consciously or unconsciously engaged in rewriting the norms and conventions of pre–1949 modern Chinese literature, converting its ideological messages while leaving the aesthetics largely intact.[13]

That Lin contributed significantly to shaping a Mainstream literary culture that answered the ethical and political demands of the Nationalist government had to do partly with her own sense of mission as a patriotic cultural worker and her genuine belief in the war against the Communists. However, neither her allegiance to the government nor her prestige in the literary field could safeguard her from being targeted for censorship, which speaks to the precarious situation in which *fukan* editors often found themselves. According to a well-circulated story, Lin allegedly published a poem suspected of implicit political criticism, leading to her resignation as chief editor of *Lianfu* in 1962. *Chunwenxue*, the journal she founded after leaving, may even be seen as a vindication, flaunting the term "*chunwenxue*" in affirmation of literature's freedom from political interference.[14] Nonetheless, unlike vocal political and cultural critics such as Boyang, who was actually incarcerated for offenses committed as a *fukan* editor, Lin largely maintained her active support of the government, saving her complaints mostly for private conversations.[15] Such voluntary support of the dominant culture by trusted cultural agents was the root of self-imposed limitations that eventually translated into accepted norms and distinctive traits of contemporary Taiwan's Mainstream literature.

Impressive individuals like Lin Haiyin undoubtedly helped to make *fukan* the dominant institution of literary production and consecration. Lin's immediate successor, Ping Xintao, steered *Lianfu* in a more popular direction at a time when elitist intellectual journals played a leading role in Taiwan's literary field. With the society's economic progress and the growing market orientation of the mass media, however, *Lianfu* again became an important player under the charismatic leadership of poet-editor Yaxian, arguably the most influential figure on Taiwan's literary scene in the last twenty years of the twentieth century. Like Lin, Yaxian guarded and promoted the politically instituted Mainstream aesthetic position with dedication and gusto, making it extremely popular among the rising bourgeois of the 1980s, while striving to preserve *fukan*'s function as a significant "ideological state apparatus" even after the government relinquished its high-handed cultural control. This phenomenon will be explored further in part 3.

CHAPTER 4

The Modernist Trend and Aestheticization of the "China Trope" in Mainstream Literature

Under authoritarian rule, with all potentially subversive artistic and cultural formations actively suppressed, the Mainstream position is by definition the one endorsed by the political authorities, and enjoys a monopoly on power to define legitimate literary discourses. Despite their privileged position and better access to government resources, however, individual Mainstream agents must still utilize their cultural capital tactfully. Competition within the government's prescribed parameters can still be fierce and dynamic.[1] This was especially the case in Taiwan when the government relaxed its aggressive literary mobilization efforts in the mid- to late 1950s, and an elitist, western-influenced literary formation championing artistic autonomy began to emerge from within the Mainstream ranks. This was the incipient Modernist literary movement, and even this early, it was able to claim a degree of cultural legitimacy.

The first part of this chapter examines the early development of the Modernist trend, paying special attention to its relationship with U.S.-influenced liberalism in the 1950s and 1960s. An English essay by Xia Ji'an, included as an appendix to the first (1961) edition of *A History of Modern Chinese Fiction* (by Xia's brother, Professor C. T. Hsia), is analyzed as an eyewitness account. Next I examine the winning strategies of two distinguished literary figures, Xia Ji'an and Yu Guangzhong, to show how the Modernists established themselves in the Mainstream-dominated literary field. Xia, the liberal-minded founder-editor of *Literary Review*, died prematurely, before the Modernist position was consolidated in the mid-1960s, but is nonetheless considered the Modernist trend's chief engineer, particularly of its fiction component. Yu Guangzhong, widely recognized as one of the greatest living Chinese poets, helped to establish the aesthetic concepts of literary modernism through his advocacy of "neoclassicism" in poetry and his

"Modernist prose" project.[2] Both of these figures were instrumental in establishing the stylistic and technical principles of the Modernist position, even while they adhered to a Mainstream political stance.

The Modernists' success is attested to not only by the high acclaim accorded their literary products but also by the far-reaching influence of their aesthetic innovations. The second part of the chapter assesses this influence through a discussion of the aesthetic transformation of the literary imagination of "China."

As the Nationalist regime began indoctrinating Taiwan into its self-legitimizing sinocentric worldview following its retreat to the island in 1949, "China" naturally emerged as an important figure in Taiwan's Mainstream literary production. In the 1960s and 1970s, however, the literary imagination of "China" changed under the influence of modernism. The signifier was gradually dissociated from its physical referent, namely the Chinese mainland, emptied of its overt political contents, and reinvented as a potent aesthetic trope. This gave the politically subordinated Mainstream position the cultural legitimacy it needed to remain competitive within Taiwan's increasingly autonomous field of cultural production. Paradoxically, this aestheticization allowed "China" to be displaced later, either by the image of a pristine Taiwan as motherland or by the emergent global imagination.

Keep in mind that although this aestheticization process is revealed partly in a discussion of three major essayists, Yu Guangzhong, Zhang Xiaofeng, and Wang Dingjun, it is the artistic positions in the literary field, rather than the cultural agents who occupy them, that are understood and compared throughout as fixed categories. In this chapter I am concerned primarily with the Mainstream and Modernist positions. Owing to the Nationalist government's pro-West stance, the relationship between them was often intimate and mutually implicating.

EMERGENCE OF A NEW AESTHETIC POSITION

In retrospect, 1956 marked an important turning point. That year, the government terminated the annual awards sponsored by the Chinese Literature and the Arts Awards Committee and, along with them, the official publication of the Chinese Writers' and Artists' Association, *Wenyi chuangzuo* [Creative writings]. These had been the two most important means of the government's direct intervention in the cultural field during the early post–1949 years. The initial loosening of political control was accompanied by the appearance of a small, independent coterie journal, *Literary Review*, which published creative writing as well as critical reviews. The journal's chief editor, Xia Ji'an, a graduate of Shanghai's St. John's University, was an English professor at National Taiwan University. The unusually high caliber (by the standards of the time) of the works published in *Literary Review* quickly earned it high prestige.

Another concurrent event caused an immediate sensation: the inaugural meeting of *Xiandai shishe* [Modernist poetry society], complete with a heretical manifesto calling for a "horizontal transplantation" of the modern western poetic tradition into the Chinese literature practiced in Taiwan at the time. The society's charismatic leader, Ji Xian, was one of the very few mainlander émigré writers who had made reputations in pre-revolution Shanghai (Ji Xian, under the western-sounding pen name of Luyishi); most established literary figures did not follow the Nationalists to Taiwan. Given that most active writers in the 1950s were just beginning to learn the trade, Ji Xian's background gave him unique cultural capital.

It was also at this time that the literary section of *Free China Review*, a highly prestigious liberal intellectual journal, entered a phase of vigorous development under the editorship of a fine writer, Nie Hualing,[3] providing another important forum for serious literary work. Meanwhile, creative literary products, in particular the subgenre of *sanwen* (the "informal essay" or "familiar essay," derived from *xiaopin wen*, a lyrical prose genre of the Qing dynasty)[4] continued to flourish in the *fukan* pages of major newspapers. Despite the fact that there was considerable overlap of cultural agents involved in all of these literary circles, a new hierarchy was clearly taking shape, with pioneers of the Modernist literary movement generally commanding greater symbolic capital than the *chunwenxue* wing of the Mainstream position.

It is important to stress that the Modernist position in contemporary Taiwan derived its unique function and identity from a context radically different from that of the various western modernist strands, one embedded in "China-versus-the-West" politics. Typical of postcolonial cases, Taiwan's Modernists regarded native literary development—at least at that time—as inferior to its western counterparts and in need of a major overhaul to "modernize" itself. Occupants of the Modernist position tended to be from a socially distinct group with superior academic capital, especially a facility in foreign, primarily western languages. Faculty and students in university English departments thus formed the core of Taiwan's Modernist literary movement.

Aesthetically, Taiwan's Modernist precursors followed formalist precepts, affirming the primacy of language and form over theme and content. Ideologically, the Modernist literary movement was an extension of the liberal trend that had enjoyed vigorous growth in Taiwan's intellectual arena in the early part of the epoch. Early Modernists followed close on the heels of liberal political critics associated with the only magazine that offered critiques of the Nationalists' political and social policies, *Free China Review*.

In *Modernism and the Nativist Resistance* I argued that, aided by borrowed authority from the hegemonic liberal discourse of the West, the Modernists in Taiwan employed liberal ideology and the concept of artistic autonomy as effective challenges to Taiwan's conservative, neotraditionalist dominant culture. However, works of fiction in the spirit of this cultural critique were mostly written later in the movement: Bai Xianyong's *Taibei ren* [Tales of Taipei characters] was published in 1971; Wang Wenxing's *Jiabian* [Family catastrophe] in 1972, *Beihai de ren (shang)* [Backed against the sea, part I] in 1981; Bai's first novel, *Niezi* [Crystal boys], in 1983; and Wang Zhenhe's *Meigui meigui wo ai ni* [Rose, rose, I love you] in 1984. Strictly speaking, West-inspired modernism influenced Taiwanese artists working in different forms at different times: painting and poetry in the 1950s, fiction in the 1960s and 1970s, and drama in the late 1970s and early 1980s. Still, a full-fledged Modernist doctrine—self-consciously elitist and potentially subversive—took shape within a decade of the movement's initial appearance, sometime in the mid-1960s.[5]

Early Orientations of the Modernist Position

To understand the lasting impact of the Modernist trend on Taiwan's literary field, greater emphasis on contextual factors is needed, rather than an exclusive focus on the contents of imported artistic doctrines, which more often than not underwent considerable modification in the hands of local artists. Modernist ideas engendered visions of alternative cultural orders among the postwar generation of intellectuals in Taiwan, who were as yet not too deeply implicated in the dominant culture's controlling mechanisms. The real or perceived inadequacies of Taiwan's historically specific cultural conditions thus ultimately determined the nature of the

Modernist influence, despite the fact that the movement's rhetoric was inevitably couched in the familiar terms of every other nonwestern society's modernity project.

At the root of most of the problems in Taiwan's post–1949 cultural environment was the reinvented country's fundamental lack of normalcy. The Nationalist government that retreated to Taiwan in 1949 brought with it not only mainlander refugees but also the military, bureaucratic, cultural, and educational institutions of the Republic of China. The new state, however, was backed by scanty material resources, and anticipation of resumed war initially discouraged long-term development plans. Consequently, many cultural institutions were established on a temporary basis, and their normalization was extremely drawn-out in some cases. Even in Academia Sinica, the country's foremost research institute, it was not until the late 1980s that a preparatory council for the Institute of Chinese Literature and Philosophy was set up.[6]

Arts and literature education, meanwhile, carried the extra burden of ideological indoctrination. The painful lesson the Nationalists had learned in the civil war resulted in such drastic measures as banning nearly all works from the Chinese new literature tradition whose authors still lived in mainland China. Lingering enmity against the Japanese, meanwhile, dictated the eradication of any legacy of Taiwanese new literature. With only this mutilated literary heritage to work with, courses on modern and contemporary literature were virtually nonexistent in university Chinese departments, and the stiflingly rigid and highly authoritarian education in a traditional cultural heritage finally sent certain branches, like creative writing and literary criticism, into long-term exile.[7]

The academic hiatus created by these circumstances magnified the influence of individual intellectuals, and the fact that Taiwan was incorporated into the U.S.-led anti-Communist coalition in the Cold War made American liberalism a major source of intellectual inspiration. While the Nationalist regime paid perfunctory respect to the principles of liberal democracy, real challenges to its authoritarian rule were not tolerated, as liberal intellectuals associated with *Free China Review* and *Wenxing* [Literary star] quickly realized after a series of arrests and crackdowns extending into the late 1960s. Across the general cultural field, however, the accessibility of American intellectual resources, facilitated by the U.S. Information Service, nourished significant cultural trends—the Modernist movement being the most prominent—while making liberal thought a powerful force in Taiwan's academic community for many decades.[8]

The extraordinary importance of Xia Ji'an's artistic vision in shaping contemporary Taiwan's literary institution is properly understood against this background.[9] In addition to his editorial work for *Literary Review*, Xia was also a charismatic teacher, whose success as an English professor in the Foreign Languages and Literature Department at National Taiwan University between the late 1950s and early 1960s was legendary. Several of his students, including writers Bai Xianyong, Wang Wenxing, Chen Ruoxi, Ouyang Zi, and Dai Tian, as well as scholars Leo Ou-fan Lee, Joseph S. M. Lau, and scholar-poet Wai-lim Yip, later became key figures in the Modernist literary movement or among its academic promoters. It is therefore worth looking at Xia's personal views on Taiwan's literary culture in the early post–1949 years, well represented in an essay appended to his brother C. T. Hsia's landmark monograph, *A History of Modern Chinese Fiction*, published by Yale University Press in 1961.

Written in an intimate style, the essay contains Xia's sensible, albeit pessimistic observations of a bleak cultural landscape in the first decade after 1949. The only positive note comes from an underlying faith in a broadly defined liberal humanism that was clearly prevalent in the country's general intellectual climate. Xia takes genuine consolation in the fact that Taiwan was spared the atrocities committed by the Communist government on the mainland, quoting Dr. Hu Shi: "Here, at least, we are enjoying the freedom of silence" (516). He blames the current cultural environment for the poor performance of Taiwan's literary field. Fiction was largely of the "escapist" type, including markedly superficial pulp romances, something the *Literary Review* vowed to fight, and to replace with down-to-earth "realist" writings. Men of letters were "notoriously gregarious," more interested in attending meetings and literary salons than in offering honest criticism to their peers. At the same time, officially designated cultural workers, members of the Chinese Writers' and Artists Association, for instance, were not given any real power, only meager support from the government.

Xia's attitude was perhaps typical of intellectuals in countries caught in the Cold War rivalry between the superpowers, when national survival and the prevention of Communist insurgency were used to justify political authoritarianism. In Taiwan, this mentality was undoubtedly more pronounced among mainlander intellectuals, many of whom were descendents of landed gentry families targeted by the Communist land reform on the mainland and felt very lucky to be in Taiwan. They willingly tolerated political constraints, placing their hopes in individual potential to overcome

unfavorable circumstances and elevate the culture. This locally and historically conditioned version of western liberalism and its aesthetic counterpart
of modernism became the ideological underpinning of the group of Xia's
students who founded the journal *Xiandai wenxue* [Modern literature] in
1960. Other values specifically endorsed by Xia, such as cultural cos-
mopolitanism, antiromanticism, and artistic autonomy, were also adopted
by his students, many of whom later became important Modernist writers.
While some ardently challenged the ethnic bias of the Nationalist dominant
culture, they otherwise tended to follow the road paved by Xia Ji'an in those
early years, channeling their intellectual discontents into the quest for professional excellence, and rationalizing political interference as unavoidable
under the historical circumstances.

Xia's death in a car accident in 1965, several years after he immigrated to the United States, prevented him from seeing his impressive legacy
flowering in Taiwan's literary arena. Part of that legacy, a western-
influenced institution of literary criticism based on the doctrines of New
Criticism, was successfully introduced in the late 1960s and 1970s by a
group of returned scholars, redressing a serious lack of professional criticism over the previous decade. Influential academic critics like Yan
Yuanshu, Zhu Limin, and Ye Weilian (Wai-lim Yip) were widely recognized as authoritative consecrating agents. Like the core group of Modernist fiction writers, a number of these academic critics were affiliated
with the Foreign Languages and Literature Department at National Taiwan University, where they had been immersed in the literary culture Xia
helped to establish.

Winning Strategies of Modernist Precursors

The strategies of the agents and institutions that are engaged in literary
struggles, that is, their position-takings (either specific, e.g. stylistic, or
not, e.g. political or ethical), depend on the *position* they occupy in the
structure of the field, that is, on the distribution of specific symbolic capital . . . and, through the mediation of the dispositions constituting their
habitus (which are relatively autonomous with respect to their position),
on the degree to which it is in their interest to preserve or transform the
structure of this distribution and thus to perpetuate or subvert the existing rules of the game. But . . . these strategies also depend on the state
of the legitimate problematic, that is, the space of possibilities inherited
from previous struggles, which tends to define the space of possible

position-takings and thus orient the search for solutions and, as a result, the evolution of production. (Bourdieu, *The Field* 183–184)

Previous scholarship has had much to offer on the artistic accomplishments of the Modernist writers as well as the partisan struggles and controversies between them and the Nativists in the 1970s. Shifting to a more contextual approach, this study focuses on a different dimension of the Modernist movement: its intimate and ambivalent relationship with Taiwan's Mainstream literature. The remainder of this section uses examples from two distinguished writer-critics, Xia Ji'an and Yu Guangzhong, to illustrate how a viable Modernist aesthetic position was established within a literary field dominated by Mainstream writers.

Knowledge and expertise in western literary traditions was undoubtedly an important form of symbolic capital for both Xia Ji'an and Yu Guangzhong, especially valuable because of its relative rarity at the time. More important, though, are the specific strategies they employed, conditioned by the "space of possibilities inherited from previous struggles," to push forward the evolution of Taiwan's literary field. In Bourdieu's words, by entering the game, they "tacitly accept[ed] the constraints and the possibilities inherent in that game (which [were] presented not in the form of rules, but rather as possible winning strategies)," while effectively affirming their own "differential deviations" (184). Xia and Yu posed themselves as challengers to the Mainstream by affirming their differences *within* the "space of possible position-takings"; Xia promoted an elitist concept of "serious literature," while Yu championed a modernistic aesthetic focusing on linguistic innovations. Working under the political constraints of their time, they succeeded in changing the distribution of symbolic capital and to a certain extent subverted, or at least altered, the existing rules of the game.

XIA JI'AN: LEGITIMATING A PRINCIPLE OF GENRE HIERARCHY AFTER THE WESTERN MODEL

In a recent article on Xia Ji'an, Christopher Lupke writes:

Within the context of Chinese literature from Taiwan, Xia has played a pivotal role. He replaced Zhang Daofan as the dominant cultural figure in Taiwan in the late 1950s. He reconfigured the structure of power in the cultural sphere by creating an autonomous space within which writers could be promoted. (61)

It is noteworthy that Xia accomplished all this largely through his editorial work—criticism, commentary, selection of works for publication, and editing of accepted works—in his capacity as chief editor of *Literary Review*. Convinced that Xia was determined to "graft Western literary modes onto modern Chinese literature" (61), Lupke devotes considerable space to his commentary on Peng Ge's novel, *Luoyue* [Setting moon] (1956), to demonstrate the particularly effective way Xia expounds on his ideas of "good literature," conceived after the western model.

Xia's choice of Peng Ge's "historical romance"[10] for meticulous textual criticism was significant in another sense. The novel represented a type of Mainstream literature extremely popular at the time.[11] Historical romances were so prevalent that even the few novels written by native Taiwanese—Liao Qingxiu's *Good Will and Revenge: A Record of Blood and Tears* and Zhong Zhaozheng's *Zhuoliu sanbuqu* [Trilogy of the murky torrent]—formally speaking belonged to the same genre. Typically love stories set in the immediate historical past, during the resistance war and the civil war in mainland China, with explicit but perfunctory patriotic themes, these middlebrow literary works conformed to the central spirit of the government's cultural policy while fulfilling the market's need for entertainment. They thrived partly because the government-sponsored consecrating agencies at the time cared more about a work's political implications than its artistic qualities. Xia, on the other hand, insisted on artistic merit. Of *Setting Moon*, he said in effect that it lacked artistic merit, but he made this criticism in a characteristically constructive manner, an earnest critical style that, in Lupke's words, succeeded in establishing "a serious attitude toward literature" in Taiwan (57). We have already heard (chapter 2) Lin Haiyin praising Xia's editorial work on her own story, suggesting the extent to which agents occupying the Mainstream position recognized his worth.

By instilling in cultural agents an aspiration to create works of higher artistic caliber, Xia transformed the literary field's distribution of symbolic capital. In his critical writing on the formal and textual qualities that distinguish "serious" literature from "popular" literature, solidly based on his knowledge of western literary tradition, Xia helped set new terms for legitimate critical discourse that lasted for a long while. Fuller establishment of these terms had to wait for a larger group of critics and writers in the 1960s, many of whom, like those in the *Modern Literature* group, received their artistic orientation directly from Xia.

YU GUANGZHONG: POSITION TAKING WITHIN THE SPACE OF POSSIBILITIES INHERITED FROM PREVIOUS STRUGGLES

The high-profile founding of the Modernist Poetry Society in 1956, with its agenda of wholesale westernization, is commonly regarded as the beginning of postwar Taiwan's Modernist literary movement. However, this effort in the restricted subfield of poetic production was more a heretical break from the literary establishment, narrowly imagined, than pursuit of a broadly defined alternative cultural vision, and probably had less to do with the larger Modernist artistic formation than is commonly assumed.

The majority of the Modernist poets sincerely subscribed to the government-endorsed cultural narrative, as well as its anti-Communist agenda, and many of them were frequent winners of government-sponsored literary prizes.[12] Judging from the careers of many of these poets later on, they constituted a primary support of the Mainstream position. Renowned poet-editor Yaxian is a good example. Undoubtedly among Taiwan's finest Modernist poets in the 1960s, Yaxian consistently observed the parameters set by the Nationalist cultural hegemony, even as he became an important champion of Mainstream *chunwenxue* while in charge of the *Lianfu* (*fukan* of the *United Daily News*) in the 1980s; not surprising, given his political affiliations and personal habitus.

By comparison, Yu Guangzhong's critical and creative activities between the late 1950s and early 1970s brought more fundamental changes to the literary field. As a student of western literature, Yu was a more thoroughgoing follower of the imported liberal tradition than most other contemporary Modernist poets. At the same time, the way he engaged with the classical Chinese and May Fourth literary traditions in his critical writing significantly reshaped literary discourse in Taiwan. His work and the symbolic capital he brought to it made him an important architect of both the aesthetic and ideological aspects of the Modernist position.

Artistically, the usual critical account credits Yu's ability to synthesize traditional and modernist aesthetics. During the Modernist poetry debates in the late 1950s he passionately confronted orthodox traditionalists, claiming that their construction of the tradition was ossified and out of date.[13] At the same time, he decried the Modernists' failure to put into practice their touted "intellectualization" (also "sensibility" or "rationality"—*zhixing*, in the terminology of the moment).[14] To distinguish himself from the ardent partisans of the Modernist Poetry Society, he joined a smaller and looser organization, *Lanxing shishe* [Blue star poetry club].

A frequently cited remark in the afterword to *Lian de lianxiang* [Associations of the lotus] (1964) exemplifies the felicity with which Yu tackled the thorny issue of "tradition and modernity":

> Viewed in an immature perspective, the "classical" and the "modern" are qualities of a drastically opposing nature. In fact, those "modernists" with a solid classical background, just like the "classicists" who have been baptized by modernism, are doubly likely to be rich and complex (*fanfu*), as well as imbued with tensile strength (*tanxing*). (*Lian de lianxiang* 160)

Yu borrowed the term "neoclassicism" from western literary history, frequently referring to figures like T. S. Eliot and Ezra Pound (160–161). His formulation of neoclassicism, moreover, privileged linguistic density and polysemic textual richness, just as in western literary modernism.[15] The persuasiveness of this particular approach to the traditional-versus-modern problematic with Yu's contemporary audience can of course be partly attributed to the fact that western literary concepts enjoyed high prestige in the postwar era, especially among the younger generation. What is unique about Yu, however, is his unusual ability to promote the aesthetic principles of his synthesis through his own creative works. Yu assimilated the imagery, diction, and rhythms of classical Chinese poetry into a poetic style deeply indebted to western modernism. His search for an ideal medium, especially his innovative use of traditionalist lyricism, reinvigorated the traditionalist mode of creative expression, contributing to a synthetic style that exerted considerable influence on the literary language of contemporary Taiwan.

The "classical" side of Yu's winning strategy drew its strength from his ability to energize a Chinese tradition that, in Taiwan's politically subordinated literary field, was rich with potential for bestowing political legitimacy. On the other hand, Yu's position on the May Fourth tradition, while attracting less scholarly attention, was significant precisely because he took issue with the officially sanctioned "selective tradition," offering his own judgments based on western-influenced Modernist aesthetics.

Following the lead of Liang Shiqiu[16]—Yu's senior colleague at National Normal University for many years—Yu revived the sino-liberal cultural ideology of the Republican era and proclaimed himself an heir to the May Fourth heritage.[17] But again, it was the way Yu situated himself between orthodoxy and heresy that allowed him to stand out from his peers. Armed with western aesthetic concepts, Yu enthusiastically promoted an artistic renaissance, working in close cooperation with promising younger Modernists. These included painters affiliated with the *Wuyue huahui* [Painters' club of May] (Liu Guosong, Zhuang Ze, etc.), poet Ye Shan (Wang Jingxian), and fiction writer Wang Wenxing, to name just a few. In essays written between the late 1950s and early 1970s, Yu announced the demise of the government's authorized version of the May Fourth tradition with youthful arrogance. He did so largely to turn attention away from tradition and toward Taiwan's Modernists. In his essay "Xia Wusi de banqi" [Lower the May Fourth banner] (1964), Yu proclaimed: "The greatest achievement of the May Fourth literary movement lies in language reform, rather than artistic revolution" (*Xiaoyao you* 2). He continued to argue that May Fourth failed to live up to the promise of a genuine "new literature movement," comparable to what Dante, Wordsworth, Hemingway, and Eliot had succeeded in bringing to western literature (2–3). In the early 1970s, Yu published a series of close-reading analyses of several famous May Fourth writers, including Zhu Ziqing and Wen Yiduo, to substantiate this claim.[18] The gist of his criticism was that, while undeniably significant in the history of modern Chinese literature, these authors had been generally overrated in terms of artistic accomplishment.[19] Yu's emphasis on structural and textual density, tension, ironic distance, and other stylistic elements exemplified the tenets of New Criticism.

Yu's verdict on May Fourth is certainly open to debate, but what matters for our purposes is that he succeeded in dismantling the prevailing order in Taiwan's early post–1949 literary scene. In order to advance a new aesthetic position, newly arrived agents must find ways to demonstrate their difference from—or superiority to—the established, already consecrated agents or traditions, making them appear "obsolete." In Bourdieu's terms, the most effective way to establish legitimacy is to identify and tackle the "legitimate problematic" in the field. Yu's criticism of the May Fourth tradition and its legacies certainly accomplished this, but even more important is the relevance of his critical remarks to the prevailing literary practices of the time. In his 1963 essay, "*Jiandiao sanwen de bianzi*" [Cutting off the pigtails of our prose], Yu aggressively faulted his fellow writers for mediocrity and disingenuousness. He reiterated this viewpoint in a 1968 article, "Women xuyao jiben shu" [We need several books], this time targeting the "prosaic, overly simplistic style" that was popularized by middle-school textbooks, *fukan*, and literary magazine editors, and valorized by university Chinese departments:

Today's most popular prose style, in essence, is still an extension of the May Fourth new literature. . . . Bingxin and . . . Zhu Ziqing still serve as models for emulation by ordinary prose writers. For decades, some *fukan* editors and compilers of Chinese-language textbooks have always subscribed to the view that their prose represents the highest achievement of modern Chinese letters. . . . Prose writings directly influenced by this May Fourth strand are especially popular among middle-school students, especially female students. Legitimized by textbooks on Chinese language, such writings have flooded all our *fukan* pages and pulp magazines. (90–91)

What made Yu's opinions unorthodox was that the literary qualities he denigrated were closely associated with many *chunwenxue* writers of the Mainstream position. Adopting the "May Fourth prose style" in their own writings, they also tended to occupy influential positions in the KMT's cultural and educational bureaucracies.

Still more crucial was the fact that Yu was able to showcase his ideal of a more original, rich, and poetical style in his own flamboyantly brilliant prose. In the afterword to his essay collection, *Xiaoyao you* [The untrammeled traveler] (1965), Yu wrote that he was consciously experimenting with "Modernist prose" in some of the pieces, including "Guiyu" [Ghost rain], "Shadan ye" [Shakespearean birthday eve], "Xiaoyao you" [The untrammeled traveler], "Jiuzhang chuang" [Nine beds], and others (208). About the modernistic aesthetic in his creative work, he said, "I tried to condense, flatten, elongate, and sharpen the Chinese language, rip it apart and piece it together again, fold it in this way and that, so that I might test its speed, density, and elasticity" (208).

The radical gestures of certain Modernists did arouse suspicion from the government, but since these writers generally supported the anti-Communist, "Free China" ideological stance, the cultural bureaucrats let them alone after some initial probes. The establishment of the Modernist aesthetic position marked an important step in the cultural field's progress toward autonomy, directing attention to stylistic, linguistic, and technical matters. Its elitist literary view effectively challenged the utilitarian discourse on literature and formed the basis of a new, widely accepted principle of cultural legitimacy in the literary field. The Modernists' substantial academic and prestige capital also quickly made them models for occupants of the Mainstream *chunwenxue* position, at least regarding the technical aspects of creative writing.

The outbreak of the Nativist debate, during which the Modernists were accused of paving the way for western capitalism to threaten Taiwan's national well-being, pushed the Modernists closer to the ruling regime and led to new alliances with Mainstream writers.[20] During the Nativist movement, the Modernists' formal experimentation and emphasis on technical aspects of creative writing were harshly criticized as superfluous conceits, and associated with a comprador mentality. The stigmatization of the Modernists in the late 1970s, however, did not prevent the literary community from keeping their' principle of artistic autonomy. Even in the *fukan*-sponsored Mainstream, "artistic autonomy" continued to inform the construction of literary excellence. Whatever its end, the Modernist movement in arts and literature successfully established a new and lasting standard of legitimate culture.

THE AESTHETIC TRANSFORMATION OF SINOCENTRIC MAINSTREAM LITERATURE

Sinocentrism was the central cultural-ideological vision to which most mainlander writers in Taiwan, liberal and conservative alike, almost unconditionally subscribed in the early post–1949 years. We have seen, for instance, that Xia Ji'an's artistic differences with the government's cultural policy makers did not detract from his sinocentric piety. Xia's generation of mainlanders, Lupke notes, "were still heavily invested in the vision of a Chinese nation-state that included Taiwan" (61). To be sure, the Mainstream writers' sinocentric sympathies served the Nationalist regime well in its pursuit of political legitimacy and cultural hegemony. For the most severe challenge faced by the Republic of China on Taiwan was the constant need to reaffirm its status as the legitimate "Chinese" government. The major difference between my approach and that of most other scholars on this subject, however, is that I am not primarily interested in the role of cultural production in the nation-building project—whether the nation is defined as "China" or "Taiwan"—or the closely related issue of identity. Rather, my focus is on the ways political and economic forces in the "general field of power," where such issues matter tremendously, are translated into forces in the "field of literary production," affecting the rules governing operations within it, and, ultimately, the distinctive quantity that is contemporary Taiwanese literature.

We already know that the political factor has been critical in modern Chinese culture. War, revolution, and other forms of military takeover have periodically accentuated its forcefulness. Immediately after 1949, forced reordering and restructuring in Taiwan included the imposition of a number of officially sanctioned modes of creative writing, from which a new set of literary norms and conventions evolved. These constituted what Peter Bürger calls "hegemonic categories," or categories that "[determine] the outlooks of subjects who participate in literature" (Hohendahl, *Building* 31).[21] I spoke to this idea first in my previous book, *Modernism and the Nativist Resistance*, using examples of several "older generation" writers—i.e., Qijun, Lin Haiyin, Zhu Xining, and Pan Renmu, who began their literary careers in the mid-1950s—to illustrate salient thematic and stylistic features of a Mainstream literature visibly marked by Taiwan's politically instituted dominant culture.

The aesthetic categories that I have associated with the Mainstream position, namely, a neotraditionalist genteel outlook, a conformist political disposition, conservative culturalism, and middlebrow tastes, were established largely though "refraction" of external—political, ethical, and aesthetic—demands from the (soft)-authoritarian Nationalist government. Because of the longevity and stability of the Nationalist cultural hegemony, which was not seriously threatened until the lifting of martial law in 1987, these categories have persisted in Mainstream literature, albeit in evolved forms, reflecting the subsequent changes in Taiwan's political and cultural context.

The term "sinocentric cultural ideology" as used here, therefore, has a broader meaning than its core reference, namely a culturalist ideology that has "China"—the Chinese land and people, its history, past tradition, and future development—as its privileged center. The phrase also refers to the intellectual, ethical, and aesthetic traditions selectively valorized by the Nationalist government to legitimize its rule, including particular strands of May Fourth, Confucianist, and classical Chinese literature. It is particularly important to note that these are "Chinese" traditions that were reinvented within the specific historical context of post–1949 Taiwan. Part and parcel of this, a sinocentric literary culture was underwritten by political authorities and supported by public resources, and gradually assumed hegemonic status in Mainstream literary production and reception.

The popular rage for mainland Chinese essayist Yu Qiuyu that broke out amid the literary market's severe depression in the early 1990s speaks to the fact that the sinocentric aesthetic nourished by the Nationalists during the martial law period survived its political sponsor. The appeal of Yu's writings—strewn with vivid cultural, historical, and geographical references from the old sinocentric aesthetic—among Taiwanese readers of various ages attests strongly to its persistence. Recognizing its lasting potency is important for understanding the complex cultural fabric of Taiwan's post–martial law period, when the China trope reemerged with new layers of political and cultural significance.

Transformations of the China Trope

Use of the China trope in literature and the arts is the most tangible manifestation of the sinocentric cultural ideology, and it has attracted considerable scholarly attention in recent years, as witnessed by the varying definitions of "Chineseness" being contested between Localist scholars within Taiwan and postmodernist scholars in transnational settings.[22] A number of sophisticated studies have explored—or made extensive references to—the remarkable metamorphosis the China trope underwent in literary, artistic, and media representations in the last two decades of the twentieth century.

Anticipating the rapid ascent of the Localist imperative in the 1980s, China as a cultural symbol was already subject to displacement and recoding during the Nativist trend of the 1970s. In his book on the campus folk song movement in the mid- to late 1970s, *Shei zai neibian chang ziji de ge* [Who are out there singing their own songs?] (1994), Zhang Zhaowei describes how "Chinese folk songs" using Yu Guangzhong's poetry as lyrics quickly gave way to "Taiwanese folk songs," with local references accentuated (ch. 2). A turning point was when young singers in Taiwan appropriated resources from the high cultural field of literature and launched on a deliberate course of indigenizing popular music.

An important focus of Liu Jihui's essays collected in *Gu'er, nüshen, fumianshuxie: Wenhua fuhao de zhengzhuang shi yuedu* [Orphan, goddess, and the writing of the negative: The performance of our symptoms] (2000) is the displacement of "China" by "Taiwan." In psychoanalytical mode, Liu discerns contradictory motives behind the use of the China/Taiwan trope in works of poetry, drama, and dance produced in Taiwan in the late 1980s and the 1990s[23]—motives, Liu argues, underpinned by the thorny issues of identity and ethnic relations.

Finally, Shu-mei Shih's English article, "The Trope of 'Mainland China' in Taiwan's Media" (1995), discusses how ideological and economic forces conditioned television travel programs about China in the early 1990s, demonstrating how "China" was objectified, exoticized, catalogued, and ultimately consumed as a commodity and appreciated as a prospective tourist destination.[24]

Using the transformation of the China trope as an index of recent cultural changes in Taiwan, these studies reveal a pivotal switch in the emblematic representation of nationhood, but their focus is largely on the activities of the challengers, with little information about the reactions and adjustments of the dominant sector in the cultural field, leaving important issues of continuity and change unaddressed. Therefore, my discussion here traces the change in the sinocentric imagination back to an earlier historical moment, the 1960s and 1970s, stressing the importance of structuring forces that were at work over the long term.

The transformation of the China trope began as soon as it appeared and became more pronounced with the passage of time. Early on, in the "literature of homesickness" (*xiangchou wenxue*), first-generation mainlander writers re-created China from their idealized memories of the mainland. After the homesickness theme ceased to be popular, the idealized image of China remained an affectively potent literary trope, and its value as symbolic capital to all cultural agents, mainlander and native Taiwanese alike, continued to grow until the Nationalist state's underlying sinocentricism was seriously contested in the mid-1980s.[25] During all that time, "China" was becoming increasingly an imaginary textual construction.

Within a decade after the 1949 retreat, it became obvious that regaining the mainland was not likely to happen soon. In the media and in public discourse "China" became more and more politically charged. It was precisely at this juncture that the Modernist trend arose and major writers like Yu Guangzhong, Zhang Xiaofeng, and Wang Dingjun, representing different literary pedigrees, began to aestheticize the China trope. Their treatment eventually effected crucial transformations of the aesthetic categories that constituted the Mainstream literary position, allowing it to remain potent in an increasingly market-driven cultural field, even as it weathered growing challenges from the Localists.

WANG DINGJUN (B. 1925)

Born in 1925 to gentry in Shangdong province, Wang Dingjun received a traditional education until he left home at the age of seventeen to attend a government-sponsored high school for refugee students from enemy-occupied areas during the Sino-Japanese war. He later joined the army briefly and, after moving to Taiwan, held a number of jobs in the KMT's cultural bureaucracy before immigrating to the United States around

1980. This gave him something in common with Taiwan's "military writers" discussed earlier. On the one hand, their experience of war and forced removal from their native place at a young age reinforced the patriotic education they received in schools run by the KMT party-military, while instilling in them a lasting homesickness. On the other hand, while government trust secured them a position in the cultural bureaucracy, it also meant continual control of their professional careers. These factors combined in nurturing a conformist disposition in many Mainstream writers.

Wang Dingjun's 1967 short story, "Tu" [Soil], shows the China trope in transition. The story's themes include changes in the public's attitudes toward nostalgia for the mainland as well as increased psychological distance between mainlanders and their lost homeland. The protagonist, Hua Di, falls seriously ill after losing a small bottle his mother has filled with soil from his mainland home. Explaining the bottle's importance, Hua Di relates to a nurse his parents' belief that those who live away from home will get seriously ill and eventually die, and that the only cure for this disease is a drink mixed with the soil from their native place. A sympathetic radio announcer broadcasts the notion, and many responses come from the audience, including a young woman who chastises Hua Di for a belief that blinds him to the beauty of the Taiwanese landscape. The bottle is finally recovered, but the cap is gone, as is a large portion of its contents. As the nurse prepares the drink, Hua Di, overjoyed, sniffs the remaining soil and sneezes, causing still more of the contents to be lost. At this point, Hua Di resolutely announces that he will keep the remaining bit of soil, forget about the drink, and trust his illness to modern medicine.

While a story like "Soil," as well as Wang's other stories in his two collections from this period, *Danshenhan de tiwen* [A bachelor's body temperature] (1970) and *Sui liuli* [Shattered crystals] (1978), may not seem particularly modernistic to western readers, the well-crafted plot and painstaking symbolism, not to mention occasional attempts at surrealism, register unmistakable influences of Taiwan's Modernist trend. The fact that Wang authored a number of literary composition manuals helps to explain his interest in adopting the Modernist techniques then in vogue. A deeper look, however, reveals some crucial differences between classical modernism and the Mainstream writers' adoption of its surface markers. Whereas classical modernism calls into question established value systems, Taiwan's Mainstream writers perforce continued to affirm the sinocentric core. Elsewhere I have discussed how another important first-generation mainlander essayist, Qijun, even when trying her hand at the modern short-story form, continues to cleave to the residual gentry-class world-view of her celebrated prose essays. This habit injects her fiction with an overwrought didacticism, a characteristic shared by many other Mainstream writers, of both prose and fiction.

This said, we must still acknowledge the aesthetic implication of "Soil," in which the Chinese homeland is rendered abstract through the author's deliberate use of symbolism, unlike its predominantly realistic representation in earlier Mainstream literature. Wang's self-reflective commentaries also deserve attention. In the preface to the 1988 *Danshen wendu* [A bachelor's temperature], a reprint of *A Bachelor's Body Temperature* with a slightly modified title, Wang relates that by the time he was writing the story the once popular homesickness motif had declined and even become something of a taboo, due to the continued hostility between Taiwan and the PRC. This suggests Wang's sensitivity to the changing political climate—especially the public's growing mistrust of the mainlanders' loyalty to Taiwan—at a relatively early time, not too surprising given his background as a veteran literary censor for the KMT. Paradoxically, however, his insider's knowledge of censorship did not prevent him from occasionally trying potentially dangerous topics, such as the lives of those who moved to Taiwan from the mainland—usually via Hong Kong—during the martial law period, few as there were, and war recollections. While insisting on following his own creative drive, Wang also exercised self-censorship, endeavoring to stay within the "permissible scope" and thus exemplifying the conformist disposition of the Mainstream writers of his generation. In the semiautobiographical stories about his mainland experience collected in *Shattered Crystals*, Wang uses "fictional reformulation," a superficial application of selected modernistic techniques, more to avoid censorship than to achieve artistic effects. Most of the stories suffer for it, turning out somewhat hollow and light-hearted adventure tales short on depth and thematic integrity.

Immigrating to New York in his mid-fifties removed some of the constraints that had impeded Wang's artistic achievement, but he has continued to write for the same Taiwanese readership, so his work is still subjected to the same consecrating agency. His collection of lyrical prose, *Zuo xinfang xuanwo* [Whirlpool of the left atrium] (1988), won the grand prize in the *China Times* literary contest, an award unquestionably deserved. Besides its freer expression of his thoughts—albeit still fairly conservative—the richly imagistic, poetical language, far superior to that of Wang's earlier work in the same genre, makes the volume exemplary of the "Modernist prose" Yu Guangzhong has advocated.[26] Of particular interest to the present discussion is a recurring motif in the essays collected in *Whirlpool*: a deep—yet greatly transformed—nostalgia for China, and memories of his mainland past intensified by his further "exile" to a western country, where he ironically enjoys greater freedom to communicate with people in China. In the first chapter of *Whirlpool*, for instance, Wang poignantly compares his parting from his native place thirty-nine years earlier to a reincarnation, with all traces of his "previous life" completely erased, as from a blackboard (3). The suppressed memory of his mainland past, however, constantly returns to haunt him at night, as in a bizarre dream in which he is separated into halves at the waist, with his lower body desperately chasing the upper one. The nightmare is triggered by something he saw earlier in the day: a row of mannequins without torsos displayed in a department store (4–5). In a letter to an intimate childhood friend in China, from whom he was separated for nearly forty years, Wang writes that now the blackboard can finally be written on again (3).

The resumed relationship with China, however, is still deeply troubled. In response to the friend's invitation to visit, Wang writes that now, to him, China is just a map on the wall, a painting that he has accidentally fallen out of. Behind his refusal to return to a home he has so intensely yearned for is a profound fear of disillusionment. In another letter Wang indignantly refutes this friend's typically nationalistic claim that "China is our mother," recounting what his Chinese friends in New York say. Twice dislocated, these new immigrants now feel that China is more like a father—mother is Taiwan, home, while China is a dream (127–129).

Enjoying relative freedom from the habit of self-censorship and from external constraints dictating conformism, Wang has become more reflective about some fundamental ideological presumptions. His new volume of inspirational essays, *Suiyuan pomi* [Following your destiny, seeing through the myth] (1997) features a more independent—even "transgressive," in the author's own mind—attitude toward conventional morality.[27] The first two (already published) volumes of Wang's memoir, *Zuotian de yun* [Clouds of yesterday] (1992) and *Numu shaonian* [Young man with a furious stare] (1995), also deserve special attention, since the wartime experiences portrayed in them are shared by a majority of Taiwan's Mainstream cultural agents of Wang's generation, most of whom also came from landowning gentry families and attended KMT-sponsored schools during the war. Among other things, the new volumes show how the right-wing government used traditionalist ideology and gentrified Confucian doctrines to forge a conservative, moralistic, and conformist dominant culture. Wang's candid and thoughtful accounts of historical events during the Sino-Japanese war, even featuring some uncharacteristically sympathetic remarks on the rise of the leftist trend toward the end of the conflict (*Numu* 327–328), show the author breaking away from the psychological confinement he abided for many decades.

YU GUANGZHONG (B. 1928)

Yu Guangzhong straddles the Mainstream and Modernist positions. With solid credentials as a student of western literature, he nevertheless had a habitus inclined toward the Mainstream, sinocentric cultural ideology. Born in 1928 in Nanjing, he spent his formative years there during the Sino-Japanese war, and shared with the older mainlanders trusted by the Nationalist regime a genuine emotional attachment to the Chinese mainland and a firm anti-Communist stance.

In 1964–66, and again in 1969–71, Yu was a Fulbright visiting professor in the United States. The experience of living on another mainland rekindled Yu's nostalgia for his homeland, especially at a time when China was being jolted by the Great Proletarian Cultural Revolution. Aesthetically powerful images of China appear in many of Yu's poems written in 1966 and collected in *Qiaoda yue* [Music percussive] (1969), including lines like these:[28]

> China O China you are a queue,
> Trademark like trailing behind you.
> . . . .
> China O China you just won't cut or shave away,
> You always choke here you're the ulcer that never heals
> —The year of Marco Polo Bridge one fancied it's healed.
> China O China what a practical joke you've played!
> You're a problem, half lost in the cigar smoke of China
> experts.
> They tell me you're raped and overdosed they say you're
> disgraced,
> Deserted, betrayed, insulted, raped again and raped.
> China O China you drive me mad.
> . . . . .
> The Yellow River flows torrential in my veins,

China is me I am China,
Her every disgrace leaves a box print on my face I am
defaced.
China O China you're a shameful disease that plagues me
thirty-eight years.
Are you my shame or are you my pride, I cannot tell.
I only know you're still a virgin though you've been raped a
thousand times.
China O China you are my qualms!
When O when
Can we ever stop our endless difference
About my cowardliness and your innocence?
                    From "Music percussive" (*The Night Watchman* 32–40)

When I am dead, lay me down between the Yangtze
And the Yellow River and pillow my head
On China, white hair against black soil,
Most beautiful O most maternal of lands,
And I will sleep my soundest taking
The whole mainland for my cradle. . . .
                    From "When I Am Dead" (*The Night Watchman* 25).

Yu also dwelled on the notion of China in essays. Of particular interest are his self-reflective comments on the abstract nature of the China
trope in his own mind:

He thus interprets the situation to himself: the China of his homesickness is neither on this side of the Taiwan Strait nor on the other. Rather
it resides in the melodies sung during the resistance war, in the vast land
that he has treaded on wearing straw sandals, in the hazily remote memories of the prewar days, as well as in the resonant ending rhymes of
classical poetry . . . his China is not geographical, but historical. ("Siyue,
zai guzhanchang" 181–182)

In many ways Yu's thinking here anticipates the more deliberately constructed notion of "cultural China" advocated by scholars like Tu Wei-
ming in the U.S. academy. What distinguishes Yu, of course, is the way he
forcefully inserts the modernistic aesthetic mode into a frame of national
imagination, finding in traditional prose and classical poetic images the

essence of "Chineseness."[29] With poetic abstraction, Yu equates China
with traditional lyrical images and uniquely Chinese ideograms:

> Apricot blossom. Spring rain. South of the Yangtze River. Six square-
> shaped characters—perhaps that's where the land called China is hidden
> . . . each single square-shaped character is a universe. ("Tingting na
> lengyu" 32)

As discussed earlier, Yu Guangzhong's identification of the struggle between the traditional and the modern as the issue of the day constituted a
successful strategy for challenging the dominant order in the literary field.
The particular way Yu synthesized the traditional and the modern in his
poetry at once affirmed and modified the prevailing aesthetic category that
privileged a traditionalist lyrical sensibility. Unlike some antitraditionalist
Modernist poets in Taiwan, Yu endeavored to incorporate traditional lyricism by transforming it. He consciously advocated a "modernist lyricism"
that departed from the lyrical sentimentalism of the more conservative
Mainstream writers who dominated the literary field at the time. Yu's lyrical rendering of sinocentric images—water lilies in his hometown in *Jiang-
nan* [South of the Yangtze River], China's ancient cultural monuments,
the humiliations and endless suffering of the Chinese people in modern
history—brought them in tune with the prevailing traditionalist taste.
However, while they recharged the outworn literary trope, the daring and
poignant analogies of his poetic evocation of "China"—for instance in
"Music Percussive" (cited above) and in the widely cited "Inflicted with
syphilis, she is still my Mother" (from "Wangchuan" [River of forget-
ting])—also posed a challenge to the conservative decorum of the neotraditionalist dominant aesthetic category. With Modernist fiction writers,[30]
Yu helped to significantly advance the evolution of literary sensibility in
the Modernist direction.

The reconceptualization of China in aesthetic, cultural terms imbued
the literary trope with true cultural legitimacy. It also relieved some of the
propagandist overtones of the sinocentric imagination, helping to reinforce its dominance. All this contributed to the popularity of sinocentric
imagery in the 1960s and 1970s with baby boomers who had never been
to the Chinese mainland but who, as aspiring young writers, adopted the
China trope as a position-taking strategy. After Localism took hold in the
mid-1980s, the trend gradually reversed itself. Sinocentric cultural ideology to some extent became a liability, and literary evocations of "cultural

China" were increasingly treated as signs of complicity with the Nationalist regime. Still, the aestheticization process in modern poetry facilitated yet another transformation of the China trope: the commodification of traditional China, marketing ancient Chinese civilization as exotic. Yu Guangzhong even began to perform his poetry accompanied by imported and locally composed folk music. Most of all, though, commodification was evident in the cultural nostalgia trend that raged in the early 1980s, when images from traditional China proliferated at all levels of cultural production and performers adopted archaic sounding names like "Yunmen wuji" [Cloudgate dance series] and "Lanling jufang" [Orchid mound theater studio].[31] Popular campus folk songs like Hou Dejian's "Longde chuanren" [Descendants of the dragon], faddish store signs like "Xiaofengxian" (or Little Phoenix Fairy, a late Qing and early Republican women's dress style, now adopted as a bridal costume), and kitschy designs on greeting cards and throw pillows with calligraphy and sketches by the unorthodox Qing dynasty figure, Zheng Banqiao (1693–1765), were all part of the same trend.[32]

The rapid vulgarization of the aesthetic category of traditionalist lyricism was largely imperceptible, like many such transformations in the age of consumerism. That it remains potent is demonstrated by the nostalgia that consumers continue to exhibit for traditional style, and appeals to this impulse are cannily embedded in many cultural products. The cultural scene in Taiwan today is rife with examples of how the China trope has been recoded in response to the reconstitution of the dominant culture and the rise of a new consumer class in the post–martial law period. At the presidential inauguration concert on May 20, 2000, Wubai, an extremely popular rock singer whose songs and style embody a masculine, rustic "Taiwanese" flavor, was the top-billed artist on the program, performing last. Wu Bai used a band called "China Blue," not what you might expect of a DPP supporter, until you understand that the name is intended more to exploit the mainland Chinese music market than to make a statement about politics.

Sediments of once-dominant sinocentric cultural ideology continue to matter to some serious artists—albeit in more subdued, even defensive forms—in Taiwan's post–martial law cultural field, in which global capitalism and an economically resurgent China are increasingly important players. Nonetheless, the heyday of Modernist lyricism as a Mainstream aesthetic mode is apparently over. Taiwanese Localism and globalization have helped to render images associated with China floating signifiers, largely divorced from the sinocentric ideological prescriptions of the martial law period.

ZHANG XIAOFENG (B. 1941)

Aside from her gender, writer and playwright Zhang Xiaofeng's particular importance in the transformation of the hegemonic sinocentric aesthetic category lies in the fact that, unlike Yu Guangzhong and Xia Ji'an, she belongs to the postwar generation of writers. Born in 1941 in mainland China, Zhang was still a young child when her family relocated to Taiwan with the Nationalist retreat. During the 1960s and 1970s she published several highly patriotic prose works. "Chouxiang shi" [Rock of homesickness] showed a longing for the mainland similar to Yu Guangzhong's. "Shiyue de yangguang" [Sunshine in October] registers her emotional reaction to the way preparations for the war to regain the mainland had been reduced to a hollow ritual ceremony on "Double-Ten Day," savored by a complacent and insensitive peacetime audience. Finally, "Hei sha" [Black armband] takes the form of a letter to her daughter expressing sorrow at the death of President Chiang Kai-shek.

Zhang is considerably less cynical than Modernists of the same generation; her work embodies the Mainstream aesthetic position's orthodox ideology. Several factors may account for this: her Christian background, the fact that she was born to a mainlander family headed by a high-ranking Nationalist military officer during the civil war, and her academic background in traditional Chinese studies. However, arriving on the literary scene just when the Modernist trend was on the rise, Zhang incorporated its aesthetic principles, if not its ideological content, into her prose. Faithful to Chinese cultural nationalism, she nonetheless expressed it in Modernist-inspired prose.

While a large number of female writers occupying the Mainstream position in Taiwan are overtly patriotic, in Zhang Xiaofeng patriotism is intricately tied to gender identification, specifically, masculine identity. The idealization of China's imperial past, more often than not identified with patriotism for the Republic of China, typically displays a right-wing, masculine militarism. For example, in her essay, "Buxia hongtan zhi hou" [After stepping down the red wedding rug], Zhang describes intense "longings for her home country" (jiaguo zhisi), and a desire to "embrace the five thousand years of history and eight hundred million Chinese people" as a violent passion deeply rooted in her being (Xiaofeng 108–109). She goes on to characterize this passion as something that cannot be contained by the "genteel education for the virtuous lady" promulgated in traditional Chinese departments (108). On the surface, this position seems to align Zhang with Modernist women writers who consciously tried to

adopt a gender-neutral identity. Denouncing generically "feminine" qualities like domesticity and sentimentalism, as well as the conservative, amateur literary culture of the 1950s, was an important drive behind the in-
tellectualized artistic project of Taiwan's Modernists in the 1960s.[33]
However, Zhang, frequently likened to the May Fourth lyrical sentimental prose writer Bingxin, obviously took a different route in rebelling
against the "feminine writings" of the 1950s. Contrary to the Modernists'
subscription to objectivity and rationality and emphasis on moral relativism, Zhang developed a heightened subjectivism, joined with sentimentalism and tinted with positivistic, voluntaristic colors. The celebration of
masculine, military power and heroism in Zhang's work is straight from
the Nationalists' official historical narrative. Drawing from traditional
Chinese culture, the nation-building experience and principles of Chiang
Kai-shek, the five-thousand-year Chinese history, and the eight-hundred-
million population of the Chinese land, she synthesizes a system of absolute values. As some feminist critics have remarked, the patriotic impulse of second-generation female mainlander writers raised in *juancun*
(the government-built housing compounds for military dependents that
became a prominent subculture in post–1949 Taiwan) is part and parcel
of their identification with the society's patriarchal order. This applies to
Zhang Xiaofeng, arguably a model for younger women writers from *juancun* who are similarly fond of using male personae and who often express
nationalistic sentiments.

Zhang's support of the Nationalist regime finds expression in another
prominent theme in her essays of the 1970s, affirming resilience and self-
sacrifice in an adverse socioeconomic environment. In many of the essays
collected in her first two books, *Ditan de nayiduan* [The other side of the
red rug] (1966) and *Geini, Yingying* [For you, Yingying] (1968), Zhang
displays stoicism toward the difficult circumstances immediately after
1949. Scornful of material scarcity, she places high value on moral forti-
tude and spiritual perseverance, at the same time cherishing life's small
pleasures—warm relationships, the beauty of the natural landscape, and
seasonal changes—with a sense of gratitude.

As time went by and Taiwan's circumstances improved, Mainstream
writers' support of the status quo gradually evolved into an ethos of complacency, or what the leftist intellectual Chen Yingzhen calls *xingfu yishi*
[consciousness of happiness], satisfaction with what the ruling regime had
achieved—stability, progress, and peaceful civilian life. Zhang's essays
from the 1980s explicitly convey this celebratory mood; and contrast with

the mainland Chinese experience of the post–1949 period reinforces her right-wing ideology.[34]

In a nutshell, Zhang Xiaofeng transformed the more cautious, subdued, self-censored patriotic rhetoric of the Nationalist loyalists represented by the *chunwenxue* group of the 1950s into a passionate affirmation of contemporary social life.[35] As she and many younger, baby-boom generation women writers demonstrated, this ethos of complacency was determined by many different factors. Paramount among these were the common background of writers whose formative years were in the heyday of the Nationalist cultural hegemony, and the encouraging progress of economic development during a particular phase of Taiwan's contemporary epoch. What merits further elaboration is the particular way Zhang instilled her characteristic assertiveness into the sinocentric literary imagination, reinforcing through aesthetic means the ultraconservative Mainstream ideological turn toward "Chinese cultural nationalism."

"Chinese cultural nationalism" is to a certain extent institutionalized in the curriculum and pedagogy of Taiwan's Chinese literature departments, contributing to a very different intellectual tradition from that of foreign (western) literature departments. Its underlying spirit found eloquent—if unscholarly—expression in a book that appeared in the mid-1970s: *Shanhe suiyue* [Mountains, rivers, and years of one's lifetime] (1975), by Hu Lancheng. Having spent most of his postwar years in Japan, Hu was an outsider to the Taiwanese literary scene until he established a close association with the group of talented young writers and would-be writers who collected around Sansan she [The double-three club] and whose admiration of Hu eventually rendered him legendary. Whereas *Mountains* obviously reached sympathetic ears in Taiwan's intellectual circle, to a westernized scholar like Yu Guangzhong, the book's unabashed cultural chauvinism was unsettling:

> Hu displays a deeply felt affection toward Chinese history, and an absolute trust in the Chinese culture. Unfortunately, this is precisely where the most serious flaw of the book, *Mountains, Rivers, and Years of One's Life*, comes from. Hu Lancheng persistently asserts the value of Chinese culture, rarely offering any criticism. Explicitly or implicitly, he proclaims that the five thousand years of Chinese culture is endowed with a degree of perfection that gives it absolute superiority—by comparison, foreign civilizations on earth are always lacking in one way or another. This type of feeling may be touching if treated as a patriotic

sentiment, and yet it can also be misleading if promulgated as rational knowledge. (*Qingqing* 262)

Yu's comments mark the dividing line between Mainstream cultural nationalists and the liberally inclined Modernists, highlighting the vast uncritical blind spot in the cultural nationalists' sinocentric ideology. While his criticism is apparently justified, note that this irrational, utopian strain is an effect of the aestheticization of the China trope by Mainstream writers like Zhang Xiaofeng in the late 1970s and 1980s.

In just one conspicuous example, an essay entitled "Dichuan, I" [The water-spring beneath the earth, part I], Zhang Xiaofeng describes her epiphany upon reading *Erya*, China's ancient dictionary/encyclopedia:

> "*Explain* exegesis, *explain* language, *explain* interpretation, *explain* parents, *explain* the *gong* tune, *explain* instrument, *explain* music, *explain* heaven, *explain* earth, *explain* hill, *explain* mountain, *explain* water, *explain* grass, *explain* tree, *explain* insect, *explain* fish, *explain* bird, *explain* beast, *explain* animal."—*Erya*
>
> As soon as I turned to the table of contents [of *Erya*], I was stunned. Nineteen "*explains*" in one breath—how come I had never in the past discerned its singular beauty? Heaven and earth of that time had feelings, and people living at that moment of history were evidently confident and full of joy. Heaven and earth; mountain and river; the sun, the moon, and the constellations; trees and grasses; fish and insects; even the most indescribable music, the most homely cow sheds and horse stables, the most intricately interwoven kinship ties, and the numerous dialects and languages of China: all of them, without exception, were comprehensible to the human mind—hence explainable. Reading *Erya*, one gets the feeling that the world was just simple and magnificent, lucid and luminous, transparent and understandable like a newborn baby. It appears that at that moment in human history, every single morning men rose from bed and were instantly met by a thoroughly friendly and familiar world. The world to them was a test for which they knew the answer from top to bottom—absolutely nothing would pose as a source of uneasiness. (*Xiaofeng* 95–96)

Notably, the lines from *Erya* cited at the beginning of this passage use a cataloguing device common to the traditional Chinese encyclopedia (*leishu*). Its archaic simplicity and symmetrical orderliness suggest an epistemology characterized by comprehensiveness and cosmic inclusion, commonly associated with the poetic subgenre *fu*, "rhyme prose" or "descriptive prose interspersed with verse." *Fu* poetry extensively employs this device, which supposedly mirrors the expansionist imperial mindset of the Han dynasty, when the poetic form gained popularity. Zhang's ecstatic empathy with the *Erya* passage, and her image of a lost cosmos populated by ancient Chinese folks, entailing a rediscovery of this archaic cosmological outlook, closely mirrors Hu Lancheng's evocation of a utopian past in *Mountains*. And Zhang was not alone among contemporary Taiwanese writers in her association of ancient Chinese culture with a national essence—the same motif pervades works like Zhu Xining's *Weiyan pian* [Chapters of minced words] (1981), though the latter work attracted less critical attention.

Once the aesthetic mode of a specific ideology is developed, it tends to take on a life of its own. Obeying the logic of the literary field and interacting with other trends, it may develop beyond the original ideological inscriptions. This explains what happened to Chinese cultural nationalism in the hands of the Double-Three Club writers. The group's conservative orientation is evident from its name: "double-three" refers to Sun Yat-sen's *Three Principles of the People* paired with the Christian notion of the Trinity.[36] Their less mature works of the period contained echoes of Zhang's tendency to fetishize classical texts that imbued ancient China's landscape with subjective desire.[37]

But the conservative culturalism ostentatiously displayed by members of the Double-Three Club in the late 1970s and early 1980s was motivated less by ideology than by youthful idealism. It underwent dramatic changes in the 1980s and 1990s, particularly difficult decades for the second-generation mainlanders in the group, who were of course the majority. Since the mid-1990s, amid the widespread KMT-bashing, criticism of the Double-Three Club has focused primarily on the reactionary, rightwing politics of its members in the earlier days. What has received less attention is the crucial role of the club in the aesthetic transformation of sinocentric Mainstream literature.

Remnants of conservative culturalist ideology, with a distinctive aesthetic touch, have informed the recent work of two core members of the Double-Three Club, Zhu Tianwen and Zhu Tianxin—both daughters of Zhu Xining, and arguably the most accomplished fiction writers of the baby-boom generation—in important ways. As the Zhu sisters will be discussed again later (in chapter 7), the examples given here focus primarily on their efforts at negotiating and displacing sinocentric ideology.

The nostalgia for Taiwan's rapidly disappearing sinocentric cultural center is an underlying motif in Zhu Tianwen's 1994 novel, *Huangren shouji* [Notes of a desolate man], one of the most celebrated works of the post–martial law period. For instance, at one point the novel's narrator, Xiao Shao, the author's alter ego, laments that soon it will be impossible to find anyone in Taiwan who speaks Mandarin with a proper accent. Elsewhere Xiao Shao admits that his youthful enchantment with China was merely a textually constructed illusion.

As noted by critics and the author herself, Zhu Tianwen's particular construction of sinocentric cultural ideals owes much to Hu Lancheng, whose vision of traditional Chinese culture invested it with transcendent value. Immediately reminiscent of Zhang Xiaofeng's piece on *Erya* (cited earlier) is Zhu's brilliant use of the cataloguing device in *Notes*. In one instance, Zhu lists archaic Chinese words for colors that run about four pages: "Terrifying green, startling green, pallid green, decadent green, fatigue green, drifting green in a windless sky. . . . Rush leaves green as the sword of Wu, looking at the Han River from afar and seeing green duck heads. . . . Vermilion from jade, complexion vermilion, two-ribbon vermilion, cannot vermilion, twice-proscribed vermilion . . . rush-to-rainbow crimson, sun crimson, sword spirit crimson, beard resentment crimson, jealous gentlemen crimson, empty desire crimson . . . (Chinese original: Zhu, *Huangren* 90–91; English translation: Chu 66–67). The flamboyant images conjured up by these colors, while aesthetically appealing in themselves, are fraught with allusions to traditional Chinese texts. Besides conveying the visual power of Chinese ideograms, the deliberately excessive pileup of old characters evokes ambivalent feelings about a lost golden age in China's idealized past.

Although critics tend to emphasize postmodernist markers in *Notes*, partly owing to the protagonist's homosexual identity, the novel resonates at least as much with classical modernist ideology. In the concluding passage, for instance, the narrator pledges to continue engaging in the act of writing, the ultimate agent of culture, in order to resist nihilistic fear of the total erasure of meaning. This acknowledgment of the redeeming power of literature is reminiscent of the hard-core aestheticism of such major Modernists as Wang Wenxing and Li Yongping.

Zhu Tianxin's encounter with sinocentric ideology has followed a different path. Partly because of her college background in history, Zhu

Tianxin's fiction features more direct consideration of contemporary sociopolitical issues. Profoundly disillusioned by political corruption and environmental pollution, including the horrendously neglected cityscape of Taipei in post–martial law Taiwan, Zhu Tianxin in her 1997 novella, *Gudu* [Ancient capital], compares her utopian vision of a pristine culture to an old map of Taipei and to modern-day Kyoto. The way she imbues both Japanese flower rites and the colonial map of Taipei with a spiritual quality, as sites where history and memory are deposited, echoes the way Double-Three Club members idolized ancient China, only with the sinocentric fetish displaced by these new objects.[38]

With Taiwan continuing to undergo rapid changes, generational logic is currently all-important. Active in the heyday of the Nationalist cultural hegemony, Wang Dingjun, Yu Guangzhong, and Zhang Xiaofeng devoted themselves to China themes with emotional urgency and assertiveness. At the same time, their receptivity to Modernist aesthetics eventually allowed them to perform a dynamic overhaul of the hegemonic aesthetic categories, keeping them relevant well beyond the time when they might otherwise have lost most of their value as cultural capital. The sinocentric carryover among Mainstream artists of the baby-boom generation working in the new political climate, however, is inevitably marked by ambivalence and self-doubt.

Meanwhile, the burgeoning phenomenon among still younger artists, as well as transnational artists around the world, recodes traditional Chinese symbols in the interests of global capitalism and a booming mainland Chinese market.[39] Taiwanese director Ang Lee's (Li An) brilliant internationally released film, *Wo hu cang long* [Crouching tiger, hidden dragon], is of particular interest. Lee was raised in Taiwan but moved to the United States in the late 1970s, after college, to study film. His hallmark culturalist approach to Chinese heritage and his skillful recoding of traditional Chinese symbols have obviously contributed to his success with mainstream film audiences around the world. More important, however, is Lee's affectionate, positive representation of values and personality traits nourished by contemporary Taiwan's sinocentric dominant culture. This thematic interest runs through his Chinese-language "father knows best" trilogy—*Tui shou* [Pushing hands] (1992); *Xiyan* [The wedding banquet] (1993); and *Yin shi nan nü* [Eat, drink, man, woman] (1994)—and is particularly pronounced in *The Wedding Banquet*. The father in the film, for instance, while playing ignorant of his son's fake marriage for the sake of securing a grandson—thus preserving the family line—also graciously accepts his son's gay lover as part of the family, performing the ritual of giving the latter a red envelope as a birthday present. Sincere respect for tradition does not prevent the father from recognizing the need to adapt to undesirable and uncontrollable factors in life, a pragmatic attitude that Lee presents in a sympathetic, favorable light.

While sinocentric imagination and the conservative, conformist dominant culture remain prominent in the work of Taiwanese baby-boom generation artists based at home and abroad, notable discrepancies between local and overseas treatments of sinocentric themes point directly to Taiwan's drastically transformed literary culture since the 1980s. This transformation, driven by both the Localist challenge and the enduring influence of the Modernist-Nativist high-culture quest, gets thorough consideration in chapter 7.

CHAPTER 5

Localist Position as a Product of Social Opposition

"Taiwanese culture should not be a marginalized segment of Chinese culture, as it is a substantial civilization with its own individuality and uniqueness," President Chen Shui-bian said yesterday. "Taiwanese literature is profound and extensive, and should be elevated to a national literature from its present status as a regional literature," Chen said. "Amid all nation-building activities, cultural cultivation is considered the most critical for a state. We can say that the genuine democracy and progress of a country depend on how much its government values its cultural roots. Everything else is temporary and shallow." The president also said that the government must devise ways to promote and educate people about local Taiwan culture.

Chen, accompanied by the Council of Cultural Affairs chairwoman Tchen Yu-hsiu, made the comments yesterday during an appearance at a seminar held for writers. The seminar, called the "Salt Belt Literary Workshop," is being held in Penmen township, Tainan county until Aug. 7.

. . .

This year marked the 22nd meeting of the workshop. The venue was chosen in the area that gave rise to several revered Taiwanese writers, such as Wu Hsin-jung and Kuo Shui-tan, whose works exemplify regional styles. Writers Yang Tzu-chiao and Huang Chin-liang, among others, organized the first workshop in 1979, when Taiwan was still under martial law.

—*Taipei Times*, Aug. 5, 2000

The highlights of this report, published in the English-language *Taipei Times* shortly after the Democratic Progressive Party assumed power, are of course President Chen Shui-bian's argument with the "regional" status of Taiwanese literature, which amounts to an indirect evocation of a "Taiwanese nation." Speaking at the Salt Belt Literature Workshop, the home base of Localist literature, Chen apparently felt free to openly criticize the former government's marginalization of a literary position commonly associated with separatist politics. The speech, of course, was mainly political rhetoric, since the "national literature" label is primarily a political designation. Nonetheless, it marked a new era for the Localist position, which had come a long way from political suspect to recipient of the government's blessing. Moreover, the fact that the president and the new Chairwoman of the Council of Cultural Affairs (the government body most directly involved in allocating funds to cultural agents) publicly debunked the formerly official sinocentric ideology indicates the intensity to which this cultural-political struggle has risen in the new political era.

Undoubtedly, the Localist struggle began long before Chen and the DPP ousted the old KMT leadership, spanning much of the contemporary era. Over time it has changed the structure of Taiwan's literary field by changing the distribution of symbolic and economic capital. In this chapter, I follow the Localist position through those changes. The first part briefly surveys the Localist position's journey from the margins to the center of Taiwan's literary field. The second section describes the situation of native Taiwanese cultural agents before the Localist position assumed a greater public presence in the 1980s, including the mechanisms that the Nationalist government used to maintain its cultural hegemony. Despite their low profile, native Taiwanese writers were coauthors of the cultural narrative prevalent in the literary field of the martial law period. The last part of the chapter compares and contrasts the diverging trajectories of two leading figures of the Mainstream and Localist positions, Yu Guangzhong and Ye Shitao (respectively), to drive home the point that ultimately what was at stake in the semiautonomous literary field of the martial law period was access to politically controlled public resources.

JOURNEY OF THE LOCALIST POSITION

Amid the strife that currently threatens to rend Taiwan's literary community along ethnic (mainlander versus native Taiwanese) and ideological (Chinese nationalism versus Taiwanese nationalism) lines, the plight of native Taiwanese writers in the early post–1949 years has frequently been a topic of heated debate. Localists recall the Nationalist regime's systematic repression of local culture and these writers, while Mainstream agents counter that the government paid due respect to the culture of Taiwan as a Chinese region and did its best to help native Taiwanese writers establish themselves after the war. In a sense, the disagreement boils down to different opinions about the legitimacy of the Nationalist government's resinicization program. To those who accept the premise that native Taiwanese had to be resinicized after the Japanese colonizers were expelled,[1] the hardships incurred to that end were necessary evils. However, the aim of this study is not to address this political question. Instead, it is concerned with how forces in Taiwan's general field of power have given rise to different artistic positions within the literary field and have affected the trajectories of those artistic positions and the cultural agents occupying them.

> The field of cultural production produces its most important effects through the play of the *homologies* between the fundamental opposition which gives the field its structure and oppositions structuring the field of power and the field of class relations. These homologies may give rise to ideological effects which are produced automatically whenever oppositions at different levels are superimposed or merged. (Bourdieu, *The Field* 44)

Whereas for Bourdieu, the main opposition that gives the cultural field its structure is between the subfield of restricted production (e.g., works produced according to the art for art's sake principle) and the subfield of large-scale production (e.g., best-sellers), in Taiwan the political factor has predominated over the economic factor in the literary field. Strictly speaking, the Localist artistic position was an effect of social opposition between Taiwan's two major ethno-ideological groups. Mainlanders were predisposed to accept the sinocentric cultural narrative endorsed by the mainlander-controlled Nationalist regime, to which their political interests were closely tied. In opposition, in the 1970s native Taiwanese began to agitate for "Taiwanese consciousness," asserting the subjectivity of a historically formed Taiwanese community. As this opposition movement developed in the 1980s, Taiwanese consciousness evolved as a more politically aimed Localist ideology, fielded especially by the Democratic Progressive Party. By the mid-1980s there appeared a rather neat correspondence between the ethno-ideological divide in the general field of power and the opposition between Mainstream and Localist artistic positions in the literary field. Cultural agents occupying the Mainstream position tended to support the government's sinocentric ideology, and agents in the Localist position joined in asserting "Taiwanese consciousness." This division would later be rendered more blurred—even while still largely tenable—and enmeshed in specific power struggles of the post–martial law period. Here I chart the long and convoluted process leading up to that pronounced division, tracing it back to the early part of the contemporary epoch.

Marginal Existence Within the Literary Field: Early Days of the Epoch

For the first fifteen years or so after 1949, the Localist opposition was at best submerged and indistinct. A number of factors prevented self-conscious identification with local Taiwanese culture and history from producing visible effects within the mainlander-dominated literary field. The most obvious was the language barrier. When the Nationalist government banned Japanese and instituted Mandarin as Taiwan's official language, middle-aged Taiwanese intellectuals who had been educated in Japanese and spoke the Minnan (Taiwanese) dialect at home were immediately handicapped. Daunted by the immense difficulty of adopting a new language as their creative medium, the majority of Taiwanese writers who had established themselves before the island's retrocession gave up on literature.[2] Repressive thought-policing practices also contributed to their silence, and all native Taiwanese intellectuals lived under the shadow of the February 28 Incident, during which many were killed or incarcerated. Some important Taiwanese literary figures were jailed during and after the incident, and therefore physically absent from the field for more than a decade.[3]

More than anything else, however, it was the official sinocentric ideology that ultimately fixed the game against native Taiwanese cultural agents. The Nationalist government had to insist on the "regional" status of Taiwan and Taiwanese culture as part of its claim to legitimate sovereignty over all China. As a result, mainlander cultural agents, who already dominated Taiwan's cultural institutions and personal networks, also brought far greater cultural capital to the literary competition. Finally, besides projecting a diminutive view of Taiwan as a regional entity, sinocentrism was overtly divisive in its attitudes toward the native population. For instance, pejoratives like *nuhua* (becoming slaves), referring to Taiwanese people's colonial experience, appeared frequently in official documents.[4] Whether the majority of the Taiwanese intellectuals actually rejected Chinese cultural identity or not is difficult to say, but the stigma attached to their Japanese experience certainly inhibited their expression, depriving Taiwanese writers of the larger part of their own history as source material. The language and cultural policies designed to resinicize postcolonial Taiwan radically devalued the cultural capital of Taiwanese writers who had come of age in the colonial period.

In a nutshell, the government's monopoly over the distribution of both economic and cultural capital most directly put native Taiwanese writers at a disadvantage early on. With the government maintaining effective control over the institutions that sponsored, consecrated, and disseminated literary products—the media (especially the *fukan*), the publishing industry, and academia—throughout the martial law period, power relations between the Mainstream and Localist positions (or at least those agents who would occupy the Localist position when it emerged later on) remained largely unchanged. Crucial to the government's grip on the cultural field was its remarkable success in education, where it cultivated new corps of consumers for the sinocentric culture.

By the early 1960s, with the coming of age of the first postwar generation and increased social and economic stability, an invigorated intellectual climate with greater critical potential began to emerge, providing the backdrop to the Modernist literary formation. Because of their different background, native Taiwanese Modernists of this generation—Ouyang Zi, Chen Ruoxi, Chen Yingzhen (the early period), Wang Zhenhe, Qideng Sheng, Ye Shan, and Lin Huaimin—did not suffer the same deficit of cultural and linguistic capital as their forebears. Some members of this group, including Chen Yingzhen and Chen Ruoxi, even became staunch Chinese nationalists, albeit in the service of leftist ideology. Thus, in 1964, when a veteran Taiwanese writer from the colonial period, Wu Zhuoliu, founded *Taiwan wenyi* [Taiwanese literature], a literary magazine with Localist leanings, he must have been motivated by a genuine sense of crisis. Two decades of Nationalist indoctrination apparently was threatening to erase the cultural memory of Taiwan's colonial past, and along with it any Taiwancentric historical perspective. The 1960s thus represented a low tide for the Localist position in Taiwan's literary field, which was captivated by imported Modernist aesthetics.

Alliance with the Nativist Literary Formation and Subsequent Departure

The 1970s was a critical turning point, beginning with the "return to the native" social ferment—a harbinger of the full-fledged Nativist literary movement—and ending with the Nativist literary debate in 1977–78. The Nativist movement was the first large-scale oppositional cultural formation in post–1949 Taiwan, but since its challenge to the KMT hegemony was couched in a leftist ideology that took the West as "Other," what "native" referred to—"China" or "Taiwan"?—was left ambiguous, at least in the movement's first few years. In fact, as became clear later, its leading advocate, Chen Yingzhen, consciously carried forward the legacy of Communist activists who were persecuted in the aftermath of the February 28 Incident and during the 1950s White Terror.[5] Chen and similar-minded Nativists, therefore, did not explicitly challenge the government's vision of a sacred, undivided "China"—instead, it was their leftist ideology that made them oppositional.

Although specifically Taiwanese identity was obviously nascent in the Nativist literary movement, the anti-West, left-leaning Chinese nationalists represented by Chen Yingzhen and Yu Tiancong were the movement's most prominent advocates, and its most articulate critics of the dominant culture. The Localist assertion of a separate Taiwanese identity directly countered state ideology, and was perceived at the time to be even more dangerous than leftism. Hence, the more Localist-minded element, like Ye Shitao, kept a low profile in the Nativist movement, for the time submerging their own agenda in the interest of combating a common enemy, the KMT hegemony.

Disagreements within the Nativist movement eventually came to a head, leading to a factional split in the early 1980s, followed immediately in 1983–84 by the Taiwan consciousness debate (*Taiwan yishi lunzhan*), which brought the ambivalent status of Taiwan vis-à-vis "China" to the fore in public discourse. The Localists emerged from this with their own, increasingly vocal movement advocating Taiwanese cultural nationalism, while the original leftist/Chinese nationalist faction became a marginalized minority in a matter of a few years. This development largely paralleled the growth of the political opposition movement in the 1980s, led first by the *dangwai* (outside the party) coalition and then by its successor, the Democratic Progressive Party.

Rising on the tide of maturing social forces and the intellectual class's growing demand for self-assertion, the Nativist movement inspired many successful artistic enterprises in the late 1970s and 1980s. It called attention to local cultural products and works inspired by native traditions with its key "return to the native" motif, but this was variously interpreted. One prominent version focused on ancient Chinese traditions. This was the choice, for instance, of the Cloudgate Dance Series, the Orchid Mound Theater Studio, and the campus folk song movement. The Nativist movement was also instrumental in instigating a moderate, left-leaning, progressive trend among younger intellectuals, mainly college students and journalists, in the mid- to late 1980s, especially through magazines like *Xiachao* [Summer tide] and *Renjian* [Human world]. This trend even had a spillover effect on some well-known Mainstream artists, explaining the romantic portrayal of 1950s leftist martyrs in Lan Bozhou's nonfiction *Huangmache zhige* [Song of the canopied chariot] (1989) and Hou Hsiao-hsien's films *Beiqing chengshi* [A city of sadness] (1989) and *Haonan haonü* [Good men, good women] (1995).

Following the left wing of the prewar literary fields of both mainland China and Taiwan, cultural agents occupying the Nativist position took "realism" as their guiding aesthetic. Nativist realism foregrounded class struggle and economic exploitation in its condemnation of the West and capitalist development.[6] Favoring a less ideologically driven, more Taiwancentric agenda, the Localists at first took a number of critical idioms and aesthetic assumptions from the Nativists, exhibiting a similar propensity for realism and themes focused on the common folk before developing a separate artistic identity. Always mindful of the past history and future fate of the Taiwanese community, however, Localist literature gradually produced a unique aesthetic signature underlined by this sense of Taiwanese cultural nationalism.

The Localist position has inspired important debates and widely disseminated its motifs in the literary field since the mid-1980s. Notable Localist works consist of a handful of *dahe xiaoshuo*, or "big-stream novels"—family sagas chronicling the early history of Taiwanese settlers, such as *Hanye* [Wintry night] (1980) by Li Qiao and *Lang tao sha* [Waves lap the sand] (1990) by Dongfang Bai—and short stories about political prisoners and the February 28 Incident.

In her recent critical collection, Chen Lifen suggests that "big-stream novels" function more as public ritual than as works of literature—few people have actually finished reading these multivolume novels, yet their prominent display in bookstores is symbolically significant (209). Her overall assessment (at least of *Waves*) concurs with the critical consensus that most Localist literary products are limited artistic achievements. While different apologies have been offered for this, and some Localist critics consider the judgment unfair, I propose an argument based on this discussion of contending legitimacy principles. Historically, the trajectory of the Localist position has been determined primarily by its struggle for political legitimacy within the dominant sinocentric literary culture. With the dramatic reversal of political power relations in the late 1980s, it finally acquired legitimacy. However, this was at the time when the whole cultural field was escaping political subjugation and gaining relative autonomy. The resulting multiplication and diversification of agencies of consecration meant that a new *cultural* principle of legitimacy was increasingly asserted over the old political principle. Seeing this, agents occupying the Mainstream position eagerly appropriated aesthetic innovations introduced by the Modernists in the 1960s and 1970s, effectively equipping the Mainstream with the cultural legitimacy it needed to remain competitive. Meanwhile, the Localists, having struggled so long from the margins, always for the old *political* legitimacy and always without the resources of the Mainstream and Modernist writers, were now caught with a deficit of appropriate *cultural* capital. Having spent all their energy winning the old race, the Localists collapsed across the finish line only to find that it had just been moved. This is the story explored in the remainder of the chapter.

Submerged Existence in the Early Part of the Epoch

The foregoing discussion introduced the development of the Localist position in outline form; here I take a closer look at its uncertain existence prior to the early 1980s, before the political opposition movement served as a catalyst for the radicalization of Localist ideology. It is important to remember that the conflict between the ideals of the officially sanctioned sinocentric culture and those of postcolonial Taiwanese intellectuals was by no means uniform and unambiguous. Even among staunch separatists, attitudes toward Chinese cultural identity have been subject to constant modification. A brief look at the careers of two native Taiwanese writers—one older, to represent the generation of native Taiwanese intellectuals who "crossed over" from the Japanese period, and one younger, to represent those who came of age in the postwar period—will illuminate some significant but frequently misunderstood features of the Localist position in the early years of the epoch.

Wu Zhuoliu (1900–1976)

Born in 1900 to gentry in central Taiwan, Wu Zhuoliu was a primary school teacher for several years before turning to journalism, and later spent time in both Japan and mainland China. From his *magnum opus*, the semiautobiographical novel *Yaxiya de gu'er* [Orphan of Asia], we know that Wu came from a Taiwanese family that maintained a strong Han Chinese identity in spite of Japanese assimilation efforts. Unlike his contemporaries, Yang Kui, Zhang Wenhuan, and Lü Heruo, who went to Tokyo and started their literary apprenticeship there, Wu also traveled to Shanghai to work and study for several years until the outbreak of the Sino-Japanese war in 1937.

Wu published no significant work until after the war, and was very much outside Taiwan's literary mainstream in the early 1940s. *Orphan of Asia*, written in secret under the surveillance of Japanese police during the last years of the Pacific War, however, made Wu an important spokesman of the Taiwanese colonial experience. The novel's straightforward theme is the dilemma of the Taiwanese colonial subject caught among multiple national and cultural identities: Chinese, Japanese, and Taiwanese.

Wu later wrote two memoirs, *Wuhuaguo* [The fig tree] and *Taiwan lianqiao* [Taiwanese forsythia], both containing eyewitness accounts of the February 28 Incident. The former was serialized in *Taiwanese Literature* in 1968, and the latter, a longer version with more forthright observations, was composed underground at great personal risk, since in the 1970s February 28 was still very much a taboo subject. Wu asked a confidant (Zhong Zhaozheng—see below) to hold the manuscript for ten years after his death before submitting it for publication. He knew well the danger involved in playing the conscientious intellectual under repressive ruling regimes, Japanese and Nationalist alike.

While much attention has been given to Wu's status as a witness of history, his other significant contribution to contemporary Taiwan's literary field was the founding of the magazine *Taiwanese Literature* in 1964. Drawing on private donations and personal savings, Wu single-handedly established the magazine and its annual literary prizes for fiction and poetry. Despite its small circulation, perennial financial difficulties, and relatively peripheral position in the field, *Taiwanese Literature* persevered, promoting a separate literary culture for native Taiwanese writers, apart from the mainlander-dominated Mainstream position. Providing a forum for Localist issues, the magazine served as a home base for networking purposes and proclaimed the existence of a distinctive Localist position.

In his writing and in private conversations Wu voiced the original Localist motive, namely a profound discontent with the way that native Taiwanese writers were relegated to a subordinate position in their own society and targeted by discriminative cultural practices. His preferred form of resistance, however, was quiet, lacking the assertiveness of later Localist cultural agents. As a member of a politically moderate gentry class, Wu maintained social connections that helped to safeguard his literary activities; this moderation was also crucial to the survival of the magazine at a time when the very term "Taiwanese literature" aroused suspicion. The fact that today Wu's writings lend themselves to use by both Chinese and Taiwanese nationalists testifies to the indeterminacy of his position on the thorny identity issue, an uncertainty that typified the Localist position and its occupants in the early part of the post–1949 era.

Wu died in 1976, and the editorship of *Taiwanese Literature* was handed down to novelist Zhong Zhaozheng, who had helped run the magazine during its first thirteen years. Zhong belongs to the first generation of Taiwanese writers who entered the literary profession after 1949. The strategies he adopted to compete in the mainlander-dominated field confirm the ambivalence of the Localist position, and shed light on the rules that governed the operations of the field.

Zhong Zhaozheng (b. 1925)

Zhong Zhaozheng's artistic achievement pales in comparison with that of his peers, notably Zhong Lihe and Ye Shitao. Zhong Lihe was arguably the most accomplished of his generation in artistic terms, but died too early to play a major role in contemporary Taiwan's literary field. Ye Shitao, on the other hand, began his literary career in the last years of the colonial period under the tutelage of a famous Japanese mentor, Nishikawa Mitsuru. Of the three, Zhong Zhaozheng is the only one who tried very hard to work with the Nationalist-engineered dominant culture in post–1949 Taiwan.

Although Zhong grew up in the Japanese period and had to switch to writing in Mandarin at the age of twenty, his initiation into literary production came after the war. While he is often credited with pioneering "big-stream novels," his *Taiwanren sanbuqu* [Trilogy of the Taiwanese] and *Zhuoliu sanbuqu* [Trilogy of the turbid stream] do not display the spirit of resistance that came to be associated with the signature Localist genre in the 1980s. Zhong's works, and the early works of postwar native Taiwanese writers in general, incorporate a number of literary tropes and plot conventions prevalent in Mainstream fiction and contain little of the ideologically informed themes that would later characterize the Localist position. This is understandable in view of the channels through which aspiring young writers attained their apprenticeship, typically by attending the workshops, training sessions, and correspondence schools sponsored by the Association of Chinese Literature and Arts and government-affiliated literary magazines. Clearly very familiar with Mainstream literary conventions, writers like Zhong, Liao Qingxiu, and Wenxin included certain elements in their own work—nationalistic sentiment, moral themes accentuating the positive side of human nature, and romantic plots—and not the "realism" stressed by later Localist works.

In 1957, Zhong found seven or eight like-minded native Taiwanese writers around the island and started a handwritten, carbon-copied monthly newsletter, the *Wenyou tongxun* [Newsletter for literary friends].[7] It lasted eighteen months, during which it served as a forum for issues of common interest to its members as well as a platform for "publishing" their literary works, which were often rejected by Mainstream magazines and *fukan*. Most of the original members became lifelong friends and comrades in the shared cause. A reprinting of the newsletters in 1983 by the journal *Literary World*, during the Taiwanese consciousness debate, is counted in recent Localist literary scholarship as a heroic record of the plight of a small number of dedicated native Taiwanese writers of the postwar generation—young adults in 1949—who just would not give up their pursuit of a literary vocation, despite extremely difficult circumstances. More to my purpose, and treated less sentimentally, the newsletters tell a great deal about the nature of the interaction between agents occupying the incipient Localist position and the Nationalist-instituted sinocentric cultural hegemony.

Staff of the *Newsletter* were a self-selected group who possessed enough of the right sort of cultural capital to give them a slight advantage in gaining acceptance in the Mainstream literary field. Zhong Lihe and Li Rongchun had both lived in mainland China for several years; Zhong had eloped with his fiancée of the same clan name, and Li was a paramilitary conscript during the Sino-Japanese war. Zhong, in particular, was a highly competent stylist of Mandarin prose and familiar with the Chinese new literature tradition. Li still struggled in Mandarin, but a novel based on his China experience, *Motherland and Compatriots*, won him a handsome grant from the Chinese Literature and the Arts Awards Committee in 1953. Liao Qingxiu and Wenxin were civil servants who attended writing workshops sponsored by the Chinese Writers' and Artists' Association, and Liao even received some tutoring from Zhao Youpei, a prominent mainlander literary figure.

Some of the *Newsletter* discussions naturally focused on the linguistic barrier faced by Taiwanese writers. At one point, Zhong Zhaozheng even initiated a discussion on whether the Taiwanese dialect should be considered an appropriate medium in creative writing. The majority of the group, however, argued for the advantages of adopting Mandarin as the standard, making arguments strikingly similar to those found in official documents (*Zhong Zhaozheng huiyilu II* 23–26; hereafter cited as *Huiyilu*). This might be interpreted as voluntary support of the sinocentric dominant culture, and given the complexities of dual identity as both Taiwanese and Chinese, this is certainly a plausible explanation. However, the *Newsletter* discussions are notable for their pragmatism. These writers wrote to be published, and to achieve that goal the best strategy was to make the linguistic switch. To gain legitimate membership in the literary field, they were prepared to play the game according to its prevailing rules.[8]

As Bourdieu says, by entering the game, cultural agents "tacitly accept the constraints and the possibilities inherent in that game (which are presented not in the form of rules, but rather as possible winning strategies)" (*The Field* 184). Even mainlander writers were subject to political constraints in those years, but the rules governing the literary field were much less favorable to native Taiwanese writers like Zhong Zhaozheng and his comrades. In this climate, Zhong blazed a pragmatic path for native writers and at the same time served uniquely as a facilitator and mediator between Mainstream and Localist cultural agents. Nationalist cultural bureaucrats adopted Zhong Zhaozheng as a token Taiwanese writer, awarding him numerous prizes and grants and putting him on various committees. Ideologically inoffensive, as early as 1965 he received financial assistance to publish twenty volumes of works by Taiwanese writers, "to commemorate the fifteenth anniversary of the retrocession of Taiwan." At the same time, he was the person to whom Wu entrusted his manuscript containing a highly sensitive eyewitness account of the February 28 Incident, *Taiwanese Forsythia*. Zhong translated the manuscript (from Japanese) and had it published about ten years after Wu's death, according to the author's will (*Huiyilu II* 106–114).

Zhong's position was complex, partly owing to what Bourdieu would call his socially constructed "habitus," which predisposed him for certain position-taking strategies. Zhong had earned his place in the field partly thanks to his dynamic personality and outgoing temperament. His class background also helped. The son of a small-town Hakka family, Zhong belonged to a conservative social group that had historically clashed less with the KMT regime than the larger Minnan dialect community. In the early days, Zhong was apparently predisposed to identify with the Nationalist dominant culture, and later he did not actively participate in the oppositional Nativist literary movement. Even in his more recent essays, Zhong repeatedly invokes the concept of *chunwenxue* to defend his professional integrity and to prove that he has no political agenda, a familiar strategy among agents occupying the Mainstream position.[9] To a great extent, Zhong's achievement is attributable to his insistent efforts to remain an active player in the game. This is especially obvious in comparison with another *Newsletter* contributor, Li Rongchun. Encouraged by the government award he received for his first novel, *Motherland and Compatriots*, Li devoted himself to literature and resorted to menial physical labor to support himself. Failing to secure a position in the literary field due to his introvert personality as well as some accidental factors (*Huiyilu II* 40–41), he led a reclusive life focused on writing. The result was pitiful—even the story collections published posthumously by his nephew failed to attract much attention. Aside from other factors, Li's near-complete isolation from the field counts as a major reason for his failure.

There were of course moments of awkwardness and uncertainty in Zhong Zhaozheng's career. For instance, in the wake of the Nativist literary debate, when works by native Taiwanese writers were suddenly in demand, Zhong was made editor-in-chief of the *Minzong ribao* [People's daily news] in the early 1980s. For publishing several politically sensitive works by native writers, he was removed as editor after eighteen months.

In his memoir, Zhong inadvertently reveals that he took chances as editor strategically—transgression of the government's boundaries was a popular play for artistic respect in those days—not for ideological reasons (*Huiyilu II*). He continued to succeed, later, by sticking to the game currently being played.

Since the early 1990s, Zhong has become one of the most celebrated Localist writers, collecting multiple honors along the way, including an appointment to the DPP President's Advisory Board and a scholarly conference dedicated to his life and work.[10] He has again returned to the Mainstream position in the literary field, which in the post–martial law period has been reconstituted in the Localist mold. Beneath the veneer of change lies continuity.[11]

Thus, while the sinocentric cultural hegemony discriminated against native Taiwanese writers, clearly there was an available choice to work within its constraints and possibilities. In making that choice, Zhong Zhaozheng may have displayed a certain degree of ideological naiveté. Others, however, feigned cooperation with the sinocentric discourse more purposefully, in order to gain a position from which to surreptitiously articulate their discontent. This tactic is exemplified by Ye Shitao, the focus of the next section.

DIVERGENT TRAJECTORIES OF TWO LEADING LITERARY FIGURES

The following incident, shortly after the political turnover in May 2000, reflects the changing power relations in today's cultural field and encapsulates the historical trajectories of the two opposite positions within it. In celebration of the millennium, the City of Kaohsiung expanded its Nineteenth Annual Award for Literature and Arts, conferring Life Achievement Awards on six eminent members of the cultural community. Yu Guangzhong, Taiwan's most celebrated Modernist poet, and Ye Shitao, the leading critic and literary historian of the Localist camp, were both honored. However, the award ceremony on July 1, attended by a number of dignitaries from the new DPP cabinet, was disrupted by two events that instantly made headlines.[12]

When the Minister of Education was about to hand the award to Yu Guangzhong, a former winner of the same award, Zhang Deben, shouted out from the audience, accusing Yu of being an enemy of Taiwanese literature. As the ceremony proceeded, the protester continued, yelling, "The wolf is here!"—apparently alluding to a controversial newspaper article Yu wrote in 1977 at the outset of the Nativist debate. The article was a public battle cry against Nativist critics' advocacy of *gongnongbing* (proletarian) literature, which, in Yu's view, menaced Taiwan by encouraging a Communist insurgence. This earned him the reputation of being a hit man for the Nationalist government.

The second surprise came as Zhong Zhaozheng, in his capacity as a newly appointed advisor to President Chen Shui-bian, delivered his speech before conferring Ye Shitao's award. Zhong first deplored the fact that the value of Taiwanese literature was never properly recognized in the age of the White Terror. He then blurted out that the site where the ceremony was being held, the Zhongzheng Cultural Center, was a place "without culture," for it still bore the name of the repressive ruler, Chiang Kai-shek ("Zhongzheng" was Chiang's honorific public name). Zhong's remark conveyed a vindictiveness to which many veteran Localists feel entitled, but it was a surprising public statement nonetheless.

No less revealing is the contrast between Yu's and Ye's demeanors at a roundtable preceding the ceremony, when the winners were invited to express opinions on promoting culture in the City of Kaohsiung using public resources. Yu cited examples of publicly funded cultural spectacles in various regions of the world (Europe, Russia, China, Hong Kong, and Singapore) and shared his own ideas for inserting poetry into commercials and producing a national park photo album. He also noted that a business group had funded the professorship he currently held. Ye, on the other hand, spoke mostly about obstacles and personal frustrations, projecting a grim outlook for literary edification in the face of engrossing materialism. A look back on the literary careers just of these two figures, Yu Guangzhong and Ye Shitao, provides a good view of the historical trajectories of the Mainstream and Localist artistic positions more generally.

Born three years apart, in 1928 and 1925 respectively, Yu in mainland China and Ye in Taiwan, both belong to the era-crossing generation who had barely entered adulthood when the Nationalist era began. With similar gentry backgrounds and precocious talent, both chose the literary vocation at an early age. Yu published poems while still a freshman at Xiamen University, while Ye was employed by the prestigious Japanese-language magazine, *Wenyi Taiwan* [Literary Taiwan], immediately after graduating from high school. The lives of both young writers were disrupted by the war. Yu was among the refugees who fled to Taiwan with the Nationalist government. Ye was enlisted by the Japanese army shortly before the war ended.

In the mainlander-dominated literary field of the 1950s, Yu Guangzhong stood out as a brilliant and energetic young poet. Actively contributing to leading journals and newspaper literary supplements, he soon became the editor of poetry features in several of these publications.[13] By the time the Modernist poetry debate broke out in 1956, Yu was established enough to take an independent stance, purporting to synthesize the traditional and the modern. After graduating from college, he earned an M.F.A. from the Iowa International Writers' Program in 1959. In the 1960s, while teaching in the English Department at National Normal University, Yu twice visited North America under the auspices of the U.S. government. By the early 1970s, he was well established, having fought and won several debates in the poetry circle and published some of his best-known works. After moving to the Chinese University of Hong Kong in 1974, Yu remained active in Taiwan's literary scene and participated in the Nativist debate from abroad. He returned to Taiwan eleven years later, this time as Dean of Liberal Arts at National Sun Yat-sen University.

Ye, on the other hand, was imprisoned for three years in the early 1950s, after being implicated in a political case involving a Taiwanese Communist organization. When he was granted amnesty and released in 1954, Ye found his family impoverished, having lost their land in the government's Land Reform program, and he had difficulty landing a job because of his poor Mandarin accent and his criminal record. In the village where he finally found employment as a primary school teacher, he did not even have regular access to current literary publications. After living under the shadow of the White Terror for a decade, Ye unexpectedly reemerged from obscurity and resumed writing, although, as a meagerly paid teacher, he had to resort to translating books from Japanese for supplemental income. Ye's fiction was not generally considered to be first-rate. A plausible excuse is that his Chinese writing ability was not up to his lofty ambition to produce an epic novel about the historical turmoil that Taiwanese of his generation experienced. What made his name in the literary field were his essays about native Taiwanese writers, both of the contemporary period and from colonial times. Most notably, in the heat of the Nativist movement, Ye wrote an article ambitiously titled "Taiwan xiangtu wenxueshi daolun" [Introduction to the history of Taiwanese nativist literature] (1977), a work later hailed as a landmark in the development of the Localist position. Though cautiously camouflaged in a sinocentric frame, the article unmistakably evoked a historically formed, independent Taiwanese subjectivity. This was immediately detected and publicly decried by the leading Nativist critic, Chinese nationalist Chen Yingzhen, as a regrettable "blind spot." The event was an early public signal of the schism to come within the ranks of the Nativists.

Ye's financial difficulty points to the unfair distribution of resources during the martial law period, but this was only part of the Localists' trouble. At an even more basic level, the ultimate violence that the Nationalist government committed against native Taiwanese writers was the complete devaluation of their knowledge and experience acquired in the Japanese period, including their language skills and their exposure to different artistic, cultural, and intellectual traditions. Yu Guangzhong was able to utilize well his knowledge and experience of the Chinese new literature tradition. Ye Shitao not only lacked access to new resources but also saw most of the cultural capital he did possess turned into a liability.[14] A disciple of comparatively harmless romantic literary visions in his early years as a protégé of the Japanese writer Nishikawa Mitsuru, Ye was ironically transformed by the Nationalist government's policies into a fighter for the repressed Localist position.

Finally, at the same award ceremony in Kaohsiung, a statement made by Chen Yuxiu (Tchen Yu-hsiu), the newly appointed Chairwoman of the Council of Cultural Affairs,[15] presents an important perspective: "The new government will pay greater respect to pluralistic cultural developments, so that the local culture can broaden its horizon and be allowed to grow in a more fertile soil." While criticizing the Nationalist government for its monolithic cultural policy, Chen indicated in the same breath that the Localist position was too narrow, something that has to be improved, and thus tacitly endorsed the forward-looking, "going global" direction that Yu had advocated earlier.

Global vision is an essential part of the DPP's new official policy line, presented as crucial to the interests of the state. Aptly putting closure to controversies surrounding the award ceremony, Chen's statement suggests that, even as the cultural politics of sinocentrism versus Localism continues to fuel fierce struggles in the literary field, another factor, the outside world and its alternative cultural visions, will also play significantly in the distribution of public resources—and thus constitute important cultural capital—in the new era.

PART 3

CHAPTER 6

Fukan-Based Literary Culture and Middle-Class Genres

Nanfang Shuo (pen name of Wang Xingqing), a renowned columnist and public intellectual, nicely sums up the momentous events in Taiwan in the 1970s and 1980s:[1]

> Chronologically speaking, for Taiwan the seventies began with the appointment of Chiang Ching-kuo as the Deputy Speaker of the Executive Yuan in June 1969, which heralded the predictable arrival of a "Chiang Ching-kuo Era"; what unmistakably punctuated the end of the decade, then, was the severing of diplomatic relations with the United States in December 1979. . . . This was a decade in which the status of Taiwan in the international arena was severely challenged. Mainland China replaced Taiwan as the legitimate Chinese government . . . [after the latter's] withdrawal from the United Nations in October 1971. . . . In addition to setbacks in the political sphere, there were also the economic fluctuations and price inflation caused by the two energy crises in the 1970s. Perhaps an even more significant event was the death of the late President Chiang Kai-shek in April 1975. (Yang, Ze *Lixiang* 118)

> The 1980s began with the trial of the Meilidao Incident in February 1980, and concluded with the skyrocketing stock market reaching ten thousand points. In between was the founding of the Democratic Progressive Party in September 1986; the lifting of martial law in 1987; and the death of Chiang Ching-kuo in 1988. The historical landscape shifted at such a breathtaking pace that people found themselves already bidding farewell to a bygone era. (Yang, Ze *Kuangbiao* 21)

The impact of events like these was comprehensive and powerful, among other things effecting definitive changes in the cultural field. The diplomatic setbacks in the 1970s, for instance, were among the immediate causes of the Nativist literary movement, the first counterhegemonic cultural trend in Taiwan after 1949. The movement effectively stigmatized Modernism as a byproduct of postwar American cultural imperialism, initiating a collective search for "subjectivity" that gripped cultural activities for the next few decades. The convoluted identity quest was then steered in a different direction by political developments. The Meilidao Incident, the martial law trial,[2] and the resulting decade-long struggle between opposition political forces and the Nationalist government were accompanied by the swift ascendance of the Localism in the cultural arena. Localists rejected the Chinese nationalism underlying the Nativist agenda and challenged the sinocentrism of the dominant culture. Meanwhile, Mainstream literary agents' resistance to direct political interference and appropriation of the Taiwanese nationalism endorsed by the Localists constituted the central dynamics of cultural activities for a large part of the 1980s. Finally, at the end of that decade, the lifting of martial law and the booming economy ushered in a new era. The withdrawal of the state from direct interference in cultural affairs, coupled with economic liberalization, brought global capitalism deeper into the country's cultural arena, and writers, editors, and publishers responded with new strategies to remain competitive in a freer, more pluralistic, and patently consumer-oriented society.

This chapter focuses on the crucial period of transition—the ten to fifteen years that preceded the "Great Divide" precipitated by the lifting of martial law—beginning in the mid-1970s, when the coterie of elitist journals that had controlled the production of "serious" literature since the 1960s ceded their leadership role to *fukan*. My account of the rise of *fukan*-based literary culture gives special attention to two major newspapers, the *China Times* and the *United Daily News*. The inspired rivalry between their *fukan* sections—*Renjian* and *Lianfu,* respectively—powerfully shaped the Mainstream literary production of baby-boom writers. The last part of the chapter is devoted to this Mainstream literature, especially its middle-class genre attributes and political conservatism, and to individual artists whose efforts exceeded its limitations.

FUKAN AND FUKAN-BASED LITERARY CULTURE

Bracketed by the Nativist literary movement in the 1970s and the lifting of martial law in the late 1980s, the last fifteen years of the martial law period were a golden age of sorts for the literary field. Many writers, critics, editors, and publishers achieved celebrity status. The *fukan* institution, riding the high tide of media expansion, emerged as the major sponsor of cultural activities, among which literature featured centrally. In addition to annual writing contests, public lectures, and creative writing workshops and youth camps, *fukan* also staged high-visibility events, special forums, and briefings on intellectual currents from the "outside world"—normally referring to the West.[3] Since the prestige and money from publishing in *fukan* were high, their editors commanded great power to dictate legitimate literary discourse and consecrate writers and critics. This was a time when Taiwan's literary field made great strides toward "relative autonomy," a process that Bourdieu describes thus:

> This process is correlated with the constant growth of a public of potential consumers, of increasing social diversity, which guarantees the producers of symbolic goods minimal conditions of economic independence and, also, a competing principle of legitimacy. It is also correlated with the constitution of an ever-growing, ever more diversified corps of producers and merchants of symbolic goods, who tend to reject all constraints apart from technical imperatives and credentials. Finally, it is correlated with the multiplication and diversification of agencies of consecration placed in a situation of competition for cultural legitimacy: not only academies and salons, but also institutions for diffusion, such as publishers and theatrical impresarios, whose selective operations are invested with a truly cultural legitimacy even if they are subordinated to economic and social constraints. (*The Field* 112)

Taiwan's steady economic development and strong public education in the postwar era supported autonomization, and the modernization and growing importance of *fukan* in the 1970s were early signs of the opening up of the cultural field. The number of positions in it increased, offering "basic resources to producers without a private income" (55). Some *fukan* gave stipends to promising young writers, and increasing numbers of creative writers found employment in the newspapers.[4] Meanwhile, the growing profitability of the literary market in the mid-1970s was attested to by the emergence of a handful of moderate-sized publishing houses—the well-known "five minors": Hongfan, Erya, Jiuge, Yuanliu, and Yuanjing—that specialized in literary products. Most of the owners of these publishing houses were either writers themselves or otherwise devoted to literature.

Rapid urbanization and the coming of age of the baby boomers in the 1980s resulted in greater social diversity and more avid cultural consumption. This decade saw the maturation of a readership among the country's growing middle and upper-middle classes, signaled by the opening of the Jinshitang [Kingstone] bookstore chain in 1983. A number of literary magazines and journals were founded, such as *Lianhe wenxue* [Unitas, a literary monthly] (1984–), *Dangdai* [Con-temporary monthly] (1986–), *Renjian* [Human world] (1985–89), and *Taiwan shehui yanjiu jikan* [Taiwan: A radical quarterly in social studies] (1988–); *Literary Star*, which was suspended in 1966, resumed publication in 1986. Several of these magazines had *fukan* affiliations, and each had its own ideological stance, ranging from conservative to liberal and radical, and content targeted at a specific audience, highbrow to more popular. This presaged further specialization and differentiation of cultural products in a more finely segregated market.

In the literary field, an unmistakable sign of the growing cultural stratification was the sudden rise to extreme popularity of certain middlebrow, quasi-literary genres, collectively known as *"lizhi wenlei"*—self-help and inspirational books, typically collections of short essays containing uplifting morals similar to those in *Reader's Digest*.[5] That some writers regarded this as betokening "the demise of pure literature" shows the extent to which a formerly dominant group in the literary field was threatened by market-oriented cultural production. But the entire cultural field was undergoing a process of professionalization. After the ban on publishing new newspapers (which also capped the number of pages existing papers could print per issue) was lifted in 1988 (Pan 90–92), press competition became more acute, causing major newspapers to explore different segments of the reading public. Book review sections, appealing to a maturing intellectual market, appeared in several major papers in the late 1980s.[6] Finally, a backflow of expatriate intellectuals from the West in the late 1980s and early 1990s contributed to the diversity and sophistication of cultural discourses, and to a mushrooming of public forums in both the print and the electronic media.

What were the effects of these transformations on the long struggle between political and cultural legitimacy? According to Bourdieu, more diversified corps of cultural producers and merchants "tend to reject all constraints apart from technical imperatives and credentials," and agencies of consecration are then forced to compete for "a truly cultural legitimacy" (*The Field* 112). This was clearly happening in Taiwan, but the process was complicated by historically specific circumstances.

Most studies have stressed immediate political causes when accounting for the transformation of the cultural field in the 1970s and 1980s, including all the events mentioned above. The story, however, is considerably more complicated, and extended explanations may be found along two lines. First, the transformation should be traced to long-term structural factors. For instance, the KMT's education policies and its success in maintaining a stable economy together created a rather homogeneous, conservative middle class, basically content with the status quo. At the same time, increasing affluence and the liberal democratic ideals promoted (albeit perfunctorily) by the government fueled middle-class desire to shed the state's authoritarian impositions. These twin impulses, to make Taiwan over as a modern civilization yet maintain stable cultural values, were manifested in two distinct types of cultural legitimacy endorsed by the key literary pacesetters of the era, the *fukan* of the *China Times* and the *United Daily News*, respectively. Second, economic and sociological factors—access to resources, market share, profit margins, and increasing professionalism—played vital roles, and merit more systematic investigation.

What follows is a preliminary step toward an extended look at the transformation that occurred in the 1970s and 1980s. It explores the interaction among the state, the market, and the literary field through a brief examination of the two major *fukan*, *Renjian* of the *China Times* and *Lianfu* of the *United Daily News*, and of the distinctive literary culture they nurtured. Individual human agency, I argue, played a prominent role. While undoubtedly constrained by political and economic forces, certain *fukan* editors were able at times to play these forces against each other, translating them into strengths.

Fukan as Cultural Forum: *Renjian* of the *China Times*

One condition that enabled *fukan* to assume such a forceful presence in Taiwan's cultural arena came, ironically, from political constraints.[7] Under martial law, daily newspapers were only allowed to print a very limited number of pages (Pan 90–92). *Fukan* pages occupied nearly one third of this space in some major newspapers. The fact that political news was routinely censored, making it predictable and unexciting, led newspapers to rely heavily on their *fukan* to attract subscribers. The literary supplements became broadly popular household reading as a consequence. This partly explains the tremendous power the charismatic and dynamic editor Gao Xinjiang wielded in the early 1970s, when he successfully transformed

Renjian of the *China Times* into a new cultural forum. Gao, who had a degree in journalism, tried to modernize the profession.[8] The government's recognition of the mass media's importance in the growing culture industry was demonstrated by its appointment of the owners of both the *China Times* and the *United Daily News* to the KMT Central Standing Committee. This gave the regime an extra surveillance mechanism at the same time that it increased the newspapers' already substantial popular influence. The major papers now performed a significant mediating role between the Nationalist regime and the public, investing *fukan* with great power.

Gao's success in developing *fukan* as a cultural forum started from the public perception of these sections, carried over from the early Republican period, as sources of both leisure reading and more serious material. The state's heavy investment in major newspapers like the *Zhongyang ribao* [Central daily news] as instruments of ideological indoctrination lent greater substance to that serious side. Gao likewise emphasized the serious, while also endeavoring to project *fukan* as providers of alternative viewpoints, albeit within the politically permissible scope. Feeding on the increasing dynamism of society and the enlightenment mentality of modern Chinese intellectuals, *fukan* presented themselves as a progressive force. The educated class, tired of the government's cultural control, naturally welcomed this. The country's isolation in the international community following its forced resignation from the United Nations (1972) and the severing of formal diplomatic relations with the United States (1979) not only triggered a need for self-assertion but also increased general awareness that liberalization and internationalization were essential and inevitable for the country's future development. It is not coincidental that Gao got his start editing the overseas section of *Renjian fukan*, which served as a window on Taiwan to the outside world before tourism was legalized. This also contributed to *Renjian*'s later focus on western high theory.[9]

The complexity of negotiating external constraints and reconfiguring cultural legitimacy is best illustrated by the delicate role *Renjian* played in the Nativist literary movement. Under Gao's direction, *Renjian* backed the Nativist critics' populist challenge with "reportage literature" documenting social injustice and environmental issues. This was an adventurous move, as investigations of class-related social issues were politically sensitive, being easily associated with leftist insurgence. However, Gao's romantic sinocentric cultural vision likely served as a balancing force. In the wake of the diplomatic setbacks of the early 1970s, both the government and the public were feeling nationalistic, and this was the primary impetus behind Nativist cultural trends. What is interesting in retrospect is the ambiguous referent of the word "China" as it appeared in Mainstream media, promulgating a rediscovery of native "Taiwanese" culture. That the notion of "China" is a discursive construction in the Foucauldian sense is nowhere more apparent than in *Renjian* in the 1970s, when advocates of sinocentrism like Gao projected their nationalistic visions onto the land and populace of Taiwan, concurring, albeit temporarily, with incipient Localist nationalism. Friction between sinocentrism and Localism (or Chinese and Taiwanese nationalisms) developed into fierce contention in the 1980s and 1990s, and the position of the Mainstream cultural agents who once ardently supported a sinocentric version of Taiwanese localism became painfully ambivalent—a situation eloquently depicted by second-generation mainlander writers like Zhu Tianxin, Zhu Tianwen, Zhang Dachun, and Luo Yijun in the post–martial law period.

The Nativist literary movement, a widely acknowledged turning point in contemporary Taiwan's cultural and social development, thus may be seen as carrying an additional set of implications. Earlier investigations of the movement in the literary studies tradition were largely concerned with conflicts between its ideological prescriptions and the aesthetics of writing. More recently, however, attention has shifted to the vehicle that carried the movement—the mass media, particularly *fukan*.[10]

The Nativist movement showcased the influence of *fukan*. They provided the main forum for the heated literary and political "debates" of the day, becoming a principal venue in the competition for cultural leadership. When the Nativist debate broke out in 1977, for instance, the *fukan* of the *United Daily News* and the *China Times* took opposite partisan stances. The former sided with conservative (pro-government) and liberal (Modernist) cultural agents, while the latter tacitly lent its assistance to the Nativists. Even as they strove to maintain the façade of neutral facilitators, the two rival newspapers engaged in a high-profile competition that became the cultural field's central dynamic for a large part of the 1980s.

The Nativist literary movement was one of many issues that raised *fukan* to the level of cultural forum. The increased affluence of the 1970s and 1980s generated confidence and an aspiration for change among the middle class. Within certain limits, the media were able to provide influential outlets for such reformist energies. *Renjian*, in particular, found its niche projecting a liberal progressive image within the confines of the mainstream. It cultivated this image by sponsoring a series of spectacular events, like the exhibition of work by native folk artist Hong Tong, that became landmarks in the history of contemporary Taiwan's social movements.[11]

As growing political opposition deconstructed the ruling Nationalist Party's political myths, idealistic intellectuals envisioned alternative political and social systems, including more liberal and more socialist versions. However, since both the *China Times* and the *United Daily News* were ultimately mainstream cultural institutions, staffed chiefly by mainlanders at the executive level and backed by government support, *Renjian* was never an organ of truly alternative, much less oppositional politics, and certainly nothing that seriously challenged sinocentrism. The cultural events that it sponsored are better understood as public rituals than as vehicles for any specific political agenda. They affirmed the value of cultural life and the sense of solidarity that shared culture promotes. Solidarity with like-minded people is an important aspect of identity construction, and the competition between the relatively progressive *Renjian* and the relatively conservative *Lianfu* played to this need. One might even argue that, in the 1970s and early 1980s, ideological differences functioned more as an index of social distinction than as politics *per se*.

Beginning in the mid-1980s and continuing in the 1990s, the Localist trend rapidly overhauled the country's dominant culture. Both *fukan* were forced to adjust. For *Lianfu,* which had relied more heavily on the Nationalist dominant culture for its identity, the transition was naturally more difficult, but *Renjian* and its affiliated cultural agents were also challenged. This and other factors, like the diversification of readership and the proliferation of consecrating cultural agencies, have removed the Mainstream *fukan* from center stage in the post–martial law era, but established *fukan* personal networks have remained important. After all, major literary publishers like Maitian [Ryefield] and Lianhe wenxue [Unitas], as well as the magazine *Unitas, a literary monthly*, had their beginnings in the two leading *fukan*.

The real importance of *fukan* culture was its role in the trend toward a more complete commercialization of the cultural sphere in the ten to fifteen years preceding the lifting of martial law. This role was strengthened, ironically, by the monopoly of public resources that supported their cultural leadership. The elegant awards ceremonies, the sumptuous parties in luxurious hotel ballrooms, and the handsome compensation for contributions to *fukan* pages created a festive atmosphere and a sense of affluence that mirrored Taiwan's transition in the 1980s from postwar "economy of scarcity" to what Guy Debord calls the "society of the spectacle" in an age of consumption.

Manufacturing a New Literary Culture: *Lianfu* of the *United Daily News*

The *United Daily News* has traditionally avoided direct ideological confrontation, striving instead to reinforce the conservative dominant culture. Under Lin Haiyin (*Lianfu*'s editor-in-chief between 1951 and 1962), *Lianfu* became a greenhouse of *chunwenxue* (a modified version of "pure literature"), and the editor's job was largely limited to reviewing, selecting, and editing submissions of creative writing. Lin's successor Ping Xintao, editor from 1963 to 1976, preserved this tradition while responding to an increasingly commercial literary environment, promoting writers of popular romance like Qiong Yao, the best known in this genre. The successful transformation of *Renjian* in the 1970s under Gao Xinjiang, however, required a similar effort by *Lianfu* to remain competitive. The new concept of "dynamic editing," for instance, required editors to engage more actively in planning content and designing special columns to address readers' concerns of the moment.

A DUAL MISSION: FROM THE POLITICAL TO THE CULTURAL

The appointment of Yaxian as editor-in-chief in October 1977 had immediate political implications. The personal profile of this fine poet of the Modernist era, whose editorship lasted almost two decades, suggests that the government was eager to maintain close control over one of the most important *fukan*. A graduate of the theater department at the KMT's Cadre School for Political Warfare, Yaxian had worked for the Chinese Youth Corp for Anti-Communism and National Salvation and served as chief editor of the party-owned magazine *Youshi wenyi* [Young lions magazine of literature and the arts] before going abroad to earn a master's degree in the United States. This training and experience in KMT orthodoxy explains obvious affinities between activities sponsored by *Lianfu* and the government's literary mobilization programs soon after 1949.

Yaxian shouldered the burden of consolidating *Lianfu*'s pro-government position and of carrying out remedial work in the midst of the highly divisive Nativist debate (1977–78). The government felt that it had to stop the Nativist literary movement to prevent the spread of leftist sentiment, but a more serious threat was the participation of native Taiwanese and the prospect of the tabooed subject of independent statehood coming into popular discussion. The Nationalist regime, by this time fully realizing the hopelessness of recapturing the Chinese mainland, wanted to set its own pace of nativization, to ease the impact of a transition to power of native Taiwanese, who constituted over 80 percent of the population. During the debate *Lianfu* was the chief government platform for attacks on the Nativists. Just before Yaxian was appointed in 1977, the supplement published several important articles reiterating the pro-government line. Yaxian's mission was to patch up the rift in literary circles and maintain the Nationalist monopoly over Taiwan's historical-cultural narrative. In his first three years at *Lianfu* several projects were undertaken to pacify and co-opt veteran native Taiwanese writers from the Japanese period, for instance, inviting them to contribute to a special fiction series, later collected in a volume called *Baodao ji* [Precious swords collection] (Huang, Wuzhong 37–42). Seminars were held and special volumes were published in a strenuous attempt to defuse the Localist position and gain co-authorship of the burgeoning nativization discourse.[12] While the official interpretation of the relationship between native Taiwanese and their Japanese colonizers was ultimately rejected in the 1980s and 1990s, these efforts succeeded temporarily in protecting the dominant position of Mainstream literary agents in the cultural field.

It would be a mistake, however, to evaluate Yaxian's exceptional accomplishments as editor of *Lianfu* in conventionally defined political terms. Even some of the projects that he launched concurrently with the political maneuvers of the late 1970s reveal a larger goal of expanding the media's influence in cultural production. Among these was an eye-catching series in 1978, *Disanlei jiechu* [The third encounter], which matched reputable people from different professions—a college professor and a popular singer, for instance—for sensational effect, engaging them in discussions of controversial social issues (like Bill Maher's *Politically Incorrect*) (Liu, Kexiang 69–75). While this kind of popular media forum would soon be pervasive, especially on television, it was entirely new in the late 1970s. Yaxian's *quanmin xiezuo* campaign, literally, "all people writing," also began in 1978 (Duye 55–60). It involved not only the *fukan* pages but also publishers affiliated with the newspaper in promoting a subgenre called *jiduanpian* (mini-short story), tailored to the busy schedules of modern men and women. In some ironic ways reminiscent of Communist "mass literature" campaigns, *jiduan pian* were instead saturated with the bourgeois utilitarianism that lay at the heart of the Nationalist government's cultural hegemony and soft-authoritarian rule. While later critics referred to the "mini-short story" as a successful commodity, at the time it could be seen as a sincere effort on Yaxian's part to negotiate between literary aspirations and commercial imperatives. The informing spirit, again, of pragmatism and compromise, was different from *Renjian*'s approach. While *Renjian* played on people's desire for political participation, *Lianfu* molded itself after the benevolent authoritarian government, cautiously broaching "change" in terms of social and economic modernization.

Many critics credit *Lianfu*'s contributions to the development of *chunwenxue* ("pure literature") in this period to Yaxian's personal commitment and artistic vision. Central to this vision was a neotraditionalist aesthetic—the term *"shuqing chuantong"* (lyrical tradition) was frequently invoked—that privileged genteel, apolitical forms of literature dealing with subjective feelings and sentiments. As previously argued, the term "pure literature" carried a political imprint in post–1949 Taiwan since it had arisen as a form of passive resistance to political mobilization practiced by Mainstream writers. The notion of pure literature remained problematic in its new incarnation within the so-called "lyrical tradition" as the literary field became increasingly commercialized. The conflict between using literature as a tool for winning newspaper readers and as a vehicle for disinterested personal expression could not always be resolved. Yet, unlike his predecessor Ping Xintao, Yaxian had a personal commitment to a high form of pure literature that seemed genuine. This inherent contradiction of the *fukan*-centered literary culture was reflected in the ambiguous position of many baby-boom generation writers, a subject that will be discussed further in the next chapter.

While the foundation of *Lianfu*'s leadership in the literary field was laid soon after 1949 under the editorship of Lin Haiyin, it was renewed and expanded in the 1970s with a number of successful new initiatives. In addition to establishing annual literary contests, *Lianfu* created a "young writers sponsorship program," through which the *United Daily News* offered a monthly stipend of NT$5,000 to ten young talents between 1976 and 1981, with the condition that they would submit their work to *Lianfu* for first consideration.[13] Judging from the distinguished accomplishments of the majority of these writers, the program must be deemed a success. Twenty years later an article in the 1997 commemorative volume, *Zhongshen de huayuan: Lianfu de lishi jiyi* [Garden of the gods: Historical memories of *Lianfu*],[14] quoted Yaxian saying the following about Wang Tiwu, owner of the *United Daily News*:

In fact, this project is something that should have been done by the government—it is definitely not one of media's responsibilities. It was out of his fondness for young people and adoration for their literary talents that Mr. Wang provided them with financial support through his newspaper's "extra-official" channel. (Jiang, Zhongming 49–50)

These words confirm that before the establishment of government agencies like the Council of Cultural Affairs the media functioned as proxies for the government in promoting cultural activities. This explains not only the perceived legitimacy of media-sponsored activities at the time but also the media's active involvement in the management of public resources for cultural affairs.

The positive side of this arrangement was that the media also functioned like the National Endowment for the Arts in the United States, promoting less popular forms of cultural production. This arrangement became increasingly difficult to sustain, but in the 1970s and 1980s a high degree of good faith among *fukan* editors and considerably less cynicism among the reading public made it work. Many participating literary agents seemed to share, more or less naïvely, a belief in *fukan*'s capacity to operate as guardians of high culture, notwithstanding the importance of the commercial market. Ample evidence of this belief can be found in the articles collected in *Garden of the Gods*. Nonetheless, the mass media's capacity to fulfill this particular mission was inevitably weakened as cultural production in Taiwan became more commercial and professional. In her survey of the *United Daily News*'s book review section between the late 1980s and early 1990s, Lu Yujia finds that its editor, Su Weizhen, was gradually forced to relinquish her initial ambition to run the section according to an orthodox model of high culture.[15]

As the society entered a more advanced stage of capitalist development in the 1980s, major newspapers competed for leadership and a larger share of the market. As *Lianfu* established peerless authority as an agency of literary consecration, through literary contests and the young writers' subsidy program, it naturally became the hub of the closely interconnected networks of writers, critics, editors, and publishers that collectively dominated the publishing business. *Unitas, a literary monthly*, a member of the *United Daily News* conglomerate, played a prominent role in Taiwan's literary field as soon as it was established in the mid-1980s. The magazine's editorial policies made it evident that, while tactfully exploiting the prestige factor of high culture, the latest generation of editors and publishers increasingly emphasized commercial viability.

A DUBIOUS PROJECT: FROM HIGH CULTURE TO THE MIDDLEBROW
In the mid- to late 1980s, the sense of political crisis that prevailed in the 1970s was replaced by a feeling of euphoria induced by dramatic economic success and boosted by the country's huge foreign reserves and the imminent prospect of political liberalization. Meanwhile, an expanding urban middle-class readership was transforming the literary culture of contemporary Taiwan. As the conservative anchor of the media, *Lianfu* always tried to consolidate its position by resorting to its archtraditionalist image. *Lianfu*'s efforts to promote the officially sanctioned culturalist ideology included sponsorship of lecture series by members of the high culture club, including eminent scholars like Qian Mu, Ye Gongchao, Liang Shiqiu, Mou Zongsan, Yu Yingshi, and Zheng Qian. The aura constructed around these scholarly figures drew its strength from the still potent Chinese literati tradition, in an updated version projecting moral integrity, erudition, and loyalty to an idealized vision of "cultural China." The high culture resort, however, did not work very well with the newspaper's bourgeois audience, just as *Renjian*'s efforts at cultivating a progressive image by introducing abstruse western intellectual discourses would not succeed. Editors at *Lianfu* thus turned to other strategies. Most notably, they actively exploited aesthetic categories nourished by the dominant culture to manufacture literary trends that catered to middle-class readers. Certain elements of the Republican era legacy proved useful in this effort. The liberal wing of the May Fourth tradition, for instance, produced cultural idols that inspired a great deal of romantic fervor. Contemporary Taiwanese readers' fascination with these figures derived partly from the fact that they were personal witnesses to a history currently taboo, enhancing the nostalgic impulse with added excitement.

The same factors lay behind the rage for Zhang Ailing, a writer from 1940s Shanghai, whose idolization also spoke to the growing importance of a more popular sector of the reading public.[16] While both academia and the media contributed to the Zhang Ailing cult in contemporary Chinese societies everywhere, the role of *fukan* was particularly significant. *Unitas* even held a "Who resembles Eileen Zhang the most?" contest, soliciting photos from female readers, to boost the magazine's subscription figures.

Prewar Shanghai became an icon in the cultural nostalgia trend of the early 1980s, as cities like Taipei and Kaohsiung metamorphosed into modern metropolises and city dwellers tried to come to terms with the tantalizing and disorienting urban lifestyle. At the same time, there was a lag of nearly a decade between the opening of China in the late 1970s and the announcement that Taiwan residents would be allowed to travel to the mainland. In this interim period the media fully exploited people's curiosity about the forbidden "homeland," to the extent that even the places that *zhiqing* (literally, "educated youths") were sent to perform manual labor during the Cultural Revolution became exotic and alluring. Amid the disintegration of the dominant culture and the consolidation of market forces in cultural production, *Lianfu* translated (appropriated) certain core values into commercially viable literary trends, many of which featured sinocentric cultural discourses. Modern and contemporary China became a site onto which the popular imagination was eagerly projected, and through which certain essential elements of the dominant culture were kept alive for a time.

In the meantime, in a society still not entirely open to the outside world, the realm of the "transnational" was always an object of public fascination. Like its competitor *Renjian*, during this period *Lianfu* staged spectacular functions playing to this enthusiasm. The annual ritual of reporting the winner of the Nobel Prize for literature, an event lavishly celebrated by *Lianfu*, served to showcase the *fukan*'s ability to globalize its personal network. Conspicuous accolades were showered on such international cultural figures as Eugene Ionesco. Jurors for *Lianfu*'s own annual literary contests typically included distinguished emissaries from abroad. In these large-scale spectacles, the distinction between high and middlebrow cultural forms naturally became blurred, or simply irrelevant. While Li Yongping received a multiyear stipend for completing *Haidongqing* [East-ocean green], a 900-page abstruse modernistic novel, Sanmao, a popular icon who rose to fame writing romantic diaries about her experiences in the Sahara dessert, received generous subsidies for travel to exotic places around the world.

THE MIDDLE-CLASS GENRES

Renjian of the *China Times* and *Lianfu* of the *United Daily News* effectively differentiated themselves—thanks partly to the different personalities of their charismatic leaders—as public forums where dominant values were challenged, defended, and negotiated. That *fukan* had historically played a part in modern China's search for new cultural values, and later served as the chief organs of KMT-endorsed official culture in early post–1949 Taiwan, helps to explain the mainstream literary supplements' eminent status in the cultural field and the way the editors fashioned their public image. Nonetheless, the undeniable reality in the 1970s and 1980s was the media's increasing susceptibility to commercial imperatives, and the new market-driven institution inevitably fostered new types of literary output. Of particular importance was the emergence of "middle class fiction," probably the most representative cultural product of the *fukan*-centered literary culture. Appearing at the same time, Taiwan *xindianying* [Taiwan new cinema] was another part of the same development.

The Evolving Genre Hierarchy: Rise of Middle-Class Cultural Genres

Sociologist Lin Fangmei sums up the impact of commercialization on literary production in Taiwan in the following manner: prior to the 1980s, the popularity of *zushudian*, or street-corner book rental shops that stocked mostly mass entertainment books, had served as an easy way to differentiate popular literature from serious literature ("Yasu"). The appearance of the large-scale Kingstone chain of franchised bookstores and its best-seller lists, however, ushered in a more advanced capitalist mode of literary distribution and consumption. This change was correlated with the marked expansion of an "upper-middle class" culture that blurred "the boundaries between high culture and popular culture," causing serious literature to lose its privileged status. It now had to "compete with the proliferation of new cultural genres and products" (50).

Lin's essay excepted, most critical studies of contemporary Taiwanese literary developments miss the big picture in this period, and even Lin underplays the contradictions and complexity of the evolving genre hierarchy. In retrospect, in addition to *fukan* literature, the burgeoning Taiwan new cinema and the mainstream theater (best represented by Lai Shengchuan's Biaoyan gongzuofang [Performance workshop]) in the early to mid-1980s also marked the arrival of market-driven middle-class cultural fare. To comprehend the totality of changes taking place in this period, a good starting point is the prominent role played by middle-class cultural consumers, and by cultural agents' responses to their emerging taste preferences.

MIDDLE-CLASS CONSUMERS: A NEW FACTOR IN
CULTURAL PRODUCTION

As *fukan* transformed from a state-sponsored cultural institution to part of a modern culture industry, the nature of the constraints on them shifted accordingly. We have seen how strict government surveillance pressed *fukan* editors to constantly exercise self-censorship; even editors as loyal to the regime as Lin Haiyin were subject to paranoid political scrutiny.[17] However, in the mid-1970s, with official oversight loosening up, a conservative reading public emerged as the source of another kind of censorship: "middle-class" taste preferences.

Consider the reception of two novels by Wang Wenxing, a devoted practitioner of literary modernism. *Family Catastrophe* was published in the scholarly journal *Zhongwai wenxue* [Chung-wai literary monthly] in 1972. An iconoclastic attack on the foundations of Confucian society—family and filial piety—the novel immediately stirred up controversy, and its author became a target of official surveillance. Wang's second novel, *Backed Against the Sea, Part I*, was initially serialized in *Renjian fukan* in 1981, but was discontinued as a result of readers' protests against its profanity. Within a decade, then, public scrutiny had taken over the state's censorship role. The cultural bureaucrats' efforts to curb the spread of a radical critique of state ideology were replaced by *fukan*'s ready compliance with a conservative reading public's reaction against literary assaults on their values and sense of propriety.

It became increasingly clear that even the more liberal sector of the media had little capacity to sponsor potentially subversive high culture products. The need for growth had become more compelling in the 1980s, and it dictated that *fukan* tailor their products to the expanding middle class, which in many cases involved creating innovative strategies and appropriating legacies from previous literary movements. These tactics are now taken for granted.[18] In the 1980s, however, literary agents struggled considerably with the increasing necessity of catering to market imperatives. Thus, while most baby-boom generation writers, who had entered the profession by winning prizes in *fukan*-sponsored literary contests, did start turning out commercially viable "middle-class literature," it was rarely labeled as such. A high culture façade was maintained against conscious acknowledgment of the ongoing commodification of the literary field.

Significant consequences of the cultural agents' ambivalent self-positioning are more fully explored in the next chapter; for now I turn to the parallel development of another middle-class artistic genre, Taiwan new cinema. The symbiosis between *fukan* literature and Taiwan new cinema, both of which spoke to the changing Mainstream literary culture in the 1980s, is remarkable in a number of ways. First, like the *fukan* fiction of the 1980s, the new cinema movement attracted the best artistic talents of the baby-boom generation, just then coming of age. Second, both genres flourished within the larger institutional frame of the thriving mainstream media, blessed by the decade's newly generated symbolic and material resources. Third, many of the early new cinema works were adapted from stories by contemporary writers, and a number of new cinema figures were also writers or literary critics, including Zhu Tianwen, Wu Nianzhen, Xiao Ye, Zhang Yi, and Zhan Hongzhi. Finally, as comparative latecomers to middle-class cultural fare, the new cinema people initially took fiction writers' earlier accomplishments as models. Thanks to film's greater translatability and Chinese cinema's sudden rise in the international arena, Taiwan new cinema soon outperformed middle-class literature in both artistic caliber and ability to address contemporary sociopolitical issues in depth. The two artistic forms' mutual implications, however, remain strong.[19]

It is commonly accepted that Taiwan new cinema came into existence in the early 1980s under the following circumstances. The domestic film industry had fallen to the lowest point of depression, due to both poor production quality and fierce competition from Hong Kong new wave cinema. As a desperate measure, the new leadership of the state-owned Central Motion Pictures Corporation decided to give some younger staff—chiefly Xiao Ye and Wu Nianzhen, both also creative writers—a freer hand in experimenting with less formulaic propaganda products. Xiao Ye and Wu mustered a group of young talents in their twenties and thirties. Their more serious, socially relevant themes and their conscious use of artistic techniques earned immediate acclaim, raising the "new cinema" banner in the media, where critics like Jiao Xiongping (Hsiung-ping Peggy Chiao), Huang Jianye, and Zhan Hongzhi enthusiastically promoted it. Fiction works by Modernist and Nativist writers of the previous decades were adapted for film, and along with them, the literary movements' high culture quest. Eager to elevate Taiwanese film above political propaganda and cheap entertainment, film critics and directors engineered a media-based mainstream cultural renaissance, caught between high culture ideals and middle-class cultural consumers.

Commercial viability is more critical in filmmaking, with its larger fiscal investment, than in literature. A few "accidental" box office successes gave new cinema a jump start, but many difficulties followed. In retro-spect, the films that significantly helped it get into the market, such as *Xiao Bi de gushi* [The story of Xiao Bi] (1983), directed by Chen Kunhou, and *Wu zheyang guo le yisheng* [Kuei-mei, a woman] (1985), by Zhang Yi, were conspicuously "middle class" in both content and formal pres-entation. The tension between high and popular culture was strong from the very beginning, and directors with high culture dispositions, like Ed-ward Yang (Yang Dechang) and Hou Hsiao-hsien, never gave up looking abroad for support. Domestic promoters of the movement also employed high culture rhetoric, both to facilitate their appeal to the intellectual com-munity and to assert the movement's legitimacy in front of "enlightened" government cultural agencies, which were lending them a sympathetic ear.

A look at the ambivalent representation of middle-class literary culture in Edward Yang's film *Kongbu fenzi* [Terrorizer] (1987) will serve to il-lustrate the awkward divide between new cinema's middle-class local au-dience base and its filmmakers' elitist artistic consciousness. Interestingly, *Terrorizer*'s parodic representation of middle-class mentality is precisely the channel through which the director's elitism is conveyed. *Fukan* fiction is a central motif in Yang's celebrated classic, attesting to both the preva-lence of middle-class fare in Taiwan's cultural field of the 1980s and the aesthetic distance that Yang tried to put between it and his own work.

A CINEMATIC REFLECTION ON MIDDLE-CLASS *FUKAN* LITERATURE
In previous work I have identified some defining characteristics of Tai-wan's middle-class fiction of the 1980s.[20] It tended to stay on safe ideo-logical ground, despite occasional radical gestures that were more sensa-tional than subversive. With subject matter revolving around domestic life, marriage, and love affairs, melodrama was pervasive. More notewor-thy is the place this fiction occupied in the rapidly expanding urban social space of the decade. *Fukan*-based literature featured so prominently in the era before cable TV that it played a significant role in shaping the ways people imagined their own positions in society. People refer to the fiction-al world for their sense of self and of what it means to be successful, for models of marital and romantic relationships, and for imagining desirable lifestyles. These also constitute the major themes of *Terrorizer*.

In *Terrorizer*, a series of episodes involving a middle-class couple make up one of the three intersecting story lines. The wife quits her regular of-fice job to devote herself to fiction writing, only to find herself sinking deeper into *ennui*. She finally leaves her pragmatic husband for an ex-boyfriend who owns a start-up business. A mischievous prank phone call to the wife from a girl associated with gangsters, insinuating that her husband is having an affair, provides artistic inspiration for a story that wins the writer-wife first prize in a *fukan*'s annual literary contest. News coverage and TV interviews follow. After someone informs the deserted husband, he immediately assumes that the fictional affair is responsible for the problems in his marriage—a pathetic mistake. He is subsequently scorned by his wife for being incapable of seeing the difference between fiction and reality. In a postmodernist double ending, the deeply humiliated husband steals a gun from a cop friend and either shoots his own boss (for failing to promote him as a result of recent events) and his wife's yuppie lover, or simply commits suicide.

The coincidental nature of the intersecting plot lines and the spatially driven cinematography work together to convey how the compartmentalization of people's lives in modern Taipei has resulted in tenuous and contingent—thus phony, meaningless, and deeply frustrating—interpersonal relationships. Each character moves about in his or her own space with clear registers of class, personality, and social position—the wife, the husband, the gangster girl, a boy with a camera from a rich family, and the cop. The office buildings are small, self-contained squares, and the city space is likewise divided into locales occupied or frequented by distinct social groups. The middle-class wife's fiction writing and the rich boy's photography become metaphors for the phoniness of this kind of life and the way it is perceived, experienced, and imagined by people confined within the well-charted urban space. The truth value of these two kinds of mimetic art is repeatedly negated in the film. The wife castigates her distressed husband for his inability to distinguish "fiction" from "reality." The rich boy disbelieves the lover's promises made to the gangster girl in front of her giant photo collage, constructed of small fragments—an homage to Antonioni's *Blowup*. The rich boy's girlfriend represents the typical young, educated female consumer of middle-class fiction, and her bedtime reading is a book (first shown in the opening scene, with recurring appearances) whose cover is immediately recognizable to the contemporary audience. The fact that she is a seasoned reader of middle-class fiction, aware of its pulp entertainment nature, does not prevent her being influenced by its behavioral models, as she demonstrates in her sensational suicide attempt after breaking up with the rich boy.

The film also comments on another important function of middle-class fiction: as an index of cultural distinction. The practical-minded middle-aged men in *Terrorizer*—the husband, his colleagues in the pharmaceutical laboratory, and the cop—speak dismissively of "women writers" and apparently do not read *fukan* literature. However, they too are being judged in the film: despised for their uncouthness in a society in which participation in the *fukan*-centered literary culture is strongly associated with sophisticated urbanity. After the wife is awarded her prize, multiple images of her being interviewed about the story appear on a row of television screens in a studio. This brings home the fundamentally middlebrow nature of *fukan* literature. Unlike the Modernists, who treated writing as a serious intellectual quest, writers in the 1980s pursued literature as a career. The TV interview is a step along the road to professional success as a producer of cultural goods for mass consumption. The sarcastic note is clear, as the scene draws attention to the gap between the wife's description of her vocation in existential terms and the truth of her careerist motivation. The film shows how frustrations with the routines of modern life are readily exploitable as raw material for middlebrow art and may function as a source of cultural snobbery.

As Frederic Jameson has suggested, Yang's central message in *Terrorizer*—that art does not imitate life, life imitates art—appears to be a "now archaic," familiar modernist theme, something of a cliché for people in the trade (123). However, Yang's repetition of this classical modernist statement, appearing at a critical juncture when Taiwan artists were just feeling the crunch of the consumer age, was quite relevant. In the same vein, the film's commentary on middlebrow art (fiction and photography) is an index of Taiwanese artists' maturation toward formal self-consciousness, toward the more complex, multifarious structure of expressive modes that constituted the emerging genre hierarchy in the market of symbolic goods.

In the "commerce or art" debate of the late 1980s (1985–87), filmmakers discussed survival strategies for new cinema, including whether or not it was necessary to cater to popular tastes and what role government ought to play.[21] Opinions were irreconcilably divided, and a manifesto was composed to that effect. Unlike the Nativist literary debate in 1977–78 and the Taiwanese consciousness debate in 1983–84, this dispute was largely confined to the film community, with few repercussions in the larger society. But the event was not without significant implications, since the same problems also confronted artists in other genres. Taiwan's *fukan*-sponsored middle-class fiction, meanwhile, faced the additional challenge of being slowed by the inertia of its own political conservatism. This, and baby-boom writers' efforts to overcome it, is discussed below.

Ideological Constraints: Fictional Representation of Political Prisoners

While drastic changes in the political arena inevitably caused writers of middle-class fiction to seriously reflect on some fundamental ideological issues, Mainstream literature was still conditioned by the conservative culture. Nevertheless, the potential existed for more progressive work, and certain artists of the Mainstream position did transcend the norm. A distinctive body of works about political prisoners illustrates the challenges posed by the conservative ideological orientation of the *fukan*-based literary culture, as well as the potential for change in the new political climate.[22]

We have seen that the *fukan* institution developed as a stronghold of the Mainstream position in the politically subjugated field of literary production before 1987. At the same time, as the society modernized and the media's role as liaison between the government and the public grew stronger in the 1980s, it increasingly came to perform the dual function of simultaneously promoting and resisting change. The two major *fukan, Lianfu* and *Renjian,* tactfully manipulated available political and cultural resources to meet the new social demands. Specifically, *Lianfu* revamped the *chunwenxue* notion by incorporating the Modernists' liberal humanism; *Renjian* harbored a Nativist agenda and played a vanguard role in the modernizing media industry. While both were pursuing a practical course of nativization, they nonetheless remained loyal to the central elements of the Mainstream position: the sinocentric frame of mind and the historical narratives it sustained. It is against this backdrop that I explore the implications of a subgenre of political literature, fiction about political prisoners. As a place where literary agents in the Mainstream position confront criticism of the ruling regime, these stories nicely foreground the ideological makeup of artists raised in the tradition of the Nationalist dominant culture.

Whereas potential Communist insurgence was considered the greatest threat in the early years, in the late 1970s and early 1980s the Nationalist government began to subtly discriminate between leftist Chinese nationalists and Taiwanese nationalists, considering the former less menacing to the foundation of its political power. *Fukan* immediately took advantage of this shift to expand the parameters of permissible literary subjects, while still avoiding the Localist cause. The appearance of such works as "Lai Suo" (1979), touching on—but keeping a critical distance from—the forbidden Taiwan independence movement, and Chen Yingzhen's confessional short story, "Shanlu" [Mountain path] (1984), reflected the changing climate. As was to be expected, the editors still made sure that a correct political outlook was conveyed. Nonetheless, breaching a longstanding taboo on political matters was an important step. In due course, the trend gave rise to a number of impressive literary and cinematic works that, while still anchored to the Mainstream position, stretched the tether.

THREE TYPES OF LITERATURE ON POLITICAL PRISONERS

The literature and public discourse on political prisoners that emerged after the lifting of martial law in 1987 have undoubtedly had a significant impact on Taiwan's democratization, helping to undermine the government's moral authority and to expose the political myths of the martial law period. I classify the literature into three categories. The first consists of works published immediately after the lifting of martial law. An unusually high number—as many as twenty-eight, according to some reports—of works of "prison literature" were published between mid-1987 and mid-1988. The authors included such well-known figures as Boyang, Yang Kui, Yao Jiawen, Lü Xiulian (Annette Lü, who became Vice President of the Republic of China in 2000), and Wang Tuo. The last three were also political opposition leaders imprisoned after the Kaohsiung Incident (or Meilidao shijian) in 1979. A closer look at these works reveals that very few of them really have much to do with the prison experience or criticism of it. Yao Jiawen's *Taiwan qi se ji* [The seven-colored account of Taiwan] is a personal reconstruction of Taiwanese history, and Lü Xiulian's novel *Zhe sange nü ren* [These three women] deals primarily with feminist issues. Boyang's book is comprised of letters written from prison to his family. Furthermore, none of these works reached a broad readership or had any great effect.

Fiction about political prisoners by Mainstream writers comprises the second category, from which I have selected three short stories about ex-political prisoners for discussion. All three are accomplished works whose authors are among the most highly regarded in contemporary Taiwan.

With the state closely monitoring literature during the martial law period, the subject of political imprisonment was naturally taboo. Thus, when "Lai Suo," a story by Huang Fan, a young, male, native Taiwanese writer of the baby-boom generation, won first prize in the *United Daily*

News fiction contest in 1979, it was immediately hailed by liberal critics as a major breakthrough. Read outside of this context, however, the sarcastic narrative can hardly be considered subversive.[23] The protagonist, Lai Suo, is a misguided native Taiwanese young man who has been implicated in the Taiwan independence conspiracy and imprisoned for twenty years. With the assistance of his elder brother, he is now settled in a comfortable middle-class life in Taipei, with a decent job and a voluptuous wife. One day, his uneventful routine is disturbed by news that the blacklisted leader of the Taiwan independence movement for whom he worked twenty years ago has returned from Japan. He has just defected to the Nationalist government and is about to make a public appearance on TV. Lai's futile attempt to speak to this big shot, rendered in a series of nicely juxtaposed flashbacks, finally brings on an attack of self-pity and belated resentment at being duped.

The next example is "Congqian congqian you ge Pudao Tailang" [Once upon a time, there was a Ura-shima-ta-roo], by Zhu Tianxin, one of the most renowned second-generation mainlander writers. Pudao Tailang (or "Ura-shima-ta-roo" in the Japanese pronunciation) is the hero of a Japanese fairy tale with a plot similar to "Rip Van Winkle." Written in the early 1990s, Zhu's story focuses on the romantic son of a Taiwanese landlord family who is imprisoned for twenty-five years for his Communist beliefs. Returning to his aged wife and grown-up children in the 1980s, the protagonist has a hard time adjusting to the drastically changed society and develops a paranoid suspicion that he is being tailed by a secret agent. The story ends on a climactic note when he discovers in a deserted corner of the house boxes of letters he sent home from prison, all unopened.

The third work is "Dai zhencao dai de mogui" [The devil with a chastity belt], written in the mid-1990s by Li Ang, a Mainstream writer who emerged as a champion of Localism and feminism in the 1990s. Li's protagonist is closely modeled on the wife of a jailed opposition movement leader who later became the chairman of the Democratic Progressive Party (Yao Jiawen). Rather than dealing with the political prisoner himself, the story focuses on the forced celibacy and repressed sexuality of the wife, who is tempted to start an affair with a younger political protégé. The situation is delicate because the wife is now a public figure, a "national mother" for the opposition group, having been elected a legislator after her husband's imprisonment.

It is important to note that these three stories were published at very different moments. "Lai Suo" appeared before the end of martial law, during the early stages of loosening political censorship when the media, backed by the market, had already grown considerably more independent. Zhu Tianwen may have used the story "Once Upon a Time" as a way of coming to terms with her own allegedly (assumed because of her mainlander background on her father's side) anti-Localist, conservative political stance. More than a decade later, and out from under martial law, Li Ang was venting her disillusionment with the DPP leadership in "Devil," and trying to fit into the commercialized literary scene. While ostensibly pursuing a sober treatment of female sexuality, she used sensationalism and topicality to win readers in a decade when serious literature was in decline. What is striking, however, is that despite the different backgrounds of their authors and publication dates, these stories display remarkable thematic continuity. Preserving the ideological outlook of the earlier dominant culture, all three authors express profound skepticism about the motives of political prisoners and present them as either seriously misguided or self-serving. While ostensibly sympathetic toward their protagonists as victims of history, the narrators maintain a distant, almost condescending attitude, and the critical theme in each case is clearly the futility of the characters' efforts and personal sacrifices.

It is interesting to compare the mistrust of political activism in these stories with the treatment of political prisoners in some fine works by non-Mainstream writers, which make up the third category. These include Chen Yingzhen's "Mountain Path" and *Zhao Nandong* (1987), Lan Bozhou's "Song of the Canopied Chariot" (1989), and Shi Mingzheng's "Kesi zhe" [The death seeker] (1980) and "Heniao zhe" [The urine drinker] (1972). Although most of these works, with the exception of *Zhao Nandong*, were also published by Mainstream enterprises, the authors occupied Nativist (Chen and Lan) and Localist (Shi) positions.

Chen Yingzhen's stories are despondent, lamenting the fate of idealistic individuals betrayed by the unpredictable course of history. They also condemn contemporary Taiwanese society for its rampant materialism and devotion to creature comfort, products of the capitalist evil corrupting people's lives. The beautifully written "Song of the Canopied Chariot," by Lan Bozhou, is a mixture of fiction and documentary based on the lives of a well-known victim of the White Terror, Zhong Haodong, and his wife Jiang Biyu. It shares with Chen's work a touching lyricism and deep admiration of the leftist martyrs. Both authors emphasize the "value" of the personal sacrifices of these ex-political prisoners. The prison experience *per se* is again a relatively marginal interest in all the stories, although more on it is found in *Zhao Nandong,* the only story that did not appear in a Mainstream publication. Shi Mingzheng's stories focus on the psychology of the protagonists, pursued in themes of betrayal and moral nihilism, and the message pertains more to human nature in general than to the particular category of political prisoners.

While undoubtedly more genuinely sympathetic, these stories exhibit some other traits in common with the whole body of Chinese literature on political prisoners, not just the Taiwanese variety. These similarities were noted recently at a 2000 conference on Chinese prison camp literature.[24] One conference participant, Jeffrey Kinkley, argued that "early classics" of PRC prison literature "were as concerned with injustices of criminal judgment and Chinese politics that led to imprisonment as with the inherent inhumanity of the camps." Perry Link similarly observed that Chinese prison literature does not usually deal squarely with the traumatic experiences that prisoners actually go through, although Shi Mingzheng's stories may be viewed as exceptions.

One may, of course, suggest different explanations for this phenomenon. My own inclination is to find answers in literary history, especially in the literary conventions available to writers at any particular moment and in accepted notions about the function of literature. The literary culture in modern Chinese and Taiwanese societies encourages and rewards writers who use literature as a means of engaging in political discourses rather than as a vehicle for reflecting upon the human condition. It is against this longstanding modern tradition of politicized literature that the achievements of some contemporary Taiwanese artists in breaking away from its limitations appear valuable.

AESTHETIC TRANSFORMATION OF THE MAINSTREAM IDEOLOGY

The Modernists in the 1960s and Taiwan new cinema participants in the 1980s are two groups of artists who consciously challenged the prevailing literary culture, transcending its limitations via different aesthetic strategies. Shi Mingzheng's breakaway short stories owe much to the Modernists' influence. Hou Hsiao-hsien's treatment of political imprisonment in his celebrated 1989 film *A City of Sadness* demonstrates the even more impressive achievement of Taiwan new cinema.

What makes *A City of Sadness* so compelling for Chinese and Taiwanese audiences is its artistic portrayal of the violence done by history to everyday life. Politics encroaches on the lives of ordinary people, here the four brothers of a Taiwanese family in a small town, in unjust and irresistible ways. A secondary, but equally important theme is conveyed by the story of the youngest brother, Wenqing, a photographer who has been deaf and mute since childhood.

Wenqing is made witness to a treacherous moment in contemporary Taiwanese history through a series of accidents. After a trip to Taipei accompanying an activist intellectual friend, Teacher Lin, Wenqing is imprisoned by the Nationalist government during the February 28 Incident. He is soon released, but only after witnessing the execution of several inmates, whose heroic composure in the face of imminent death deeply affects him. Wenqing thus accepts the task of secretly delivering the letters these martyrs wrote to their families before their execution. During a visit by one of the surviving family members, Wenqing discloses a personal decision: from then on, he will dedicate his life to those who have sacrificed their lives in prison. After his request to join the activists in their mountain hideout is rejected, Wenqing secretly supports them financially, and is arrested following a crackdown on the rebellious group, leaving behind his wife and a young child.

It is evident that Wenqing's conversion to political activism is motivated neither by ideology nor by idealism about "the people" or "the mother country," both of which the martyrs referred to in their letters.[25] Rather, his behavior springs from instinct—a basic human response to extreme violence done to other human beings, from the psychological needs to remember and mourn, and from the "survivor's guilt" that continues to haunt him. That Hou Hsiao-hsien rejects putting ideology before instinctive humanism in this critical part of the story supports the argument that his artistry is rooted in Taiwan's conservative Mainstream literary culture, even as it escapes that culture's boundaries. Nor should this conclusion be surprising, as Hou's scriptwriters, Zhu Tianwen and Wu Nianzhen, are established Mainstream writers, and the central thematic thrust of *A City of Sadness* is consonant with the Nationalist government's antiradical culturalism. There is a crucial difference, though. Like the Mainstream writers discussed above, Hou protests the unjust way politics makes individual citizens its involuntary pawns, but he does this without a trace of cynicism. And while he admires the romantic idealism and noble heroism of the leftist martyrs, he also rejects ideological dogma by refusing to endorse any side's political agenda in the film.

A City of Sadness portrays the awakening of a "bystander" to history who transforms himself into an active participant. Made in the late 1980s, immediately following the lifting of martial law, this cinematic representation of political activism is especially meaningful in its historical context. The majority of the film's domestic audience consisted of the very same politically apathetic middle-class residents of Taiwan whom Chen Yingzhen reproached in his stories, but precisely at the moment when they were undergoing a major transformation into more politically engaged citizens of a modern, newly democratic country.

Hou's film shows the interaction and synthesis of the previous two categories, the conservative culturalist ideology and the high culture progressive model. The limitations of a conservative middle-class mentality actually serve as artistic inspiration, the basis of a humanistic assertion of the mundane life of ordinary people by artists involved in the Taiwan new cinema movement of the 1980s. As we will see in the next chapter, Hou Hsiao-hsien, with considerable input from screenwriter Zhu Tianwen, continued to advance the high culture model in the 1990s. *A City of Sadness* marked the end of the golden age of *fukan*-based literary culture, presaging the division of the cultural field into two opposing camps, pursuing elitist and popular goals, respectively, both in a more self-conscious manner.

CHAPTER 7

High Culture Aspirations and Transformations of Mainstream Fiction

The previous chapter established that a middle-class genre emerged in and dominated the Taiwan literary field between the late 1970s and late 1980s, and that the Mainstream writers active at this time were politically conservative. This chapter explores some other aspects of the period's literary culture that complicated the post–martial law development of Mainstream literature. Most significant were the lingering high culture aspirations of many Mainstream writers. In Taiwan, high/low literary hierarchies were established during the Modernist literary movement that began in the late 1950s and flourished in the 1960s. In the 1960s and 1970s, scholars from various foreign language and literature departments successfully promoted "New Critical" tenets that likewise privileged a high/low genre distinction and gained considerable authority in the literary field. Though the Nativists of the 1970s attacked the Modernists' aesthetic elitism, their own socialist agenda was serious stuff, and primarily a property of the society's educated elite. Nativists and Modernists alike, then, subscribed to a high culture principle, at least to the extent that both demanded a commitment to serious literary content.

In this *fukan*-dominated literary culture, the juries of media-sponsored literary contests were important arbiters, promoting a mixture of Modernist and Nativist notions about what constituted "serious literature." This was because most of the jurors were invited from pools of established literary figures and expatriate scholars who were advocates, or at least contemporaries, of the two influential literary movements. Despite its increasing commercialization, therefore, literary production in the 1980s carried the legacy of the preceding decades' established criteria. Although the Modernist movement had been tarnished by Nativist critics, the artistic techniques it introduced had been broadly assimilated, and its modified notion of "artistic autonomy" continued to be the key measure of cultural legitimacy. At the same time, and in spite of the government's efforts to slow it down, the Nativist effort to promote socially engaged literature and literature about the "Taiwanese homeland" continued to make gains in the public sphere. The result was mixed. On the one hand, in the consumer-oriented, *fukan*-based literary climate, legacies of the Modernist and Nativist movements were carried forward in a selective and fragmented manner, often dissociated from the informing spirit of the originals. On the other hand, elitist literary ideals still influenced the creation and consecration of cultural products. While this mix did not fundamentally alter the conservative character of middle-class fiction, it did push authors to write more complex works than they might have otherwise, and sometimes to transcend the usual limitations of a consumer-oriented genre.

Following Bourdieu, in this discussion of the hybrid genre characteristics of Mainstream fiction in this period, I am particularly interested in the way these traits bore out new operational laws in the considerably more autonomous literary field. I argue that forces in the larger social space (the general field of power) and legacies of previous intellectual/cultural movements affected literary agents primarily through the mediation of these new laws. A look at the classifying schemes employed by Mainstream consecrating agents will illuminate this point.

In an article written in 1980, influential critic and editor Zhan Hongzhi proposed a taxonomy of contemporary fiction that registered a binary opposition between two kinds of "*wenxue xinling*," or "literary gestalts":[1]

> There is one type of writer, whom we may call "writers with ideas" . . . [whose] works contain specific messages and values; the authors want people not only to read their stories but also to share their opinions. A second type of writer (sorry, I find many of them to be of the female gender) could be labeled as "writers with feelings." Their works might also carry some messages, but the authors themselves are not entirely sure what they would like to say. And even if they are, they cannot say it clearly—their real strength lies in acute observations of the minute details of everyday life and the nuances of people's emotions; they are moreover capable of representing these through a language marked by X ray-like precision. ("Liangzhong" 49)

Simplistic as it seems, this distinction is apt, and mirrors the divergent positioning of the more conservative, traditionalist *Lianfu* of the *United*

Daily News and the more progressive, socially engaged *Renjian* of the *China Times*. Of course, both newspapers were agencies of the Nationalist cultural front, and the literature they sponsored in their respective *fukan* sections came from the Mainstream position in the literary field. However, their relative differences cannot be dismissed, because from the late 1970s through the 1980s their competitive dynamic exerted a significant impact on the ideological engagement of the emerging middle-class literature. While neither of these positions seriously deviated from official ideology, different factions and alliances formed around them, generating real competition within the Mainstream. In Bourdieu's terms, this competition derived from a structural opposition within the field, and functioned as an essential productive force, moving literature further from political constraints and closer to reflecting the internal structure of the field, the measure of increasing autonomy.

This leads to another important point: the mediated (or "refractive," in Bourdieu's terms) relationship between the general field of power and the field of literary production. Taiwan society weathered momentous changes in the 1970s and 1980s: accelerated urbanization, a dramatic rise in social affluence, rapid disintegration of the KMT hegemony, mounting pressures for democratization, more diversified trade relations with the outside world, and resumed civilian contacts with mainland China. These changes inevitably affected cultural development, but largely in an indirect manner. With greater freedom from political interference, agents in the more autonomous literary field were increasingly competing for a different prize, what Bourdieu calls "properly cultural legitimacy." The remainder of this chapter explores the different ways that Mainstream writers of middle-class fiction negotiated the forces that were competing to define "properly cultural legitimacy" in Taiwan: the lingering high culture impulse, market demands, and changes in the larger social space.

In a stark demonstration of changing conditions, sometime in the mid- to late 1980s, just before martial law was lifted, several important fiction writers of the baby-boom generation made a conscious choice to move closer to one polar extreme or the other in the genre hierarchy: some began to seriously pursue high culture, while others consciously adopted a more professional, market-savvy creative approach. Coupled with parallel shifts in Taiwan new cinema, this new clarity helped to redefine the Mainstream position as it moved into the post–martial law period, while enabling Taiwan's Mainstream artists to interact productively with cultural agents in other regions of the Greater China market.

To get a better feel for the different currents in this tidal change, I move now to a detailed account of two particular developments: the appearance of "boudoir literature," a subgenre of women's fiction centered on romance, marriage, and extramarital affairs that flourished in the early part of the period (the late 1970s and early 1980s); and the emergence of a "neo-Nativist" position among Zhan Hongzhi's "writers with ideas," most obviously in the mid- to late 1980s. While a handful of writers occupying Modernist, Nativist, and Localist positions were still active throughout this period (some of their works also appeared in Mainstream publications), the focus is on the Mainstream literature produced by writers of the baby-boom generation.[2]

From "Boudoir Literature" to the "Aesthetic of the Commonplace"

That young women writers constituted the main force on the literary scene of the late 1970s and early 1980s is a phenomenon that has received much attention from critics and scholars, and a slightly pejorative label, *guixiu wenxue* [boudoir literature], has been attached to their work. The list of women writers active at the time is indeed quite impressive, including Jiang Xiaoyun, Yuan Qiongqiong, Su Weizhen, Zheng Baojuan, Xiao Sa, Liao Huiying, Xu Taiying, Xiao Lihong, Zhu Tianwen, Zhu Tianxin, and Zhong Xiaoyang (a Hong Kong writer who was active in Taiwan's *fukan* literary culture), among others. While early critics slighted boudoir literature for its domestic triviality and escapism, some more recent critics have found in it traces of "feminist awakening." In her introduction to *Riju yilai Taiwan nüzuojia xiaoshuo xuandu* [Anthology of fiction by Taiwanese women writers since the Japanese period], scholar-critic Qiu Guifen laments boudoir literature's lack of a progressive vision, even as she acknowledges critic Yang Zhao's plausible suggestion that it offered an antidote to the excessively militant Nativist politics (34–35) (there was a brief overlap between the two: works of boudoir literature began to be published concurrently with the staging of the "Nativist debate," the grand finale of the decade-long oppositional literary movement).

Lü Zhenghui, a disciple of the neo-Marxist literary theories (especially of Georg Lukács) that gained popularity in Taiwan in the wake of the Nativist literary movement, interpreted the flurry of lighthearted romance fiction as a political conspiracy, engineered by pro-government literary agents to diffuse the lingering Nativist influence (*"Fenlie de"*). Given that the majority of these women writers (except Xiao Lihong and Liao Huiying) were second-generation mainlanders raised in military housing compounds, it is tempting to accept Lü's hypothesis. Chapters 2 and 3 revealed a close link between the Nationalist regime's cultural policy and the reputedly "apolitical" *chunwenxue*, or "pure literature," touted by Mainstream writers in the early part of Taiwan's contemporary era (the 1950s and 1960s). Continuing complicity between the authoritarian state and the state-supported cultural institution, however, cannot fully explain the behavior of boudoir writers and their receptive readership in the rapidly commercializing and liberalizing society of the 1980s. By then the cultural field had undeniably assumed greater independence, and this was apparent in the absolute range of available ideological content, which now extended from the relatively uncritical representation of middle-class values found in boudoir literature to the explicit condemnations of capitalist-induced moral degeneration found in the works of leftist writers like Chen Yingzhen. So while the Nationalist government was still anxious to maintain its political and cultural hegemony, the process through which forces in the society at large were translated into forces in the literary field had become much more complex.

The appearance of boudoir literature, I argue, marked this departure. This subjective, sentimentalist genre still clearly corresponded to sociopolitical elements in the larger historical context, but unlike the politically forced literature of the authoritarian past, it was much more a product of the literary field's own internal forces and operational laws, including the changing nature of the clientele in the cultural marketplace, positional competition between the two major *fukan* sections, and the collective "habitus" (or socially constructed personal dispositions) of baby-boom writers, as well as the lingering, if somewhat diffused and latent, high culture impulse. The examples below will give a clearer picture.

Yuan Qiongqiong: Transitions to a Professional Writing Career

Taiwan's women writers of the 1980s borrowed their signature trait, a sentimentalized appreciation of everyday life, from Zhang Ailing, the 1940s Shanghai writer who captivated Taiwan's literary scene in the 1970s and 1980s. There was, however, a crucial difference between Zhang and her followers, as I have argued elsewhere (Chang, "Yuan Qiongqiong"). Born into an aristocratic family, Zhang nonetheless embraced the plebian and folk culture. Her deliberate affirmation of the ordinary was meant partly to overcome her own deeply ingrained sense of social marginality. Taiwan's women writers were, for the most part, solidly middle-class. The Zhang Ailing cult instilled a romantic element into their middle-class imagination, and set a model for them of writing consciously to please a popular audience, a practice for which Zhang was known.

Stories by Jiang Xiaoyun and Yuan Qiongqiong represent the finest of boudoir literature, rendered with vivacity, stylistic charm, and a genuine appreciation of middle class life. Jiang, however, quit writing soon after winning the top prize in the first literary contest sponsored by the *United Daily News*, so Yuan will be our guide to the extended evolution of boudoir literature.

Subtle observation of social manners and a world seen through women's eyes give Yuan's stories collected in *Ziji de tiankong* [A space of one's own] (1981) a flavor of Katherine Mansfield or Jane Austen. The cool-headed portrayal of her characters' obsessive romantic fantasies and the impeccable psychological realism, reminiscent of Zhang Ailing but with less sarcasm, made stories like "A Space of One's Own" and "Cangsang" [The mulberry sea] (1984) among the most celebrated in the *fukan* catalog. For my purposes, however, it is what Yuan and her stories shared with other boudoir authors that needs more attention. First is the preoccupation with women's lives—their aspirations and anxieties, their roles in the family and the workplace, and their romantic relationships; writers of boudoir literature catered to the tastes and concerns of young female readers, a new consumer class produced by economic growth and rapid urbanization. Second, their works usually contain (perhaps unintentionally) a subtext registering the overall improvement in economic conditions.[3]

In Yuan's best-known story, "A Space of One's Own," the protagonist, Jingmin, is a stereotypically traditional character. Contented and submissive, so sentimental as to easily become tearful, she arranges her life entirely around her husband, and appears to be good only at domestic tasks. As the story begins, Jingmin is humiliated when her husband's family asks her to move out of the house temporarily while her husband's mistress has his baby there. Without carefully assessing the possible consequences, Jingmin rejects the arrangement and chooses divorce instead, surprising even herself. Unexpectedly, Jingmin finds freedom and independence as a single woman, even becoming a competent insurance sales agent. Given a feminist reading by most critics, "Space" is praised for exemplifying women's personal growth outside marriage. At the same time, quite a few critics have complained of a "flaw" later in the story, when Jingmin takes a married man for her lover.

In fact, Yuan seems more interested in portraying the society's changing values than in conveying a feminist message. Paramount among the new qualities Jingmin possesses are self-confidence and aggressiveness, as well as the ability to manage social situations to her own advantage. Running into her ex-husband in a restaurant a few years after her divorce, for instance, Jingmin casually teases him in front of his new wife, causing the couple to be greatly embarrassed. Unlike their moralizing critics, boudoir writers treat their characters' transgressive behaviors with nonjudgmental pragmatism. Furthermore, the women in boudoir stories achieve financial independence with considerable facility, reflecting the burgeoning urban economy of the moment. Indeed, celebration of middle-class financial striving is a prevalent subtext in boudoir literature.

Most examples of this appreciative fictional treatment of Taiwan's thriving economy and middle class come from "older" baby boomers who were born between 1945 and 1955 and possessed vivid memories of the material scarcity of the immediate postwar years. Having grown up at a time when the authoritarian Nationalist rule was unchallenged, they had a relatively positive experience of political and cultural indoctrination, and many had internalized the ideological assumptions of the dominant culture, which made them and their writing initially conservative. Sometime in the mid-1980s, however, as market forces began to exceed all others, this natural conservatism yielded to the growing demand for more immediately mass-appealing content, to which several writers obviously responded. The oft-cited examples are the later works of Liao Huiying and Xiao Lihong, which contained large doses of sexual allusion, local color, and different types of romantic fantasy.

Yuan Qiongqiong answered to the new market imperatives in particularly deliberate fashion. She first explored sensational murder and abnormal psychology in her collection *The Mulberry Sea*, featuring scenes like these: a mother deliberately coaxes her toddler son to walk on the terrace railing of her high-rise apartment, evoking terror in fascinated onlookers; a possessive wife refuses to take her husband to the hospital and derives satisfaction from watching him die helplessly; and a mother adopts two young girls as sex partners for her retarded son and later murders one of them when she refuses to bear her a grandchild. Yuan's talent for crafting tightly knit, suspense-ridden narratives served her well as she branched out into *jiduanpian*, or "mini-short stories," a new form promoted by the *fukan* of the *United Daily News*. Even Yuan's semiautobiographical novel *Jinsheng yuan* [Affinities of this life] (1988), known for its thematic focus on second-generation mainlanders' identity quest, is punctuated by climaxes in a manner reminiscent of television drama series, and calculated to achieve the same attention-holding effect. In fact, Yuan left print to work as a television writer from the late 1980s to the mid-1990s. After a decade away from the literary scene, Yuan published a new collection in 1997, *Kongbu shidai* [The age of horror], which contains full-blown thrillers and sensational murders bordering on surrealism. By now a mature writer of pop fiction, Yuan has a career very much in keeping with the general direction of the literary field.

As mentioned earlier, there was a definite point in the mid- to late 1980s when serious literature and pop fiction went their separate ways. If Yuan Qiongqiong represents the pop trend, two slightly younger baby-boom generation writers, Zhu Tianwen and Zhu Tianxin, took the other path. The daughters of a distinguished literary couple, fiction writer Zhu Xining and translator Liu Musha, the Zhu sisters gradually emerged as the finest writers of their generation in the late 1980s and early 1990s. Below I focus largely on the older sister, Tianwen, as an example of the high culture route taken by some writers of boudoir literature.

Zhu Tianwen's High Culture Quest

The Zhu sisters were among the first winners of *fukan* literary prizes in the late 1970s. Born in 1955 and 1957, they were several years younger than the average boudoir author, barely in their twenties when they published their first story collections. In chapter 4, I discussed how the older Mainstream writers' dedication to the sinocentric cultural narrative was carried on by writers of the baby-boom generation, most notably by the coterie associated with the Double-Three Club, who came under the influence of Hu Lancheng, former husband of the legendary Zhang Ailing and a visiting lecturer at the College of Chinese Culture in the late 1970s. Amid rising tension between Taiwan's two major population groups in the early 1990s, considerable critical attention was given to Zhu Tianwen's role as a key member of the club and to the unique influence Hu exerted on her, allegedly shaping the arcane gender concepts that inform her important novel, *Notes of a Desolate Man*.[4] Here, however, I am interested in how Hu's ultraconservative culturalism influenced Zhu's work. Hu's flamboyant, high-flown literati style and the scintillating, idealized image of ancient

China communicated in his sentimentalized vision clearly made a powerful impression on Zhu Tianwen. His personal influence and the Double-Three Club experience made her a more ambitious and idealistic writer than most other boudoir authors.

Zhu was also influenced by her close contact with key figures of the Taiwan new cinema movement. In the mid- to late 1980s Zhu wrote several screenplays for director Hou Hsiao-hsien.[5] New cinema's high culture aspirations are echoed in Zhu's fiction works of the same period. Her two short-story collections, *Yanxia zhi du* [Summer capital inferno] (1987) and *Shijimo de huali* [Fin-de-siècle splendor] (1990), assume an intellectual pose reminiscent of the Modernists, and the sentimentality of the Double-Three phase is tempered by modernist aesthetics. At the same time, and again like many in new cinema, Zhu is also apparently inspired by Nativist Chen Yingzhen's progressivism, especially his efforts to revisit Taiwanese history.[6] Despite Zhu's native conservatism, Chen's indictment of rampant materialism and courageous treatment of taboo subjects, like the leftist martyrs and victims of the White Terror in the 1940s and 1950s, find many echoes in Zhu's own stories and in her new cinema screenplays.

A prominent theme in *Summer Capital Inferno* and *Fin-de-siècle Splendor* is the rapid transformation of cities like Taipei and Kaohsiung, and their manifold corruption—rampant materialism, rising crime rates, and blind expansion on top of large-scale demolition. The characters in her stories are both fascinated and overwhelmed by the monstrosity of this phenomenon. The biblical allusion to Sodom and Gomorrah in the film version of Zhu's story, "Daughter of the Nile," in particular, resonates with Chen Yingzhen's condemnation of creature comfort that leads to moral degeneration, albeit without Chen's explicit socialism.[7] Zhu shares boudoir literature's sentimental appreciation of and attention to emotional nuances and the details of daily life. At the same time, a mildly cynical and increasingly melancholy tone unmistakably begins to move her work away from the middle-class genre.

In the early 1990s, Zhu Tianwen once again broke new ground. With Taiwan's intellectual circles fast at work indigenizing progressive western and global cultural trends, some Mainstream writers also began to take an interest in ideas like postmodern deconstruction, gender and sexuality, gay and lesbian rights, and the plight of Taiwan's aborigines. Zhu Tianwen's novel *Notes of a Desolate Man* included extensive allusions to Foucault, Levi Strauss, and gay rights. Importantly, however, Zhu incorporated these ideas without subscribing to the radical politics that had overrun

Taiwan's cultural circles. The narrator in *Notes* articulates a conservative worldview, including profound skepticism about the gay rights activism by which his best friend, Ah Yao, is suddenly captivated. Meanwhile, he thinks about progressive cultural theories in highly subjective, sentimental terms, empathizing with the loneliness of Foucault in his last days and admiring Strauss's kinship codes of the primitive tribe for their beauty and sense of order. Zhu's endeavor in *Notes* to combine serious content with a distinctive aesthetic style clearly moved her to the high culture end of the genre hierarchy.

Zhang Ailing and the "Aesthetic of the Commonplace"

Zhu Tianwen's later work deserves special attention for another reason. While moving boudoir literature beyond the confines of its middle-class generic characteristics, she also participated in an ongoing trend promoting the "aesthetic of the commonplace," an idea traceable to Zhang Ailing's influence. Zhang Ailing's works of the 1940s and 1950s have affected Chinese artists everywhere, including writers of both elite and popular genres, and her literary style has been imitated frequently over the last three decades. While the city in Zhang Ailing's writings was primarily China's first metropolis, prerevolution Shanghai, it has been reincarnated many times over in the work of later Chinese artists from different regions. These include an impressive number of celebrated literary and cinematic works produced in the last few years of the twentieth century by people like Yim Ho (*Gungun hongchen* [Red dust], 1990), Stanley Kwan (*Hong meigui, bai meigui* [Red rose, white rose], 1994), Peter Chan (*Tian mi mi* [Comrades, almost a love story], 1996), Ann Hui (*Bansheng yuan* [Eighteen springs], 1997), Wang Anyi (*Changhen ge* [Song of everlasting sorrow], 1996), Hou Hsiao-hsien (*Haishang hua* [Flowers of Shanghai], 1998), and Wong Kar-wai (*Huayang nianhua* [In the mood for love], 2001).[8]

Taiwanese writers' fascination with new forms of desire, decadence, and urban sophistication was doubled by their weariness of the early martial law period's disciplinarian approach to community life, modeled after the Nationalist New Life movement of the 1930s. Moreover, as I argued in "Yuan Qiongqiong and the Rage for Eileen Zhang Among Taiwan's *Feminine* Writers," the idolization of Zhang Ailing was symptomatic of the surge of "cultural nostalgia" in the early 1980s. This trend was driven partly by second-generation mainlanders' homesickness for an imaginary China of the past, and partly by increasing demand for cultural commodities of all sorts in the booming domestic market. Thanks to the backward-looking Nationalist historical narrative and the reopening of mainland China, pre-revolution Shanghai became an object of popular cultural fantasy.

The oft-repeated renewal of the Zhang Ailing legend is a complex, mul-tifaceted phenomenon in which the emerging Chinese metropolis—Hong Kong, Taipei, and post–Mao Shanghai—clearly plays a central role. In these modern and modernizing Chinese cities, modern Chinese literati si-multaneously experience pride (especially contrasted with the colonial or semicolonial experience) and mixed feelings of fascination and uneasiness. Zhang Ailing's archetypal tales provide them with a special way of imag-ining themselves vis-à-vis this disorienting, potentially alienating urban life. Of particular interest, though, is this distinct disposition, the "aes-thetic of the commonplace," that also has grown out of Zhang's influence. As I will demonstrate below, using two short pieces by well-known main-land Chinese writers, this aesthetic traces an interesting path across the still notably tangible borders of the greater Chinese cultural sphere.

The first piece is "Qingtang guashui bushi yu" [Watery soup, and no fish] (1994), by Zhong Acheng, an acclaimed writer of China's "root-seeking" school. In 1986, with his short stories "Qi wang" [King of chess] (1984) and "Haizi wang" [King of children] (1984), Zhong became the first active PRC writer to be published in Taiwan after 1949.[9] He subse-quently developed a friendship with the two generations of writers in the Zhu family, with whom he also shared an expressed admiration for Zhang Ailing. "Watery Soup" was a bitterly sardonic condemnation of the ultra-left, totalitarian Communist reign that deprived people of the most basic forms of individual freedom, completely exterminating private space—or, in Zhong's Daoism-flavored phrase, *ziwei de shijie*—"the realm in which one does as one pleases." During the Cultural Revolution, Zhong says, people enjoyed privacy only during the brief moment when they stopped working to smoke a cigarette; otherwise, only the mentally retarded halfwits on rural streets were free from the watertight surveillance of the omnipresent state machine. The government's obsession with creating a "new" society and achieving the "extraordinary" is a psychology that leads to disaster. Zhong counters this by insisting on the basic humanity and value of the "ordinary life," eloquently articulating the political im-plications of the "aesthetic of the commonplace" that underlay a number of works from both sides of the Taiwan Strait in the mid- to late 1980s.[10]

Another dimension of the "aesthetic of the commonplace" is brilliant-ly expressed in a short essay by Wang Anyi, one of the finest fiction writers in China today, published in the Hong Kong–based magazine *Ming-bao yuekan* [Ming pao monthly] in 1999 (*"Jiachang"*). Describing urban scenes from contemporary Shanghai, Wang elaborates on *jiachang*, or "that which is familiar to ordinary people in the context of everyday life," a term that Wang attributes to veteran May Fourth writer Shen Congwen. The gorgeous dance halls we see in the movie *Temptress Moon* are misleading, Wang argues. Genuine luxury is rare in overcrowded Shanghai, where surface sumptuousness often hides gritty conditions underneath. Wang's nearly opposite passion for lush description of prosaic realities betrays a sentimentality characteristic of Zhang Ailing and shared by Taiwan's "boudoir" writers. Meanwhile, Wang's tribute to Shen Congwen, who reemerged in the post–Mao era as an icon of the right wing of the May Fourth movement that was suppressed during Mao's tenure, is also significant. It suggests a common inheritance from the lyrical-sentimental strand of May Fourth new literature behind the "aesthetic of the commonplace" shared by baby-boom generation Chinese writers in China and Taiwan.

Given the range of artists who have drawn inspiration from Zhang Ailing, the "aesthetic of the commonplace" is naturally configured differently in individual works. One of the latest examples, *Flowers of Shanghai* (1998), a film directed by Hou Hsiao-hsien and written by Zhu Tianwen, deserves special attention for its determinedly high culture rendition of this aesthetic. *Flowers* is adapted from *Haishang hua liezhuan* [Biographies of the flowers of the sea] by Han Bangqing (1856–1894), a novel of the late Qing dynasty originally written in the Wu dialect (close to today's Shanghainese) and translated into Mandarin by Zhang Ailing. In spite of a marketing campaign that played up the story's romantic triangles involving courtesans and their wealthy patrons in the high-class brothels of Shanghai's British concessions, the film does not cater to popular tastes. Many in the mass audience find it unbearably tedious and trivial. Art-film lovers, on the other hand, have been impressed by its fine craft, exquisitely transforming an exotic world into something intimately familiar. The daily routines of the brothels are seen to include ordinary household and business activities, revealing the quotidian reality behind the suggestive, elegant atmosphere. The modernistic effect of aesthetic defamiliarization is unmistakable. At the same time, a certain sentimentality about these mundane activities is apparent in the meticulous attention to nuances of female psychology and mannerisms, reminiscent of the *Honglou meng* [Dream of the red chamber], a Chinese classic worshipped by all Zhang Ailing fans. So

the film is a solid high culture effort, even as it verges into popular sentimentality, fully registering the various influences that have energized contemporary Taiwan's literary culture over the last few decades.

NEO-NATIVISM, WESTERN CULTURAL TRENDS, AND THE "CHINA COMPLEX"

In the preface to *Death in the Cornfield*, a collection of English translations of Taiwanese short stories from the 1980s, editors Ching-Hsi Perng
and Chiu-kuei Wang highlight the writers' ability to capture "the dramatic—some would say unprecedented—transformations in the political,
economic, and social scenes in Taiwan of the 1980s" (v).[11] This privileging of literature's capacity to reflect sociopolitical reality clearly echoes
the dominant critical discourse of the 1980s, itself a prominent legacy of
the Nativist literary movement. Several of the anthologized writers—
Chen Yingzhen, Zhang Xiguo, Liu Daren, Huang Fan, and Ping Lu—
were known for being articulate on sociopolitical issues, while the
women writers associated with boudoir literature generally were not. If
we add a few more names—Li Ang and Dong Nian, for instance—then
the list virtually encompasses all the Mainstream writers active in the
1980s whom Zhan Hongzhi might call "writers with ideas."[12] Notably,
however, their stories do not entirely fit the classical model of Nativist literature. Instead, their appropriation of the classical Nativist agenda implies a critique from a moderate political stance characteristic of the
Mainstream, while accentuating a "native" motif.[13] It is in this sense that
the term "neo-Nativist" is useful.

Unlike the terms "Nativism," "Localism," and "boudoir literature,"
"neo-Nativism" has not been widely used.[14] I employ it here to call attention to the fact that, while the legacy of the 1970s Nativist literary
movement was assimilated by Mainstream cultural agents in the 1980s, it
was significantly altered in response to multiple changes in the external environment. Backed by growing political organization, certain Nativist
propositions had gained substantial legitimacy, and writers were now
obliged to address the immediate claims of a rapidly transforming sociopolitical reality. "Realism" replaced "modernism" as the privileged literary mode, but neo-Nativism developed as an essentially emotional identification with Taiwan as "homeland," unattached to the broad
ideological programs that had divided the earlier Nativist movement be-

tween leftists and Localists. This identification was complicated by the impact of transnational cultural flows, the reemergence of the PRC in the international arena, and the Localist debunking of contemporary Taiwan's sinocentric dominant culture, all of which made what constituted the "Other" a moving target. The old Nativists' call to resist western cultural imperialism was rendered moot by the fact that western intellectual trends were being avidly appropriated for prestige. Meanwhile, as previously forbidden knowledge about mainland China became accessible, the "China" at the core of the sinocentric cultural ideology was destabilized, forcing Mainstream writers to readjust.

These changes were necessarily played out in the literary field through interactions with its internal operational laws. The following discussion singles out two aspects of this process for elaboration: how writers negotiated the impact of the transnational cultural flows, which tended to aggravate critics' propensity to impose high culture criteria, and the role played by the shared "habitus" (socially constructed personal disposition) of the baby-boom generation Mainstream writers in their adjustment to Taiwan's new (imagined) relationship with "China."

Cultural Flows and Elitist Criticism

Reeling from the effects of events at the end of the 1970s—the Nativist debate and U.S. recognition of the PRC—in the 1980s the Nationalist government actively promoted "internationalization and liberalization" in its foreign and economic policies, creating a climate particularly favorable to western cultural influences.

Scholars have long acknowledged the important role played by "returned students" in Chinese intellectual life since early in the twentieth century. The first significant literary movement in post–1949 Taiwan, Modernism, was closely tied to a group of students who had pursued graduate studies in the United States, some through U.S. Information Service (USIS) programs. The fact that the number of literary agents with such experience was relatively small partly explains the elitist nature of the Modernist movement in Taiwan. The situation was quite different in the 1980s, when transnational cultural flows surged as a result of cheaper travel, a receding Cold War, and improved telecommunications. Increasing numbers of returned students joined expatriate intellectuals in transforming the cultural field within Taiwan. U.S.-trained critics like Liu Shaoming (Joseph S. M. Lau), Zheng Shusen (William Tay), Cai

Yuanhuang, Wang Dewei (David Der-wei Wang), Long Yingtai, Jiao Xiongping, Dan Hanzhang, Qi Longren, and Liu Senyao were able to steer literary and film criticism in new directions. Overseas experience became so prevalent that friction and factional competition often developed between scholars associated with different U.S. schools and returning to Taiwan at different times.[15]

Beginning in the mid-1970s and throughout the 1980s, *fukan* played a prominent, but also rather dubious role in this new wave of transnational cultural flow. They maintained close relationships with writers and scholars in the Chinese diaspora, depending heavily on their input to build a progressive image. *Renjian fukan*'s enthusiastic introduction of western "high theory" under the relatively short editorship of Jin Hengwei—who in 1986 founded Taiwan's best known highbrow intellectual magazine *Con-temporary Monthly*—is just one prominent example. Unfortunately, the succession of "theory booms"—structuralism, deconstruction, neo-Marxist critical theory, postmodernism—found the majority of local writers and critics ill prepared to deal with the typically muddled translations of high theory.

More important is the attitude that valorized such elitist knowledge. The Modernist movement had baptized a whole generation of Taiwanese intellectuals into the high culture faith between the 1950s and the 1970s, and they were now established members of the literary field who played influential roles in the *fukan* literary contest selections. As Taiwan's westernization advanced, fewer and fewer people listened seriously to the Nativist critics' denunciations of American cultural imperialism. On the contrary, the general climate strongly favored western influences. The theory boom "-isms" mentioned above not only lent prestige to literary critics and scholars but also refueled writers' zeal to catch up with the latest thing in the global cultural arena. By the mid-1980s, more and more Mainstream literary agents, including the writers of boudoir literature, came under their influence.

Writers in the 1980s who incorporated trendy western theories still perfunctorily adhered to the "nativist" imperative, consciously depicting the unique contemporary realities of Taiwan, in particular the social changes caused by urbanization.[16] Given the increased autonomy of the literary field, Mainstream writers were primarily interested in producing "good" works that would earn them critical acclaim. This made them mindful of currently valorized criteria and the consecrating agents who controlled them—literary contest jurors, book reviewers, and *fukan* editors. Long-term aesthetic and intellectual pursuits became secondary, since these were not immediately recognizable in the anonymous award-selection process. Meanwhile, aspiring writers eagerly catered to the preferences of specific critics or jurors. When New Criticism enjoyed a long spell of popularity with jurors, for instance, writers tried to conform to its tenets.

This award- and popular press-driven consecrating system weighed against critical standards conceived in high culture terms. Furthermore, as "Taiwanese" literature was still a politically taboo subject in academia, critics in the 1980s devoted most of their energy to evaluating individual works, at the expense of developing broader generalizations about the status of old and new genres. Shadowed by elitist conceptions and without the benefit of systematic scholarly inquiries, many critics adopted analytical categories unwarranted by the texts they examined. Under these conditions, writers were often caught between critics pulling in one direction and the commercializing market pulling in the opposite direction. The career of Zhang Dachun, one of Taiwan's foremost baby-boom generation writers, speaks eloquently to this phenomenon.

Zhang Dachun and Competing Critical Protocols

While the general decline of *fukan* literature in the 1990s caused a number of baby-boom generation authors to stop writing, Zhang Dachun has been a prominent exception. Zhang's impressive productivity over the last decade attests to his ability to adjust to the changing rules of a literary field moving toward greater professionalism. Working through a succession of narrative forms, he has tried to meet both the field's elitist ambitions and its popular requirements, gradually slipping toward the stronger pull of the latter. Zhang's shifting forward movement—particularly through his trademark experiments with postmodernism—reflects the evolutionary pattern of the larger field and its consecrating system. His extended engagement with the postmodern discourse has had more to do with the internal dynamics of the literary field than with any intellectual or ideological choice.

Zhang is a great storyteller, with a powerful linguistic facility, encyclopedic knowledge, and technical virtuosity. When he entered the literary scene in the late 1980s, his brilliant application of trendy postmodern devices to socially relevant subjects immediately earned him high critical acclaim. Imported literary fashions, as we have observed, were routinely equated with serious artistic endeavor during the reign of elitist critics in the

1980s. However, the disparity between Zhang's fantastic narratives and the canons of high culture did not escape critical notice, for instance in commentaries by Cai Yuanhuang and Zhan Hongzhi on the stories collected in *Sixi youguo* [Sixi worries about his country] (1988). Citing their affinities to *chuanqi*, or traditional Chinese "wonder tales," Cai identifies the stories' plot-oriented, "popular" nature. Zhan, meanwhile, finds Zhang's flights of fancy lacking in comparison to Gabriel García Márquez's use of "magical realism" to convey serious humanistic themes.

Still, many other critics were calling Zhang a promising "postmodern writer." He earned this reputation in the late 1980s and early 1990s with works like *Da shuohuang jia* [The big liar] (1989) and *Meiren xiexin gei shangxiao* [No one wrote the letter to Colonel] (1994), each ostensibly treating postmodern themes like the celebration of irony and the problematization of "truth." The stark reality of the dwindling readership for *fukan* literature, however, dictated a turn to more straightforward material. Zhang complied, and demonstrated his commercial acumen, by turning out the "Big Head Chun Trilogy," *Shaonian Datouchun de shenghuo zhouji* [Weekly journals of a boy named Big Head Chun] (1992), *Wo meimei* [My kid sister] (1993), and *Ye Haizi* [Wild kids] (1996)—phenomenally popular stories targeted at the teenage market. This success contributed to a new trend, as more and more writers cultivated niche markets—teen, queer, feminist, ethnic, etc.—and exoticized history and the society's subcultures. Hesitant critical reactions to these works signaled a gradual parting of ways between mainstream literature and the elitist critical regime.

What has even more seriously offended the elitist sensibility is Zhang's methodical adaptation of postmodern devices to a creative agenda directed toward professional success rather than high culture objectives. Zhang achieves this by mixing his postmodernism with his Chinese literary heritage (he is aided by an M.A. in Chinese literature).

In the following incident, for instance, Zhang's interest in postmodern polemics and his ideas on narratology referred back to native sources. Playing a prank on the local scholarly community, Zhang once faked a research article purporting to trace the origins of the Monkey, the protagonist of the classic novel *Xiyou ji* [Journey to the west]. The essay was published in a major newspaper on New Year's Day 1992, the Year of the Monkey. Later, he announced that the original essay and two subsequent rebuttals were intellectual gags (Zhang *Benshi* 180–212).

The target of this joke was the *kaozheng*, or textual verification school, which has notoriously dominated traditional Chinese scholarship in Taiwan. Zhang was taking issue with the positivistic assumptions and empirical zealotry of this scholarship, but while he was making fun he also betrayed his own preoccupation with the notion of originality, an interest that drives a number of his postmodern works, including *The Big Liar, No One Wrote the Letter to Colonel, Sahuang de xintu* [The disciple of the liar] (1996), and especially the stories in *Benshi* [Pseudo-knowledge] (1998). In all of these works Zhang deliberately weaves together simulated and authentic texts with the somewhat mischievous intention of making it impossible for readers to distinguish between the "real" and the "look-alike." This appears to be an explicitly postmodern ploy, but in Zhang's work it doesn't go the whole distance. Concerned with how the effects of truth are produced within discourses, an important postmodern proposition holds that discourses are neither true nor false in themselves, suspending the knowability of "truth." By comparison, Zhang's fictional exercises are mere feints, playfully manufacturing "fake" versions of an unproblematized, even tacitly acknowledged "original" text. His interest is not in bringing the original text's truth into question but in exploiting the intellectual cachet of a fashionable concept and displaying his consummate skills of imitation, both of original texts and of postmodern techniques. The truth is that Zhang lives by the same empirically minded epistemology that he lampooned in his fake research article, and harbors greater interest in the narrative act itself than the philosophical notion of originality.

Next, Zhang utilized his Chinese heritage in a more straightforward fashion, to build suspense in plot-oriented popular novels that require culturally familiar cues. In the last few years Zhang has written several lengthy popular novels in the traditional vein, including *Chengbang baoli tuan* [Gang of the city state] (1999–2000) and the yet-to-be-completed *Wulin waishi* [Unofficial history of the knights-errant]. Playing again with the "origins" idea, he situates an elusive, forever receding "origin," in the form of a piece of missing information, at the core of the endlessly proliferating, tangentially related plot lines that run through these detective-mystery stories.

The most genuinely postmodern aspect of Zhang's work has been its fluidity in exploiting the very notion of "postmodernism." Zhang dressed his work in postmodern clothing first for its prestige value in Taiwan's contemporary literary discourse, and then for its popular culture-friendly licensing of his favorite resort to pastiches of traditional cultural forms that would otherwise look anachronistic. While elitist critics still nag him about a lack of compassion and cynical evasion of serious themes, their views no longer count for as much as they did in the 1980s. Now ranked among Taiwan's most prominent cultural celebrities—he currently hosts a popular radio talk show, having presided over a couple of TV programs— he is also a seasoned professional writer consciously trying to retain and expand creative control. In recent years Zhang has been personally involved in multimedia productions of his stories and increasingly active in the commercial distribution of his works. His latest novel, composed in the style of Haruki Murakami, the Japanese popular writer who has captivated younger readers in Taiwan in the last decade, has allegedly attracted interest from NHK, the Japanese media giant. As Zhang's case demonstrates, the shadow of high culture imperatives has receded almost entirely under the high noon of Taiwan's commercial literary market, making professional success a more straightforward objective.

Mainstream Writers' Ambivalent Relationship with "China" and New Self-Positioning

Finally, as western products saturated Taiwan's cultural market in the 1980s, the role of the "West" as Other diminished, considerably overshadowed by the reemerging "China." Mainland China's return to the international community suddenly rendered untenable Taiwan's claim to "authentic Chinese" identity. After the initial shock, most Mainstream cultural agents shifted their loyalties away from the Nationalist orthodoxy's imaginary "China" toward Taiwan itself, the natural choice for a generation of artists born and raised on the island. At the same time, deeply imbued with old cultural ideology, Mainstream writers did not necessarily sympathize with the Localist position that was just beginning to make strides in the cultural arena of the mid- to late 1980s.

The Localist cultural formation was essentially a post-Nativist development. Unlike the Nativists, who considered western cultural imperialism the primary threat to national identity, the Localists in the 1980s engaged in renouncing "China," including the "Chinese within us" nourished by the KMT's sinocentric cultural ideology. The 1983–84 "Taiwanese consciousness debate" was a landmark event. Localist champions of Taiwanese nationalism, like Chen Fangming, began to campaign for a process of "desinicization," while veteran Nativist Chen Yingzhen and expatriate historian Dai Guohui strove to either defend Chinese nationalism on a socialist ideological premise or chart the evolutionary path of the ascending

"Taiwanese consciousness."[17] Localists denounced the government's claim that mainland China, rather than Taiwan, was the real "motherland" of the Taiwanese people, and criticized its lack of public acknowledgment of "ethnic conflicts" on the island, as well as its marginalization of the history and culture of the aboriginal population. Stressing the imperialist nature of the "Chinese Empire" (*huaxia diguo*), the Localists urged Taiwan's rejection of subordinate status as a necessary precondition for establishing its own subject position.[18] While the debate took place mainly in fringe publications, its noise reached the mainstream media, stirring up lively discussions about the "China complex" versus the "Taiwan complex." It presaged further attacks on sinocentrism in public discourse and initiated the precipitous decline of the Nativist left wing headed by Chen Yingzhen, whose pro–People's Republic stance became increasingly unpopular.

Starting in the realm of domestic cultural politics, the Localist line initially gained momentum from the so-called "Frontier Literature Incident." This began as a storm of furious protest against a 1980 essay by Zhan Hongzhi in which Zhan expressed doubt that future critics would find much of real value in the first thirty years of contemporary Taiwanese literature—except its significance as "Frontier Literature." Later, by Zhan's own account, the reaction developed into a debate over "Taiwanese literary subjectivity," a hot topic that contributed to the strife between the "Third World Literature" (North) wing of the Nativist camp and the "Taiwanese Localist Literature" (South) wing (*Lianzhong* 10–11).

Mainstream cultural agents' restraint in the aftermath of this event deserves special attention. In a moderate rebuttal, published in the overseas edition of *China Times* in 1982, Zhan urged inclusiveness and relativism in considering the relationship between Taiwanese identity and the sinocentric notion of "China." "Chinese consciousness" and "Taiwanese consciousness," he said, can be the same thing or different, depending on context (*Liangzhong* 76), repeating an argument popular among Mainstream literary agents at the time.

At least on the surface, Mainstream cultural interpretations like Zhan's still enjoyed substantial legitimacy, thanks partly to the abiding shelter of state institutions. In reality, however, a great deal of rethinking, especially about Taiwan's relationship with mainland China and the official version of modern Chinese history, was taking place. In Zhang Dachun's celebrated "Jiangjun bei" [General's monument], for example, a son replies to his KMT war hero father's lecture on Chinese history, "That's *your* history,

Father." The tone of the story is cynical, registering a general erosion of faith in the official history among second-generation mainlanders. Latent tension of the same sort also features in Zhu Tianwen's *Fin-de-Siècle Splendor* collection. Accompanying her mother on a family reunion trip to mainland China, the protagonist in "Dai wo qu ba, yueguang" [Take me with you, moonlight] stops her trip at its doorway, Hong Kong. Harboring no interest in her "ancestors' homeland," she is more attracted to the shopping opportunities in the international metropolis.

Ambivalently situated between Taiwan and mainland China, Mainstream writers were making subtle attempts at asserting an independent identity.[19] This theme was most eloquently expressed in the film *A City of Sadness*, made in the wake of the lifting of martial law, which took on the taboo subject of the February 28 Incident. Judging from the backgrounds of the filmmakers,[20] I argue that the film was part of a self-positioning effort by Mainstream baby-boom artists in the late 1980s. This is most apparent in *City*'s emphasis on Taiwan's hybrid, multilingual cultural reality, and the characters' ambivalent relations with their Japanese colonizers and the Chinese "motherland."

The KMT-supported cultural infrastructure remained largely intact until the end of the 1980s, despite all the challenges to its orthodoxy coming from a changing public discourse. The lifting of martial law changed everything. Afterward, the mounting Localist trend swiftly forced a reconstitution of the dominant culture. Tension between the two major population groups, native Taiwanese and mainlanders, came to a rapid boil, eventually effecting a dramatic power reversal, and this extended to the institutional structure of cultural production. As identity politics gripped the cultural field in the 1990s, Mainstream writers became divided among themselves, frequently along the same native Taiwanese/mainlander lines.

Naturally, native Taiwanese were in the minority among Mainstream writers. A representative case was Li Ang, a Mainstream writer who reclaimed her native Taiwanese identity and repudiated sinocentrism. Her novel *Mi yuan* [Lost garden] (1992) features a symbolic reconstruction of the genealogy of Taiwanese ethnicity (discussed further in the last chapter). The majority of Mainstream writers were second-generation mainlanders, and they reacted very differently to the political and cultural upheavals. Zhang Dachun's satires aggressively targeted both the old and the new political administrations. The Zhu sisters' fiction registered an inward turn, reflecting upon the imprints of their upbringing. This introspection contributed to a melancholy mood: picturing the mainlanders' plight, Zhu Tianxin poignantly remarked that it was indeed hard for them to consider Taiwan their "homeland," as they have no ancestral tombs to sweep during the Qingming Festival (*Xiangwo* 78–79). And yet there is clearly no other place to which they can now "return."

The apparently divergent politics of these reactions should not obscure what is faced by both groups of baby-boom generation Mainstream writers, namely the vacuum created by the debunking of the sinocentric dominant culture of their formative years. Meanwhile, the common consequence of this loss is that all Mainstream writers have embarked on a search for a new locus of idealized human civilization.

While abiding by Localist imperatives, Li Ang's fiction of the last decade simultaneously engages in redefining the Chinese heritage, even if in negative terms. A main thrust of the *Lost Garden* is how Taiwanese had to uproot the "Chineseness within" in order to assert their Taiwanese identity. The heroine's father resolutely replaces all the "Chinese trees" in Hanyuan, an aristocratic Chinese-style garden he built earlier with the family fortune, with native species after being put under house arrest by Nationalist secret agents. Identity formation assumes even greater prominence in Li's 2000 novel *Zizhuan no xiaoshuo* [Fiction: An autobiography], based on the life of Xie Xuehong, the legendary founder of the Taiwanese Communist Party. Taiwan, Japan, and mainland China are all crucial to Xie's experience, highlighting the notion of hybridity in her own identity.

A profound ambivalence underscores the quest for a new civilizational ideal in Zhu Tianxin's stories in *Ancient Capital* and *Manyouzhe* [The wanderer] (2001). The narrator in "Wuyue de lanse yueliang" [Blue moon in May], an obvious persona of the author, travels abroad to various real and imaginary locales in Asia, the Middle East, Europe, Africa, etc., feeling in each a sense of *déjà vu* that makes clear by odd contrast the narrator's unsettling sense of alienation at home. A similar sense of estrangement is powerfully present in "Ancient Capital." The narrator in this story, accidentally mistaken for a Japanese tourist upon arriving at the Chiang Kai-shek Airport, decides on a whim to take a make-believe tour of her hometown Taipei, following a Japanese guide map printed with place names from the colonial period. The uncanny experience of viewing what is thoroughly familiar through a borrowed looking glass turns out to be a psychological journey into deep recesses of personal as well as collective memories.

CHAPTER 8

New Developments in the Post–Martial Law Period

The lifting of martial law in 1987 divides Taiwan's post–1949 era into two drastically different periods. Although a clearer picture of the latest period seems to be emerging now, various cultural forces are still busily negotiating. Returning to Raymond Williams's tripartite structure of cultural formations (dominant, alternative, oppositional), the ongoing developments in Taiwan's cultural field may be described as follows.

With sinocentrism under attack, the dominant culture of the martial law period and the corresponding Mainstream position in the literary field are seriously undermined. Localism, which used to play the oppositional role, is now contending for the dominant position in the cultural field, with less accumulated cultural capital but powerful support from rising Taiwanese nationalism—and thus, increasing public resources. At the same time, a broadly defined "Postmodern" trend, promulgated by radical intellectual groups, has replaced Modernism as the main source of alternative cultural visions and inspired iconoclastic movements in various social spheres, although it is also showing susceptibility to assimilation by the new mainstream.

The literary field has sustained significant changes. For good or for ill, the mode of literary production in post–martial law Taiwan is now closer to that in other advanced capitalist societies. Following the universal logic that leads to greater differentiation and professionalization, the field has assumed greater autonomy, and individual agents have become more conscious of its changing operational laws.

As a rule, contemporary studies like this one face a unique challenge: most of the phenomena under examination are still unfolding; their long-term implications remain unclear. This chapter therefore contains more descriptive accounts than conclusive analyses of trends and developments that appear to have significant bearings on literary history. The chapter first outlines literary agents' contribution to new transformations of the Localist discourse, then introduces the development of various radical cultural trends, subsumed under Postmodernism, that have held the limelight since the early 1990s. There follow preliminary observations on the more specialized, professionalized literary vocation, using examples from contemporary fiction. The final section focuses on a well-publicized, controversial media event held in spring 1999—the Selection of Taiwanese Literary Classics, co-sponsored by the *United Daily News* and the Council of Cultural Affairs.[1] Participated in by a broad range of literary agents and readers, the event is a lens through which the dynamic interplay of different positions in the literary field can be glimpsed.

TRANSFORMATIONS OF LOCALIST DISCOURSE

There is a consensus about what constitutes the core of the new dominant culture in the post–martial law period—it is the spirit of *bentu*, or a Localist imperative that Taiwan be treated as the "center" in cultural mapping. The reconstitution of Taiwan's dominant culture has resulted primarily from the momentous political changes since the lifting of martial law. Treating Taiwan as the center, however, still leaves open the question of contents, or how to define the distinctive features of the culture, a question still very much under discussion and development in academic institutions, in the press and in the media, and among intellectual elites.

An important focus of the evolving Localist discourse is national/ethnic identity, long the central subject of political maneuvering. In the early decades after 1949, for instance, the political needs of the ruling Nationalist regime were served by the promotion of a sinocentric cultural ideology. Government practices that protected the interests of the mainlanders, originally a rather diverse group from many different provinces, virtually re-created them as a single ethnic group (Rigger 6). Exiled political proponents of the Taiwan independence movement, on the other hand, have long proclaimed that "Taiwanese" is a racially mixed nationality with Malayo-Polynesian, Dutch, Portuguese, Japanese, and Han components, a view frequently echoed in Localist discourse within Taiwan, particularly in the late martial law period. Rather than proposing a scientifically based new ethnic discourse, this claim was primarily conceived to subvert the legitimacy of sinocentrism, a major obstacle to building a "Taiwanese nation."

Since the lifting of martial law, the intense power negotiation between the two major population groups and the rising menace of the People's Republic of China have called for a rehashing of the term "Localism" according to current sociopolitical realities. With increasing acknowledgment of the hybrid nature of the island's culture, the latest effort to redefine a distinctive "Taiwanese ethnicity" in the public sphere has focused on shared historical experience, designating mainlanders as *xin zhumin* (new settlers) or *xin Taiwanren* (new Taiwanese), the latter a term favorably evoked in many recent election campaigns.

However, Localist writers, such as Wu Zhuoliu, Ye Shitao, Li Qiao, and Dongfang Bai, began to reimagine the Taiwanese community—interpreting its history in the fashion of what Raymond Williams calls the "selective tradition"—much earlier. Their successors in the post–martial law period have revived this activity and contributed significantly to transforming public perceptions. Much cited in recent literary discourse is Wu Zhuoliu's statement in his 1979 memoir *The Fig Tree* about the "agrarian community spirit" among rural Han settlers in Taiwan, suggesting that the will to protect the land that their ancestors had cultivated with blood and sweat against outside invaders formed the basis of a "Taiwanese consciousness" (38–39). It was this that enabled the Taiwanese Han settlers to fight off the aboriginal tribes and to put up a foolish but stout resistance to the Japanese takeover at the end of the nineteenth century. Also receiving renewed attention are Ye Shitao's earlier works. In his 1977 landmark essay "Introduction to the History of Nativist Literature," for instance, Ye suggested that Taiwan's semitropical weather and other geographical features helped to shape a distinctive Taiwanese literature. Then, Li Qiao's and Dong Fangbai's multivolume sagas, *Wintry Night* and *Waves Lap the Sand* (written in the 1970s and 1980s, respectively), chronicling the history of migration and land cultivation by early Han settlers in Taiwan, clearly served as alternative national epics.

The post–martial law Localist discourse also features a new emphasis on the pragmatic and dynamic dimensions of the "Taiwanese character." The screening of the PRC television documentary *Heshang* [River elegy] (1988) in Taiwan unexpectedly triggered a new Taiwanese ethnic discourse, inspired by the idea that, as an island, Taiwan has always been a mercantile society heavily dependent on import-export trade. Therefore, it long ago developed an "oceanic" civilization different from mainland China's "agrarian" model. This new narrative clearly underscores Li Ang's *Lost Garden*, which features an origin myth suggesting that Taiwanese descended from a pirate ancestor whose uncouth adventurous energy is inherited by modern-day Taiwanese entrepreneurs. Another book, *Xinxing minzu* [An emergent nation] (1995)—part of DPP presidential candidate Xu Xinliang's campaign propaganda, ghost-written by a group of younger intellectuals, including writer-critic Yang Zhao—makes an even more explicit attempt at forging a new identity on a capitalist anvil. Departing from the "sadness" (or *beiqing*) motif that stresses the traumatic experience of Taiwanese as colonial subjects,[2] the book's characterization of the modern Taiwanese as an energetic and smart entrepreneur operating with special aplomb in the transnational business world draws on the island's economic boom of the 1970s and 1980s.

Although initially the majority of mainlanders felt excluded by the Localist politics, an increasing number of them have actively participated in constructing a new Taiwanese identity. Literary scholar Liao Xianhao, for instance, applies Benedict Anderson's *Imagined Communities* concept to Taiwan's ethno-linguistic problems. Urging a more flexible approach, Liao takes issue with the inherent bias of the "Taiwanese consciousness" discourse and insists that the mainlanders, as new settlers on the island, ought to be included as "Taiwanese" without discrimination. Such voices have undoubtedly contributed to the appearance of more inclusive Localist discourses in the post–martial law period.

POSTMODERN TRENDS AS A NEW ALTERNATIVE CULTURAL FORMATION

In 1994, English professor He Chunrui's highly engaging book advocating sexual liberation, *Haoshuang nüren* [The untrammeled woman], created a great stir. Eloquently demystifying traditional gender ideology and urging women to actively explore carnal pleasure, the book was a clarion call for a sexual revolution that had already been fermenting on college campuses for a few years. Adding to the sensation, on International Women's Day in the same year, a group of women intellectuals and professionals spontaneously shouted out the slogan, "We want orgasm, not harassment," in a street demonstration triggered by a notorious case of sexual harassment in one of Taiwan's most prestigious universities. In November 1996, a shocking news story shook the entire society: Peng Wanru, a well-respected feminist scholar and director of the DPP Division on Women's Development, was stabbed to death after being sexually assaulted in a taxi one night after a meeting in Kaohsiung. The tragedy provided an occasion for various women's organizations to unite in pursuit of a common cause, the promotion of women's safety and general welfare, leading to the establishment of the Peng Wan-Ru Foundation in 1999. Between the mid- and late 1990s, the radical wing of feminist activists engaged in a number of highly visible social activities. In 1997, for instance, backing the appeal from Taipei's legal prostitutes to postpone the abolishment of the government-operated brothels for two years (to allow them to find new jobs), they sponsored public symposia including international activist groups of sex workers and supporters. In the last couple years of the decade, the tremendous vitality of the Postmodern feminist trend seemed to be wearing down, especially with the rift between the more radical and the more moderate feminist factions, which inevitably caused some negative repercussions.[3] Nonetheless, it has effected a profound change in ideas about gender, and this is particularly evident in the behavior patterns of young people.

Feminism is just one prominent example of the numerous radical cultural formations that emerged in the 1990s. In their overall contribution, Taiwan's Postmodern activists have significantly altered the conceptual framework and analytic categories with which people perceive contemporary culture. For one thing, they have expanded the conventional definition of "politics," bringing in elements of a more purely cultural nature, making popular in Taiwan's contemporary intellectual discourse such terms as "gender politics," "cultural politics," and "identity politics." Harboring their own interventionist agenda, the Postmodern activists alternately rival and cooperate with the Localists, whose political opposition is of a more traditional kind. While the Localists in the 1990s—prior to 2000, when the DPP became the ruling party—targeted their attacks chiefly at the KMT's political rule, the radical Postmodern cultural trends have been challenging the conservative social norms of the martial law period, performing a historically specific function. As the successor of the earlier alternative cultural formation, the Modernist movement, the Postmodern trend offered correctives to Taiwan's conservative dominant culture by drawing strengths from imported progressive ideologies.

Of course, that dominant culture had already begun to disintegrate in the 1980s. The marked increase in affluence, the growing independence of the media, and the government's own "liberalization and internationalization" program aimed at reducing Taiwan's diplomatic isolation following the U.S. recognition of the PRC in 1979 all worked to erode the social norms of the passing era. Outward symptoms of this disintegration surfaced within a couple of years before martial law was lifted. The Nationalist regime, beset by serious financial and political scandals, came under severe attacks from the oppositional political force, accompanied by an outburst of social agitation. "Self-help" demonstrations addressing various civil rights issues, environmental activism, campus protests by student groups, veterans' demonstrations pushing for legalization of visits to the mainland, etc., complemented the DPP's increasingly successful challenges to the KMT in local and national elections. The activist impulse was apparently feeding on the social discontent accumulated over forty years of authoritarian rule, which also explains the idealism of intellectual groups interested in community regeneration. Within the intellectual circle, the independent image projected by such cohorts like Cheng she [The clarity club], which advocates liberal political reform, and a more progressive coterie centered around the journal *Taiwan: A Radical Quarterly of Social Studies*, exemplified the idealism of this phase in Taiwan's contemporary society.

After the lifting of martial law, intellectual formations began to take on a new look. Incorporating the progressive agenda of such discourses as postmodernism, postcolonialism, the new left, and cultural studies, they became more active in reaching out to the public and the media. Manned primarily by intellectuals who had recently returned from abroad and occupied prestigious academic positions, the Postmodernists built their base on college campuses, establishing new centers and radical magazines, engaging in public lectures, symposia, and street demonstrations, and forming alliances with emerging popular movements on an ad hoc basis. The Chengxiang yanjiusuo [Graduate institute of urban-rural studies] at National Taiwan University, the Liangxing yanjiu shi [Center for gender studies] at National Tsing Hua University, the cultural section of *Zili wanbao* [Independence evening post], the academic journal *Taiwan: A Radical Quarterly in Social Studies*, and the slightly later, more avant-gardist magazine *Daoyu bianyuan* [Isle margin] were among the best known bases. As previously noted, in the mid-1980s new theoretical concepts from the West flooded Taiwan's cultural field in greater quantity than before. However, most local intellectuals and students had little opportunity to digest the new cultural theories and more often than not treated them as fashionable markers. As a group, the Postmodernists of the post–martial law period have been a great deal more successful at indigenizing and popularizing imported theories, as exemplified by the Postmodern feminist activists cited earlier.

Viewed from the perspective of a longer time span, the historical significance of the Postmodern trend is its effective challenge to the conservative/liberal hegemony in Taiwan's cultural spheres in the entire post–1949 era. While outspoken liberal intellectuals were persecuted in the 1950s and 1960s, as more technocrats and "enlightened" U.S.-trained liberals—best represented by James Soong, now chairman of the People First Party—entered the government ranks in later decades, the dominance of U.S. liberalism was consolidated at the expense of genuine intellectual pluralism. In a significant sense, it was the lack of legitimate forums for radical intellectual strands in Taiwan's post–1949 era, as well as the sudden release of pent-up social energy after the end of martial law, that gave the Postmodern cultural formation its special niche and popular appeal.

There was, to be sure, a notable precedent of intellectual groups' challenge to the liberal-conservative hegemony in post–1949 Taiwan; it came from the leftist faction of the Nativists in the 1970s—led by Chen Yingzhen—and caused much alarm to the Nationalist ruling regime at the time. The doctrines promoted by the Nativist "old left," intermixed with sentimental nostalgia for prerevolutionary China, paled in comparison with those of the Postmodern "new left" in terms of intellectual sophistication. And yet, the old left's historical contribution cannot be ignored. After the Nativist movement was officially suppressed, veteran advocates of socialist ideals received substantial support from the 1980s liberalizing and expanding media, and continued to work effectively on educating the public about issues like industrial pollution, exploitation of the aboriginal community, legitimacy of the student movement, and gay rights. The pictorial magazine *Human World* operated by Chen Yingzhen and his associates, for instance, was a remarkably successful platform for progressive ideas.[4] Chen's insistence on returning to the fate of early postwar Communist martyrs and victims of the 1950s White Terror also complicates the historical narratives projected by both the Mainstream and the Localist agents. More significantly, these efforts helped assuage the public's paranoia about radical ideology, paving the way for the across-the-board "radical turn" in Taiwan's intellectual sphere in the early 1990s.

The post–martial law radical cultural formation benefited greatly from the proliferation of public forums in the 1990s, spurred by dramatically increased freedom of speech, intellectual pluralism, and new forms of competition within a more autonomous cultural field. As noted, trendy western theories had been flooding in since the mid-1980s, but were mostly undigested. The Postmodernist group has been the exception, integrating these theories thanks to the higher quality of introductory work done by scholars recently returned from abroad, whose number grew considerably in the 1990s. Theorist Arjun Appadurai singles out the electronic media and mass migration as two essential factors that helped to shape today's transnational cultural economy. The backflow of emigrant intellectuals certainly contributed to the Postmodern surge in Taiwan. This group includes several theater people from New York who played crucial roles in starting the Little Theater movement; left-leaning professors who endorsed and participated in various street protests, including younger intellectuals advocating a "new oppositional movement"; and key leaders of the feminist/sexual revolution movement and gender studies. This new development has resulted in a significantly enhanced synchronization of local intellectual movements with international discourses. Keeping abreast of cutting-edge trends in the West, Taiwan's Postmodern intellectuals generally subscribe to an interventionist, populist approach, are sensitive to the hybrid nature of local cultural production, and are prone to wage wars against the conservative forces through smartly engineered strategies. In this regard, they depart from intellectuals baptized in the Modernist movement. The Modernists are more self-consciously elitist, are relatively uncritical of western "neocolonialism," and shoulder a liberal agenda seeking to modernize Taiwan by reforming and professionalizing its institutions.

Friction is inevitable between the Modernists and the Postmodernists owing to basic differences in their theoretical presumptions. Viewed within Taiwan's historical context, however, these two alternative cultural formations show unmistakable family resemblances. Both trends took root on college campuses before spreading into broader social spheres. This elitist starting point made both more susceptible to mainstream appropriation of their potentially subversive agendas. Both also came onto the scene at momentous historical junctures. The Modernists appeared at the beginning of Taiwan's economic takeoff, when the first generation educated under the Nationalist regime was coming of age and the government first relaxed its authoritarian grip a little. The Postmodernist formation was directly associated with the lifting of martial law, and benefited especially from the return of emigrant intellectuals, partly attracted by the late 1980s booming economy. So despite their divergent intellectual agendas, the Taiwanese versions of Modernism and Postmodernism have followed similar trajectories of development and served essentially the same function, challenging the politically instituted, conservative, neotraditionalist, and conformist dominant culture.

The Postmodernists, in particular, have played a crucial role in the post–martial law era in liberating the public from the social inhibitions of the authoritarian past. Making successful inroads into the mainstream media in the mid-1990s strengthened the Postmodernists at the same time that it changed their nature. As charismatic leaders of the group became media icons, their radical agenda lost much of its subversive edge. In their own words, the forces of resistance have been "co-opted" (*shoubian*) by mainstream institutions. This process has been aided by the intense competition ensuing from the new era's redistribution of public resources among cultural agents of different ethnic backgrounds, and the revaluation of politically authorized cultural and symbolic capital—among the most obvious, the elevation of the Minnan dialect (Taiwanese) and Taiwancentric motifs at the expense of Mandarin and sinocentric themes. The latest round of restructuring in the field of cultural production is thus inevitably attended by fierce partisan struggles.

As the Postmodernist formation heavily relies on input from the outside world for renewal, it cannot but undergo rapid change, for the new era's liberated cultural environment and advanced stage of globalization have greatly accelerated the interaction between local and international intellectual communities. Direct contact with the "center" of the western cultural hegemony has steadily increased in recent decades, and even the new DPP government is stressing the importance of internationalizing Taiwan's cultural sectors.[5] While this has facilitated real-time assimilation of the latest western theories (Stuart Hall, Benedict Anderson, Judith Butler, Slavoj Zizek, Charles Taylor, etc. are all familiar to graduate students) and stimulated higher academic performance among local scholars, it has inevitably diluted the radical agenda of the original Postmodern cultural formation, moving it away from local issues and hard targets toward generic global issues and pure theory. Moreover, in the last few years a financial crunch has hit some of the key players, including the pioneering lesbian publication, *Nüpengyou* [Girlfriends] (Zheng, Meili), and Nüshudian, or the Feminist bookstore, an important base for feminist writing and coordination. In the meantime, street activism has declined, and other signs likewise suggest that the movement has entered a new phase.

For instance, the Cultural Studies Association, founded in 1998, has absorbed several Postmodern factions into its institutional structure. Its recent (June 2002) summer-study camp featured prominent postcolonial theorists from the First World, including Homi Bhabha, Gayatri Spivak, and Rey Chow. Homi Bhabha's lecture tour also included stops in Beijing and Hong Kong, and the whole event, despite its thematic focus on resistance strategies of nonwestern intellectuals, cannot but remind us of the old Modernist "high culture quest." In any case, it seems indisputable that Taiwan's Postmodern radical formation has already been assimilated by the country's academic mainstream. Its future development, therefore, is likely to have greater impact within the increasingly professionalized academic world than on the society at large.

New Developments in the Post–Martial Law Literary Field

While the politics of Chinese versus Taiwanese nationalism gets more attention, it is important to remember that other factors also play into the identity complex of contemporary Taiwan residents. In 1997, two important demonstrations were held, on May 4 and May 18, that had little to do with competing nationalisms. Instead, these were protests against bureaucratic incompetence and the perceived failure of the government to prevent a general deterioration of living conditions and social well-being in Taiwan. The protesters were mostly people who normally dislike street activism, including many housewives. The organizers were mostly "opinion makers" interested in educational reform, women's rights, environmental issues, and welfare for the handicapped. Explicitly nonpartisan, the demonstrators forcefully demanded greater efficiency and accountability from the country's civil servants. Considering that public demonstrations were a recent phenomenon in Taiwan, the sophistication displayed was remarkable. More important for our purposes is the fact that the appeals came from the middle class, and focused on quality-of-life issues.

The alliance across party affiliations is also notable. Middle-class interests featured in the election platform of the China New Party, a spinoff from the KMT in the 1990s, and its supporters came mainly from the urban areas of northern Taiwan, which are more heavily populated by mainlanders. However, multiple political factions cooperated in the May 1997 demonstrations, indicating new awareness of the importance of separating social issues from party politics and "provincial identity" conflicts.

The greater presence of the middle class in Taiwan's sociopolitical space has not translated into notable growth of the "middle-class *fukan* literature" that thrived in the 1980s. Instead, developments in the post–martial law literary field appear to parallel the maturation of the middle class in another way: literary agents have been remarkably adaptive to the rules of a more advanced capitalist society, displaying greater professionalism and a pragmatic openness in preserving self-interest.

The Great Divide

Literary readership has noticeably dipped in recent decades for a number of reasons, above all, the dramatic increase in both volume and diversity of popular cultural products from the global market. High-quality mass culture products like pop music from Hong Kong, Japanese comics and popular fiction, Hollywood films, and Japanese and Korean soap operas are easily available and have been drawing away potential consumers of *fukan* literature. Literary production itself is also more subject to market imperatives. Taiwan's post–martial law government has steadily withdrawn from direct interference in cultural activities. Old and new state agencies have eased their endeavors at political indoctrination and adopted a more modern, managerial approach, paying more attention to cost efficiency than ideology. The responsibility of such bodies as the Government Information Office, the Council of Cultural Affairs, the Council of National Sciences, and even the Cultural Bureaus of the Municipal and County Governments has shifted away from transmitting centrally designed cultural policies toward sound management and effective distribution of public resources. While this process is inevitably susceptible to the politics of the day, especially the identity politics between the two major population groups, substantial freedom from official control means greater responsibility to the market.

A turning point, in the late 1980s and early 1990s, was marked by a series of pronouncements declaring the death of this or that cultural phenomenon: *chunwenxue* ("pure literature"), Taiwan new cinema, and Little Theater, among others. These gestures of alarm made it evident that the post–martial law sea change was taking its toll on the previous decade's cultural momentum, precipitating a shared sense of crisis among cultural producers. What awaited them was a new cultural order. Most important, the same imperatives that sparked middle-class activism in May 1997 have also fostered a more specialized, differentiated, and professionalized mode of literary production. The influence of *fukan* and their annual literary contests has sharply declined, giving way to more specialized publishing houses (Unitas and Ryefield are important new players) and newspaper book-review sections (most importantly in the *China*

Times and the *United Daily News*). The new agencies of literary consecration are transforming the standards by which literature is appreciated
and evaluated. Writers are likewise compelled to conform to the new standards and to professionalize their approach to the craft. Everywhere we
see a paradigmatic shift: more consideration is given to the popular reception of literary products, while high moral ambitions and elitist assumptions about the arts are now treated with greater cynicism. At the
same time, the new climate is emphatically at odds with the spirit of engagement propagated by the progressive Postmodern ferment. It is instead
a frank coming to terms with the new rules of the game.

Before the 1990s, literary discourse in Taiwan was dominated by a liberal humanist view that stressed the "intrinsic" artistic qualities of literary
texts, predicated on a separation of politics and art. With its focus on
"high culture," literary criticism conspicuously omitted the market factor,
except for associating it with philistinism.

Influenced by the progressive spirit of Postmodernism, literary criticism
in the 1990s responded negatively to the ascendance of naked market
forces, bemoaning the "commodification" of literature in terms supplied
by neo-Marxist and critical theories. But creative writers had to cope with
the immediate problem of survival and thus reacted to the new environment more pragmatically. There has been a gradual turnabout in attitudes
toward "high" and "popular" literatures. Where once there was regret
about the decline of "serious" and "pure" literature, there is now considerable skepticism about self-appointed cultural guardians. The predominant tendency among literary agents now is to denigrate "self-indulgent"
aesthetic practices in favor of commercial viability. All signs suggest that
the "high culture quest" is over.[6]

Fiction Writing in the Post–Martial Law Period

This section offers some preliminary observations on fiction writing in the
post–martial law period as it moves toward greater professionalism. It is
worth noting that in spite of its accomplishments, fiction since the mid-
1980s does not occupy the same vanguard position that it once did in
Taiwan. During the tumultuous closing years of the 1980s and the opening years of the present era, with DPP supporters, progressive student organizations, and social activists launching attacks on KMT political institutions, the recently released energy found its main cultural outlets in the
Postmodern Little Theater movement, Localist historical reconstruction

efforts, and Taiwan new cinema. Fiction from the period was comparatively unremarkable, its treatment of such popular but volatile subjects as the February 28 Incident, the White Terror, and KMT factional politics restrained and cautious. Mainstream fiction by second-generation mainlanders tended to be reflective, with a touch of cynicism and disenchantment. Meanwhile, Localist "big-stream" novels exuded a constructive spirit of cultural nationalism and an eagerness for community regeneration. Neither genre reflected the iconoclastic spirit of the day.

NEW WINNING STRATEGIES

Farther into the 1990s, new genres of "middlebrow" literature began to emerge. Generally speaking, these works are technically adroit, ostensibly topical, and often targeted at niche markets. It is worth noting that the Postmodern radical formation of the same period made only a limited—and frequently superficial—appearance in fiction writing. For instance, although the vigorous queer discourse inspired a host of works on gay and lesbian themes,[7] witnessing the belated acknowledgment of homosexuality in Taiwan society, it did so largely without breaking new ground on gender ideology or advancing artistic development. Among the most notable queer writers, Qiu Miaojin's tragic suicide ended prematurely her brilliant but brief literary career, and the success with which Ji Dawei carved an image for himself as a queer writer owed much to his versatility—he had also written impressive futuristic fiction (Mo [Membrane], 1996) and intelligent commentaries on Taiwan's queer phenomenon in his edited twin volumes Ku'er qishi lu [Queer archipelago] and Ku'er kuanghuan jie [Queer carnival] (1997). Furthermore, the fact that for several years in the mid-1990s stories constructed on queer themes inundated the desks of fukan editors and annual fiction contest jurors suggests how aspiring writers simply used this radical cultural trend to identify niche markets for promoting a literary career.

As dictated by the new rules of the game, publishers and writers in the post–martial law era are actively exploring new markets. The impressive sales figures for Zhang Dachun's Weekly Journals of Big Head Chun, a mildly iconoclastic adolescent story reminiscent of Catcher in the Rye, are said to have benefited from a successful marketing strategy that encouraged middle-school teachers to assign the book as extracurricular summer reading. While daring sexual descriptions and sensational subjects have always guaranteed a certain degree of popularity for Li Ang's fiction, the media-hyped scandal surrounding Beigang xianglu renren cha [Everyone puts their incense sticks in the Pei-kang incense burner] (1997), which pairs explicit sex with allusions to a real female celebrity and well-known political figure, gave the novel a huge boost. By the late 1990s, such practices as media interviews, colorful photos on book covers, and press conferences for new releases had been routinely adopted to package creative writers as cultural icons—a familiar production-promotion strategy in advanced capitalist societies.

As writers become more pragmatic about the market, they also make more calculated efforts at improving the "quality" of their products. Of particular interest is that many now make conscious attempts to imitate proven successes. This often leads to eclectic use of techniques and aesthetic modes associated with different artistic positions in the field, thus softening the boundaries between them. For instance, as we have already seen, the Zhu sisters have incorporated Modernist and Postmodernist elements that move their work closer to "high art" genres. Li Ang, a baby-boom Mainstream writer who has regularly shifted positions, returns to something like "classical modernism" in her recent books, *Pei-kang Incense Burner* and *Fiction: An Autobiography*, fully exploring sensuality's transgressive potential to create the "shock effect." Ping Lu, best known for intellectually challenging stories, shifts gears in her latest collection, *Ningzhi wenquan* [Jadelike skin in hot springs] (2000), to a more subtly "feminine" style reminiscent of the 1980s sentimental school of women writers. The tendency is even more pronounced among younger writers. As a rule, those entering the profession in the 1990s have followed closely conventions established by baby-boom generation authors, such as the witty and playful portrayal of the yuppie culture (Cheng Yingshu, Luo Yijun, Ji Dawei, Zhu Guozhen) and sentimental love stories featuring sensuously detailed depictions of the female psyche (Hao Yuxiang, Zhang Yingtai).

Topicality, rather than ideological commitment, rules the day. Li Ang's *Lost Garden* provides an excellent example, deploying an impressive array of trendy topics, including Taiwanese ethnic identity, female sexuality, political persecution during the White Terror, and the vital but vulgar business culture of self-made millionaires in Taiwan's economic boom. Writers who have entered the field in the last decade, amid overheated identity politics, show a particular predilection for drawing their subjects from the distinctive subcultures in contemporary Taiwan—the queer community (Ji Dawei, Chen Xue), the youth culture of the post–baby boom generation raised on Japanese *manga* and anime (Hong Ling), and the ethnic subgroup of second-generation mainlanders brought up in the now largely demolished *juancun* (military housing compounds) (Luo Yijun, Zhang Qijiang). Of course, the current cultural climate dictates new treatment of old subjects: the complacency of the 1980s *juancun* stories is replaced by emphasis on the self-positioning problems faced by the former residents of *juancun*; and in place of pervasive accounts of the Sino-Japanese war on the mainland are now more, and rather deliberate, references to the Pacific War during the Japanese period in Taiwan.

Greater professionalism is manifested in fiction writers' willingness to invest more time and energy in archival research. The number of full-length novels has notably increased, many resulting from extensive research efforts. This is a conspicuous departure from the 1980s, when the short story prevailed, limited by the space available in *fukan* pages, and longer works were often merely expanded versions of short stories. In fact, quite a few impressive novels have appeared recently, including Ping Lu's *Xinglu tianya* [A journey to the end of the world] (1995), a fictional account of the love story between Sun Yat-sen and Song Qingling; Wu Jiwen's *Shijimo shaonian'ai duben* [Pamphlet on the love of young boys in the fin de siècle] (1996), a rewriting of *Pinghua baojian* [Precious mirror that ranks the beauties], a Qing dynasty novel on homosexual eroticism; Shi Shuqing's *Xianggang sanbuqu* [The Hong Kong trilogy] (1993, 1995, 1997), a historical romance set in colonial Hong Kong; Wuhe's *Yusheng* [Remains of life] (1999), which evokes the unrecorded feuds and massacres in the recent history of Taiwan's aboriginal tribes; Zhang Dachun's *Gang of the City State*, featuring the dealings between criminal gangs and Nationalist secret service agents during the 1949 retreat; and Li Ang's *Fiction: An Autobiography*, based on the life of Xie Xuehong, the legendary female leader of the Taiwanese Communists.

THE INWARD-POINTING REFLEXIVITY

Baby-boom generation writers still active in the post–martial law period are a self-selected group of earnest *litterateurs*, as evidenced by the recurrence in their works of self-reflexive statements on the act of writing. As we have seen, Zhu Tianwen concludes her *Notes of a Desolate Man* by affirming the redemptive quality of literary writing. The shifting back and forth between the narrator's present tense and reenacted historical events in recent novels by Ping Lu, Li Ang, and Zhang Dachun unmistakably functions as a self-referential device that foregrounds the narrative act. While such techniques are clearly inspired by foreign models, they are also indicative of the writers' self-conscious identification with their vocation.

Fittingly, it is only in the last decade that the label *zhuanye zuojia*, or "professional writers," has gained greater prestige, increasingly defining Taiwanese writers' self-perception.

Finally, two recent novels by a newly consecrated baby-boom generation writer, Wuhe, provide an occasion to reflect upon Taiwanese fiction's trajectory between two important models, the Modernist and the Postmodernist. Both novels appeared in 2000: the previously mentioned *Remains of Life*, and *Gui'er yu ayao* [Queer and Ayao], a parodic work on contemporary Taipei's queer scene that is strewn with explicit sexual descriptions. Quaintly esoteric, the books are written with superlative linguistic skill, sophisticated narrative techniques, and unruly, if not fully coherent, themes—a rare combination. Wuhe's work, in fact, makes an excellent first example supporting the proposition that Taiwanese fiction writing has been testing a new paradigm.

As I tried to demonstrate in *Modernism and the Nativist Resistance*, Taiwan's Modernist fiction is essentially framed within a humanist ideology, interested in the existential meaning of life, the nature of human suffering, and the complex problem of interpersonal ethical responsibilities in Taiwan's specific historical context. This seems true of the three novels published in the 1990s by veteran Modernists: Wang Wenxing's *Beihai de ren (xia)* [Backed against the sea, part II] (1999), and Li Yongping's *Haidongqing: Taibei de yize yuyan* [East ocean green: A parable of Taipei] (1992) and *Zhu Ling manyou xianjing* [Zhu Ling in wonderland] (1998). With all its obscurantism, Li's work is anchored in a coherent moral vision—albeit couched in a highly personalized, ultraconservative nationalism. A firm intellectual commitment is clear in these works' high modernist aestheticism, a commitment to challenge prevalent ethical and artistic conventions. While these authors flaunt their belief in the literary art's self-sufficiency, they conceive their practices within a "master narrative" of sorts, or what Linda Hutcheon would call "totalizing systems" of meaning.

In contrast, judged by Hutcheon's criteria in *A Poetics of Postmodernism: History, Theory, Fiction*, Wuhe's novels are "decentered" in their deliberate deconstruction of totalizing systems. The justifications the narrators give for their idiosyncratic courses of action are patently flimsy, and the thematic structure of the stories insistently operates on a depthless surface. In *Remains of Life*, the narrator's search for truths behind the bloodthirsty feuding of two aboriginal tribes in a none-too-remote past finds no answer, nor are there any plausible symbolic resolutions in sight. In *Queer and Ayao*, sexual fulfillment is attainable, but there is emphatically no pretense that it means anything more than physical gratification, and a touch of nihilism lurks behind the impenetrable mask the narrator wears. The first novel exhibits postmodern traits classed by Hutcheon under "historiographical metafiction" (92). The imaginative reconstruction of historical records is revealed to be ultimately inconsequential, thus assuming the status of parody. *Queer* also exudes intertextuality (127–133), building its central thesis around caricatures of prevalent queer discourses as well as their trendy subscribers, who imagine themselves as practitioners of utopian sex. Again following Hutcheon, one might discern in Wuhe a dual intention to simultaneously subvert those discourses and make use of them for "what they are worth" (133). Both novels contain an explicit element of metafiction—not only in the author/narrator's self-referential remarks but also in their carrying to the extreme the modernist aesthetics of "autotelic self-reflection" (i.e., self-reflection as an end in itself) (40)—making them devoid of any intention to validate meaning structures outside of the work.

To conclude, the more professionalized, differentiated, and specialized cultural climate of the post–martial law period is reflected in certain new tendencies in literary production. Literary agents have geared their efforts toward winning in the competitive market, using more diverse marketing strategies, searching for niche markets, imitating proven successes, focusing on topical issues, and investing more in research. However, just as writers become more self-conscious about their commitment to the vocation, their works become increasingly self-reflexive, fraught with meta-commentaries pointing to their own creative acts, the conventions of the literary genres in which they write, and the very rules governing today's field of cultural production.

The Legitimacy Question: An Analysis of a Media Event

Commissioned by the Council of Cultural Affairs, the *United Daily News* announced over the 1999 new year holiday that it would hold a public selection of *"Taiwan wenxue jingdian"* [Literary classics of Taiwan]. The selection process combined cultural elitism with procedural democracy: the seven-member Selection Committee made an initial recommendation of 150 works in five categories: fiction, poetry, drama, prose, and criticism. Ballots accompanied by a questionnaire were first mailed to 100 Taiwanese literature instructors at colleges and high schools across the island,

and the committee made its final selection of 30 classics in each category based on the votes returned (approximately 70 percent of the original recipients responded). A report of the discussion at the selection meeting was published in the *United Daily News* (Jian). The event concluded with a three-day scholarly conference on the selected works.[8]

To the surprise of the seasoned *Lianfu* organizers and their well-intentioned sponsor (the CCA), the event turned into chaotic public theater and a political shouting match. In the considerably restructured literary field of the post–martial law period, the tension between political and cultural legitimacy not only continues but also takes a more openly confrontational form. Before addressing that issue, there are some other telling points to be highlighted.

In his opening remarks, Chen Yizhi, chief editor of *Lianfu*, summoned the notion of *chunwenxue* ("pure literature"), the old totem of the Mainstream position, against commercial vulgarization and new brands of theme-centered critical discourses, proclaiming that the goal of the selection was precisely to restore "purity" and "dignity" to literature ("Xu" 6–8). As we have seen, *chunwenxue* has never been an innocent, ideology-free entity. In a positive sense, it served as a haven from the chore of serving political purposes. It could also be camouflage, however, serving to legitimize the dominant culture and conservative instincts. Both functions have become largely obsolete in the new era's liberalized politics and radicalized cultural climate. Chen's statement, therefore, represented an effort by Mainstream literary agents to imbue *chunwenxue* with new significance.

The outcome of the selection also confirmed the Modernists' strong claim to cultural legitimacy in contemporary Taiwan's literary field. Despite the fact that its ideology had been discredited in public discourse since the late 1970s, the majority of winners—especially the undisputed ones—received their artistic training in Taiwan's Modernist literary movement.[9] Despite increased activism in the new era, many literary agents still cleave to a principle that separates aesthetics from politics, a belief that underpins the Modernist position. Even some Localist participants harshly criticized the overly politicized cultural climate.[10]

The fact that only one of the selected fiction works, *Whirlwind*, owes much to traditional Chinese vernacular fiction serves as a reminder that in fiction, western-patterned products overwhelmingly outperform the more traditional types. Although they have received little attention, such clues from the selection point to an ongoing struggle between indigenous and imported literary genres and aesthetic conceptions. Since the battlegrounds are normally the collectively established genre hierarchy and categories of critical analysis, the selection, a consummate activity of literary evaluation, is the best occasion yet to examine where things are headed.

Issues like the above that are pertinent to a conventionally defined "literary history" of contemporary Taiwan, however, were largely submerged in the immediate controversies surrounding the selection. While unquestionably one of the largest *fukan* spectacles in a decade, without the high-profile protest it provoked, the event might not have excited so much attention. The protest was launched by a coalition of Localist literary groups led by the Taiwanese PEN Association and joined by leading scholars (Chen, Wenfen). A public demonstration, a press conference, a formal, signed complaint, and a series of critical essays in *Taiwan shibao* [Taiwan times] all made the point.[11]

At the core of the contention was the ultimate legitimacy question: Which writers and which works qualify as Taiwanese? Pressing the issue, Localist protesters complained that native Taiwanese authors were grossly underrepresented, noting in particular the absence of such key figures as Lai He, the "father of Taiwanese new literature," and many other artistically accomplished writers from both the prewar and postwar eras. Troubled by the fact that some of the selected mainlander writers are openly anti-Taiwancentric, they proclaimed that since these writers have maintained that they are "Chinese" rather than "Taiwanese," their works should be disqualified. Another dispute concerned whether Zhang Ailing, who had never resided in Taiwan, ought to be considered a "Taiwanese writer." Zhang's representative works also were mostly written in 1940s wartime Shanghai, and thus fall outside the "contemporary" time frame of most of the other selected works (with one exception, Wu Zhuoliu's *Orphan of Asia*). (In the current political climate, it is unsurprising that few raised this issue, along with the sensitive question of linguistic medium, with regard to *Orphan of Asia*, written by Wu Zhuoliu in the 1940s during the Pacific War, originally in Japanese.)

Zhang's defenders argued that the exceptional influence she has exerted on contemporary Taiwanese writers makes her an important part of Taiwanese literary history; the Localists countered: Suppose we say that Shakespeare and Hemingway have significantly influenced Taiwanese writers—does this mean that they are also eligible for the Taiwanese classics competition? The challenge to Zhang's inclusion also touched a raw nerve among some older mainlanders. Although Zhang left the mainland for Hong Kong and then the United States, not Taiwan, after the Communist takeover, her experience is otherwise essentially the same as theirs. Qi Bangyuan, a prominent critic from this generation, maintained that a "doubly exiled" Chinese like Zhang Ailing ought to be considered "one of us," a view consistent with the Nationalist regime's official stance recognizing overseas Chinese as citizens (Lai).

The boundary between prewar and postwar Taiwanese and Chinese literature is another hotly contested topic, intricately tied to the nationhood question. The selection revealed that as of 1999, although the history of the colonial period is no longer a political taboo, it has yet to be widely accepted as a legitimate part of Taiwan's cultural tradition. While the public consciousness of Taiwan's history has already changed since 1999, some deep-seated presuppositions that surfaced at the selection continue to affect the literary field of the new era.

Mainstream literary agents remained evasive on the central issues, opting instead to focus on defending the logistics of the selection procedure and to plead for nonpartisan, open-minded pluralism. They might have felt that they had already made significant concessions to the Localist imperative, since ten years earlier a similar event would mostly likely have been called the "Selection of *Chinese* Literary Classics." Obviously not quite prepared to relinquish the literary genealogy established under the sinocentric cultural narrative of the old authoritarian regime—one that is traced back to the "new literature movement" in China's Republican era ("Xu" 7)—Chen Yizhi nonetheless proclaimed that the event was intended to select and honor "Taiwan-centered literary classics" (6–7), thus making his position intrinsically dubious.

A closer look at the Localist protesters reveals latent issues on their side as well, including some simplistic assumptions about art, mostly inherited from the Nativist literary movement of the 1970s. To be sure, the Localists differ from the Nativists on the crucial issue of Taiwanese versus Chinese nationalism. Yet, like the Nativists, the Localists endorse a "simple reflection theory" of literature's mission to speak for the common folk, an idea originally introduced to Taiwan by the leftists of the prewar period that reinforces the traditional didactic views on literature. The more sophisticated contemporary audience in Taiwan today, however, is predisposed to maintain a certain distance between art and politics, so this theory, like much of what the Localists learned from the Nativists in the 1970s, does not fly so well.

This failure to keep up with contemporary tastes has a great deal to do with the historical marginality of the Localist position and the lack of cultural and academic capital of its agents, who over the years spent tremendous energy struggling for political legitimacy in the field. This historical disadvantage was an important focus of the 1999 protest. In her essay published in *Taiwan Times*, Yang Cui, granddaughter of Yang Kui, a much-respected left-wing writer of the Japanese period, accused the organizers of having "usurped" the capital accrued to the term "Taiwanese literature," for which the oppositional cultural alliances had fought hard and made many sacrifices. Worse still, she argued, Mainstream literary agents should be considered accomplices of the KMT in its repression of Taiwanese Localism. A more moderate expression of the same view came from Lin Ruiming, a history professor and pioneer of the Lai He study; laying the blame on structural factors, he suggested that the selection agents' bias was a vestige of the historical exclusion of Taiwanese literature from the education system until very recently (Chen, Wenfen).

Ultimately, of course, the dispute was about the distribution of public resources as well as symbolic capital. While the protesters attacked the sponsoring government agency, the CCA, they never challenged the foundation of its authority, only its misuse. Claiming that the selection was skewed by an "anti-Localist" stance, they were upset less by the government's involvement than by its choice of the "reactionary" media organizer, the *United Daily News*, as co-sponsor (Chen, Wenfen).[12] Rather than questioning the government's right to interfere with cultural affairs, they remonstrated with it for failing to choose the right sponsor for such an important event in Taiwan's literary development. In effect, then, they reconfirmed the state's authority to supervise cultural activities.

While the amount of public resources allocated to Localist projects has dramatically increased since the mid-1990s, there is also the matter of who has actually benefited from this redistribution. At least part of the Localists' grievance came from the fact that the symbolic capital accrued to the term "Taiwanese literature" had been distributed too broadly. Cultural agents of various ideological persuasions had been sharing the benefits flowing from the state's promotion of Localism, at the expense of what the protesters considered to be the "genuine" Localist cause.[13]

The selection also provided an occasion for venting frustration with the media, starting with skepticism about their self-appointed role as arbiters of legitimate literary discourse. Critics questioned the pseudo-democratic manner in which literary canons were established. Some found fault with the habitually inflated use of descriptive terms, including the word "classics," which still retains for some an immediate association with the lofty Confucian canon, the "Four Books and Five Classics" (*sishu wujing*). If the purpose of the selection was to recognize the achievement of Taiwanese writers within a specific time span, why couldn't the organizers adopt a less pretentious title for the event, such as the "Thirty Best Books from Taiwan in the Last Fifty Years"? After all, American publisher Random House's "100 Best Books of the 20th Century" was an obvious inspiration for the event, constantly referred to. All the criticism suggested increased concern about the media's exploitation of culture for profit.

The selection and all the controversy that it provoked provide an excellent map of the various positions in the literary field of the new era and the players' position-taking strategies. Agents in the field are moving to new positions, building new symbolic capital, and negotiating new terms with the internalized values and belief systems of the past. The investment of creative energy in these transformations, potentially divisive as they may be, constitutes the central dynamics of Taiwan's literary field today.

The event vividly showcased how the politically authorized "Mainstream position" became a fiercely contested space in the post–martial law era. This, along with the trend of professionalization fostered by a new set of socioeconomic forces, spells disintegration of the particular literary culture that grew into maturity during Taiwan's extended (four-decade-long) martial law period—a literary culture that accounts for many of the presently recognized accomplishments of Taiwan's contemporary literature, as well as its new wave cinema.

INTRODUCTION

1. Some insightful discussions are found in Jing Wang's *High Culture Fever: Politics, Aesthetics, and Ideology in Deng's China*, Xudong Zhang's *Chinese Modernism in the Era of Reforms: Cultural Fever, Avant-garde Fiction, and the New Chinese Cinema*, Ben Xu's *Disenchanted Democracy: Chinese Cultural Criticism After 1989*, and Zha Jianying's *China Pop: How Soap Operas, Tabloids, and Bestsellers Are Transforming a Culture*.

2. Good examples are Perry Link's *The Uses of Literature: Life in the Socialist Chinese Literary System* and Ban Wang's *The Sublime Figure of History: Aesthetics and Politics in Twentieth-Century China*.

3. Postmodern trends and their more limited influence on literature are addressed in chapters 7 and 8.

4. Besides *fukan*-sponsored fiction, other types of middle-class cultural production included the Mainstream theater group Biaoyan gongzuofang [Performance workshop] founded by Lai Shengchuan et al., and the majority of the early films of the Taiwan New Cinema movement. These representative works by artists of the baby-boom generation frequently featured nostalgic themes that looked back on the hardships of life in the early decades of Taiwan's post–1949 era and implicitly celebrated the social affluence of the 1980s.

5. A clash between native Taiwanese demonstrators and KMT troops sent to stop them in Kaohsiung on International Human Rights Day in 1979 that resulted in the arrest of fifteen of Taiwan's most important opposition leaders. The well-publicized trial and sentencing of these political activists in military court caused a great stir, reminding people of the lack of real democracy in Taiwan. The event became a turning point in Taiwan's postwar history.

6. Although the government has launched various "Taiwanization" programs, such as the "Ten Major Constructions," as early as the mid-1970s, in the Chiang Ching-kuo era, the Taiwan-born Lee Teng-hui was the one who successfully "Taiwanized" the KMT by endorsing, albeit ambivalently, a Localist ideology and empowering Localist factions within the party.

1. ACADEMIC CONTEXTS AND CONCEPTUAL FRAMEWORKS

1. Grant applications from organizations like NEH, ACLS, and SSRC used to specify that Taiwan and Hong Kong were acceptable sites for research projects on China, since applicants would have no access to the mainland.

2. Although Thomas Gold's *State and Society in the Taiwan Miracle* (1986) still considers Taiwan's economic success an "alternative form of Chinese modernization" (xi), it also explicitly contrasts Taiwan with Latin American countries, situating it in a global context and making it a good example of the "case study" approach. This approach has gained popularity among scholars interested in contemporary Taiwan in recent years.

3. Many anthologies that include literary works or critical essays from both mainland China and Taiwan fail to provide an adequate account of the different historical contexts of the two regions, especially the Japanese colonial period in Taiwan. This is also true of my own book, *Modernism and the Nativist Resistance*, which may be faulted for bracketing Taiwan's pre–1949 literary history in its referential frame.

4. The actual sovereignty of the Republic of China includes Taiwan and a few offshore islands near the Chinese mainland.

5. Anthropologists who participated in the "Taiwan Studies at the Millennium: State of the Field" symposium held on August 17–18, 2001, at the University of Texas at Austin, brought some alarming statistical evidence of this trend. Similarly, whereas Taiwan's economic miracle and peaceful democratization process attracted considerable interest from social scientists in the 1980s, many of the same people have moved on to China as it enters its own period of unprecedented growth and socioeconomic transformation.

6. A recent proliferation of studies of "Chinese-language" cinema, media, and popular culture typically treat China, Taiwan, and Hong Kong as a generic industry and audience. A similar equation frequently occurs in the growing literature on "global cities," which include Taipei and Hong Kong as well as Beijing, Shanghai, and other coastal cities in the PRC.

7. Xiaobing Tang's article "On the Concept of Taiwan Literature" illustrates the point, surveying the controversies over the meaning of the term *Taiwan wenxue* in the 1980s and 1990s and venturing into questions about the project of Chinese modernity and the legacies of the May Fourth intellectual tradition.

8. I do not treat separately the progress in research on Taiwanese literature outside of Taiwan during this same period because of its extremely small scale. Despite new individual and institutional efforts, progress outside pales in comparison with the exceptionally vigorous development of the field within Taiwan.

9. In fall 2002, the first academic department of Taiwanese literature was founded at National Cheng Kung University, Tainan. Even the president, Mr. Chen Shui-bian, attended the ceremony in celebration of this landmark event.

10. The study of contemporary Taiwanese literature in the U.S. academy began with C. T. Hsia's essay on the novel *The Whirlwind* by Jiang Gui (Chiang Kuei), which appeared in an appendix to the 1962 edition of *History of Modern Chinese Fiction*. Joseph S. M. Lau's articles on Chen Yingzhen (Ch'en Yingchen) and Bai Xianyong (Pai Hsien-yung), published in the *Journal of Asian Studies* in 1973 and 1975 respectively, then helped to constitute Taiwanese literature as a recognized subfield of Chinese literary studies in the United States.

11. "Traveling theory" has since featured prominently in Taiwan's cultural landscape. Structuralism, deconstruction, neo-Marxism, the Frankfurt School, feminism, postcolonialism, postmodernism, cultural studies, queer theory—each has enjoyed its fifteen minutes of fame.

12. The much discussed *Chung-wai Literary Monthly* debate on issues of Taiwanese literature and Taiwanese identity between 1994 and 1995 is a good example of how institutional affiliation and scholarly orientation are tied in with individuals' stands on unification versus independence. For a detailed analysis of the debate in English, see Marshall McArthur's dissertation of 1999 (ch. 3, sec. 2).

13. See Liao's article "Taiwan wenxue zhong de sizhong xiandai xing," as well as chapters in his book *Linglei xiandai qing*.

14. As will be further demonstrated in this work, views from expatriate scholars often form an important part of the local critical discourse in contemporary Taiwan. In the case of David D. Wang, while he has taught in the United States since the mid-1980s, he is simultaneously a full-fledged member of Taiwan's literary field through his numerous Chinese publications as well as influential work in literary publishing there during the last decade.

15. A good example of this type of ideologically informed, reductionistic interpretation is Chen Yingzhen's 1997 essay "Jiyue de qingchun." Another notable event is the impassioned exchanges of literary views between Chen Yingzhen and Chen Fangming, advocating Chinese nationalism/leftist ideology and Taiwanese nationalism/postcolonialist viewpoints respectively. The debate was carried out in Taiwan's leading literary magazine *Lianhe wenxue* [Unitas, a literary monthly] in 2000 and lasted for several months.

16. By and large, because of the lack of official channels, cultural exchange in the 1980s and 1990s between Taiwan and mainland China was left to the selection of the market. It thus provides excellent clues to "average" Chinese taste preferences.

17. These comments were made on a private occasion. Wang expressed similar views publicly at a roundtable during the same visit ("Informal Roundtable").

18. For commentaries on the event, see "Wang Shuo vs Jin Yong," a special section in the Dec. 1999 issue of *Mingbao yuekan*. A Web site, "Jin Yong he Wang Shuo teji," collects an even larger number of commentaries.

19. Wang originally made this comment in an interview with *Beijing qingnian bao* [Beijing youth daily].

20. I have treated issues related to Taiwanese literature in the Japanese period in "Beyond Cultural and National Identities." For an English survey of debates on the term "*Taiwan wenxue*" among local intellectuals in the 1980s and 1990s, see Xiaobing Tang's article.

21. Williams briefly defines the term "hegemony" in *Marxism and Literature* as follows: "Hegemony is . . . not only the articulate upper level of 'ideology,' nor are its forms of control only those ordinarily seen as 'manipulation' or 'indoctrination.' It is a whole body of practices and expectations, over the whole of living: our senses and assignments of energy, our shaping perceptions of ourselves and our world" (110).

22. Moishe Postone et al. explicates Bourdieu's definition of "habitus" as follows: "The notion of *habitus* is central to Bourdieu's theory of practice, which seeks to transcend the opposition between theories that grasp practice solely as constitut*ing* . . . and those that view practice solely as constitut*ed*. . . . To this end, Bourdieu treats social life as a mutually constituting interaction of structures, dispositions, and actions whereby social sturctures and embodied (therefore situated) knowledge of those structures produce enduring orientations to action, which, in turn, are constitutive of social structures. Hence, these orientations are at once 'structuring structures' and 'structured structures'; they shape and are shaped by social practice. . . . This capacity for structured improvisation is what Bourdieu terms the 'habitus'" (4).

2. POLITICAL AND MARKET FACTORS IN THE LITERARY FIELD

1. See, for example, Chen Sihe's discussion of the evolution of contemporary Chinese intellectuals' self-valuation and self-positioning ("Lun zhishifenzi").

2. These views are also found in Link's new book, *The Uses of Literature: Life in the Socialist Chinese Literary System* (2000).

3. The awarded novels were: *Enchou xielei ji* [Good will and revenge: A record of blood and tears] (1952) by Liao Qingxiu, *Zuguo yu tongbao* [Motherland and compatriots] (1953) by Li Rongchun, and *Lishan nongchang* [A farm on Li Mountain] (1956) by Zhong Lihe.

4. Li's literary writing, which amounts to over two million words, was largely unpublished during his lifetime. After his death his nephew found the manuscripts in Li's closet and began to publish them. The first collection, *Huai mu* [Remembering my mother], appeared in 1997.

5. See Leo Ou-fan Lee, *The Romantic Generation of Modern Chinese Writers*, in particular chapter 1, "The Emergence of the Literary Scene," and chapter 2, "The Phenomenon of Wen-t'an and Wen-jen."

6. The most important argument Laughlin has made is that the transformation of the mode of literary production from commercial industry to "a form of regimented social participation and education" (98) during wartime does not signal the victory of ideology, but the emergence of a new aesthetics. He goes

on to assert that "many of the collective campaigns' assumptions about the creation and reception of art under these [wartime] conditions went on to influence cultural life in the People's Republic, regardless of doctrine and outside influence" (100).

7. Zhang Daofan (1896–1968), who was in charge of the KMT Propaganda Bureau in the 1940s, rose to the top of the party bureaucracy when he became Speaker of the Legislative Yuan in 1952. Zhang was the most powerful figure in the government-controlled cultural sphere in the early post–1949 years, simultaneously chairing several important organizations and committees, including the Chinese Writers' and Artists' Association and the Chinese Literature and the Arts Awards Committee.

8. The entry on Chiang Ching-kuo (1909–88) in the sixth edition of *The Columbia Encyclopedia* (2001) has the following: "eldest son of Chiang Kai-shek, Chinese Nationalist leader, and president of Taiwan. Returning after 12 years in the Soviet Union (1937), he served in minor Chinese government posts until the Nationalist retreat to Taiwan (1949). Afterward he rose to control the armed forces, the intelligence agencies, and became powerful within the Kuomintang party. He was defense minister (1965–72) and premier (1972–78) before becoming president in 1978, a post he held until his death. In his last years he oversaw significant democratization in Taiwan."

9. The Anti-Communist Youth Corp for National Salvation (*Fangong qingnian jiuguotuan*), led by the Chiang Ching-kuo faction, was a good example. It was extremely active between the 1960s and 1980s, sponsoring all types of summer camps and leisure activities for school-age youths.

10. Based on an interview with Mr. Wang Dingjun, a writer and veteran cultural bureaucrat who worked for the China Broadcasting Corporation and the party-owned literary magazine *Youshi wenyi* [Young lions magazine of literature and the arts] in the 1950s and 1960s.

11. Well-known military writers include Yaxian, Luo Fu, Zhu Xining, and Duan Caihua.

12. See Wang Dingjun's autobiographies, *Zuori de yun* [Clouds of yesterday] and *Numu shaonian* [Young man with a furious stare], written in the 1990s, for touching accounts of events in his own life that exemplify this phenomenon.

13. During this period Chiang served as premier (1972–1978) and president (1978–1988).

14. This is not to say that political, ideological, and factional struggles were not also at play, e.g., the personal strife between Zhou Yang and Lu Xun.

15. For a discussion of the symbolic expression of Japanese colonial power in Taipei's architectural style, see chapter 2 of Jason C. Kuo's book *Art and Cultural Politics in Postwar Taiwan* (2000).

16. In the same article, "Head and Body," Shi describes the appearance in Taiwanese fiction of a new breed of intellectuals. Many of them studied in Japan

or had just returned from there, and harbored a sense of nostalgia for the Japanese metropolis. This "double-homelands in a cultural sense" (*wenhua shang de shuangxiang*) significantly separated these intellectuals from their immediate predecessors, who had dedicated themselves to social reform (216).

17. Excessive critical attention to Zhang Ailing is the best example of this. Interestingly, it has been mainly in the hands of feminist critics (Rey Chow, Qiu Guifen, and Deborah Tze-lan Sang) that the popular elements of Zhang's work have received more adequate treatment.

18. The reputation of *Whirlwind* as an "exemplary" anti-Communist novel for the scholarly community was established by C. T. Hsia, who also praised the work for its artistic excellence in the Chinese narrative tradition. In his paper at the conference following the 1999 Selection of Taiwanese Literary Classics, Wang Dewei carried forward this critical approach—while giving it a sophisticated twist—by arguing that the novel represents a major breakthrough of the anti-Communist fiction genre in that its author "sexualizes politics and politicizes sexual desires" ("Cangtai" 26). Instead of justifying the novel as a representative work of "anti-Communist literature," Wang highlighted its difference from typical propagandist works in that category, and appears to have narrowly spared it from becoming the subject of crude political charges at that event.

19. For a critical reexamination of representative anti-Communist fiction from Taiwan, see Wang Dewei's article, "Yizhong shiqu de wenxue?".

20. Hu was then the President of the Academia Sinica and the Nationalist government's former Ambassador to the United States.

21. Hsia's comment appeared in 1961, in an appendix to his *A History of Modern Chinese Fiction*. More recently, David Wang further underscores the continuity between *Whirlwind* and a particular strand of Chinese narrative tradition in terms of a macabre historical vision ("The Monster That Is History").

22. Jiang reputedly led a dissolute, irresponsible life, once even being sued for negligence of his bedridden wife, which led to her death.

23. Wang even supports his argument by citing as an example the prevalence of tabloid journalism at the time: pages of even the major newspapers were filled with sensational social scandals, such as love murders, etc., side by side with heavily censored political news.

3. SOFT-AUTHORITARIAN RULE AND THE MAINSTREAM POSITION

1. The only observation the narrator makes in reference to the mourners is characteristically pragmatic, noting that the autocratic leader "revitalized the island's economy and gave its people a new stake in their future."

2. Bourdieu defines "habitus" as "not only a structuring structure, which organizes practices and practices and the perception of practices, but also a structured structure: the principle of division into logical classes which organizes

the perception of the social world is itself the product of internalization of the division into social class" (*Distinction* 170). See also note 22 in chapter 1.

3. The "Japanization" assimilation program was already in force in the second half of the colonial period. It should be distinguished from the coercive *Kominka* campaign for transforming Taiwanese into imperial subjects during the Pacific War.

4. In literature and film, this took place slightly earlier, in the 1980s, a phenomenon addressed in chapter 7.

5. Working for the China Broadcasting Corporation at the time, Wang recalls that one day they were ordered to go shopping for recordings of popular music, which the corporation did not have in stock because its radio stations were only allowed to broadcast military, patriotic songs. Feng-huang Ying's dissertation also mentions how a well-known advocate of anti-Communist literature like Sun Ling lost favor because of his hard-line stand (56–59).

6. For more details see chapter 3 of Feng-huang Ying's dissertation, which also mentions that between 1954 and 1956 *Free China Review* even carried critical discussions on the government's policies on arts and culture (98–101).

7. A group of women editors—such as Wu Yueqing of the *Zhongyang ribao* [Central daily news] *fukan*, Lin Haiyin of *Lianfu*, and Nie Hualing of *Free China Review*—found their niche promoting women's writing. The 1950s became the golden age of lyrical prose and familiar essays, with such women authors as Zhang Xiuya, Ai Wen, Zhong Meiyin, Xu Zhongpei, Meng Yao, etc. occupying center stage. As Wang Dingjun has emphasized, this was also part of the softer anti-Communist strategy engineered by more farsighted cultural policy makers in the party.

8. These included such well-known figures as Lin Haiyin, Wang Dingjun, Wang Lan, and Peng Ge, fine writers who also served as literary bureaucrats or as editors of officially sponsored magazines or *fukan* sections.

9. The other two being the Xiandai shishe [Modernist poetry society] and Lanxing shishe [Blue star poetry club].

10. A conference volume, *Shijie zhongwen baozhi fukanxue zonglun* [Essays on *fukan* in Chinese newspapers of the world] (1997), edited by Yaxian and Chen Yizhi, is dedicated to the subject of *fukan*, particularly *fukan* in postwar Taiwan.

11. All these qualities also aided in Lin's role in reviving the *wentan* in post–1949 Taiwan, as discussed in the previous chapter.

12. There were also more popular magazines edited by people closely affiliated with the government, such as *Changliu* [Free flows], *Wentan* [Literary arena], and to a lesser extent, *Yefeng* [Wild wind].

13. For further analysis of this phenomenon, see chapter 2 of Sung-sheng Yvonne Chang, *Modernism and the Nativist Resistance: Contemporary Chinese Fiction from Taiwan*.

14. Lin founded the literary journal, *Chunwenxue yuekan* [Pure literature monthly], in 1967 with friends. She also served as its chief editor between 1967 and 1971.

15. Only very rarely did Lin refer to this kind of political interference in her writing, as she did in her essay, "Liushui shi nian jian—zhubian *Lianfu* zayi" [Ten years like flowing water—my life as *Lianfu* editor], where she wrote that this kind of fault-ferreting was "totally uncalled for" (279).

4. THE MODERNIST TREND AND AESTHETICIZATION OF THE "CHINA TROPE" IN MAINSTREAM LITERATURE

1. The numerous debates among Taiwan's Modernist poets in the late 1950s, for instance, were highly polemical.

2. While another important poet and essayist, Yang Mu, also exemplifies the neo-classicist aesthetic approach, compared to Yu's, his position is more unambiguously that of the "Modernist" rather than the "Mainstream."

3. Nie later immigrated to the United States for political reasons. She married Paul Engle, English professor at the University of Iowa, and her affiliation with the Iowa Writers' Workshop boosted Taiwanese writers' presence in this program.

4. Charles Laughlin's ongoing project featues a comprehensive treatment of this important literary subgenre in modern China. Edward Gunn also mentions the resurgence of the traditionalist essay form in occupied cities like Beijing and Shanghai during the Sino-Japanese war in his book, *The Unwelcome Muse*.

5. This was manifested in the popularization of imported concepts like existentialist agony, alienation, and moral relativism in both literature and public discourse.

6. The Preparatory Council for the Institute of Chinese Literature and Philosophy was founded to complement the existing Institute of History and Language in the late 1980s. Yet the Institute of a Division of American Studies was already in place in the early post–1949 years, demonstrating the unusual importance of the country's chief postwar ally.

7. Thus, when the modernist trend hit the country in the late 1950s, artists first directed their attack at this atrophied version of Chinese tradition. Only later did several important figures return to Chinese tradition with fresh perspectives.

8. As documented in Xiao Baixing's paper, the liberal inclination of a single professor, Jin Changming, in the Department of Architecture at National Cheng Kung University (formerly the Provincial College of Engineering) largely determined the academic outlook of his department, which in turn had a significant impact on the direction of the entire architectural field in contemporary Taiwan. Parallel situations were found in many other academic fields.

9. It is in this sense that we may understand the special roles played by such people as Xia Ji'an, Ji Xian, Yu Guangzhong, Liu Guosong, and Yan Yuanshu, among others, in different cultural spheres.

10. The term is Lupke's.

11. Other works in the same category include Pan Renmu's *My Cousin Lianyi*, Wang Lan's *Lan yu hei* [Blue and black], Xu Su's *Xingxing yueliang taiyang* [The star, the moon, and the sun], Xu Xu's *Feng xiaoxiao* [Sound of the wind] and *Qi zheng piao piao* [The flag is waving in the wind], Yang Nianci's *Feiyuan jiushi* [Old stories from the abandoned garden] and *Heiniu yu baishe* [Black cow and white snake], Fan Lu's *Xiangrikui* [The sunflower], and Feng Feng's *Weixi* [Dim sunlight] from a slighter later period. Some of these writers, such as Xu Su and Xu Xu, resided in Hong Kong, but since their works were popular in Taiwan and conformed to the state's ideology, they can be properly considered participants in Taiwan's literary field.

12. See Michelle Yeh's article and chapter 4 of Feng-huang Ying's dissertation.

13. In one well-known debate, Yu criticized the rigid conception of "tradition" underlying the arguments of his opponent, Yan Xi, who represented the more conservative faction in the literary field of the day.

14. This is the main point in Yu's criticism of Ji Xian.

15. A formulation promulgated by Yu and several leading figures in the late 1950s to early 1970s, including Xia Ji'an, Yan Yuanshu, and Zhu Limin.

16. Liang, a former member of the Crescent Moon Society, was one of the most important scholars/writers who followed the Nationalists to Taiwan, and enjoyed great respect in contemporary Taiwan's literary field.

17. This view appears in a number of Yu's essays. See also his 1963 essay, "Feng, ya, chun" [Phoenix, crow, and quail] in *Xiaoyao you* [The untrammeled traveler] (47–61).

18. These essays were collected in the 1977 collection, *Qingqing bianchou* [Homesick border blues].

19. At this time, Yu had begun teaching in the Chinese department at the Chinese University of Hong Kong, where he stayed for eleven years before returning to Taiwan. The critical essays were supposedly written for a course he taught on Chinese new literature. The essay, "Lun Zhu Ziqing de sanwen" [On the prose of Zhu Ziqing], was extremely harsh, and received much criticism after it was published.

20. The Nativist attack abruptly and effectively pushed even the most radical of the Modernists to the right on the ideological spectrum, earning the government's trust and giving them a more conservative public image.

21. Bürger's notion of "hegemonic categories" can also be related to what Bourdieu describes as the category through which works of art are perceived and appreciated. As Bourdieu says, "All agents, writers, artists or intellectuals construct their own creative project according, first of all, to their perception of the available possibilities afforded by the categories of perception and appreciation inscribed in their habitus through a certain trajectory and, secondly, to their predisposition to take advantage of or reject those possibilities in accordance with the interests associated with their position in the

game" (*The Field* 184). Obviously, for Bourdieu the formation of such categories is intimately tied to a person's habitus, or disposition, which in turn has to do with his or her position within the structure of the field of power. Such categories also play determinant roles in cultural agents' position-taking strategies, conditioning the way agents perceive "available possibilities" in the game.

22. Some good examples of the latter include Rey Chow's edited volume for *Boundary 2* (1998), later republished as *Modern Chinese Literary and Cultural Studies in the Age of Theory: Reimagining a Field* (2000), and two articles by Allen Chun, "From Nationalism to Nationalizing" (1994) and "Fuck Chineseness" (1996).

23. Particularly noteworthy is Liu's discussion of modern theater, which refers to work by the well-known playwright-directors, Wang Qimei and Lai Shengchuan, and modern dance choreographer Lin Huaimin.

24. In more recent years, the China-Taiwan role switching has taken intriguing forms. An interesting example is given in Lifen Chen's book, *Xiandai wenxue yu wenhua xiangxiang: cong Taiwan dao Xianggang* [Modern literature and cultural imagination: From Taiwan to Hong Kong] (2000). Lifen Chen teases out the many ironic twists in Taiwanese literary scholars' treatment of Zhang Ailing, the legendary prerevolution Shanghai writer idolized in Taiwan's literary circle years before a similar rage for Zhang appeared in post–Mao China, and whom many Localist critics refuse to recognize as a "Taiwanese writer" (despite her tremendous influence there, Zhang never resided in Taiwan). These scholars (chiefly Chen Fangming), Lifen Chen writes, claimed that because of her resistance to the patriarchal Chinese society—which they equated with "old China"—and her experience of marginalization and exile, Zhang shares much with "colonized" Taiwanese writers (169). They even credited Taiwan for having "resuscitated" Zhang when she was rejected by the People's Republic of China following the Communist Revolution (169). Interestingly, as I have argued elsewhere, in the 1980s second-generation mainlander writers adored Zhang as a symbol of "old China," while in today's Localist-dominated Taiwanese literary field, Zhang's honorary position in Taiwanese literary history is justified by asserting that she is "anti-China."

25. A poem, "Fangfu zai junfu de chengbang" [As if residing in the country of the father], by Yang Ze, a well-known native Taiwanese poet of the baby-boom generation, has been discussed as an example of even Taiwanese writers' subscription to the sinocentric ideology before awakening to its problematic political implications.

26. Another collection of Wang's lyrical prose is *Qingren yan* [Lover's eyes], published in 1977. Although Wang has always been considered a stylist, with a solid background in classical Chinese, the majority of his writings are not literary in nature. The more purely literary works include *A Bachelor's Body*

Temprature; *Shattered Crystals*; *Lover's Eyes*; and *Whirlpool of the Left Atrium*—the first two are short-story collections, and the latter two lyrical essays. The originality of imagery and stylistic precision found in *Whirlpool* definitely surpass those of his earlier literary works.

27. According to Wang, the essays were written in 1989, but he hesitated to publish them on account of their "offensive" content.

28. The following lines are cited from *The Night Watchman*, a bilingual collection of Yu Guangzhong's poems written between 1958 and 1992. The English translations are by the poet himself.

29. In a different thematic frame, Liu Jihui also observes the aesthetic abstraction of the China image in Yu Guangzhong's poetry, where "China" is objectified as a thing of the past, crystallized in poetic images of the treasures in the Palace Museum. See Liu's book *Orphan, Goddess, and the Writing of the Negative*.

30. Similar aesthetic challenges were made by Modernist fiction writers like Bai Xianyong, Wang Wenxing, Qideng Sheng, and Shi Shuqing.

31. *Lanling* and *yunmen* are both taken from classical Chinese texts. That troops of Modernist artists chose classical names suggests the popularity of synthesizing the modern and the traditional in the wake of the Nativist literary movement.

32. This is also part of the broader cultural nostalgia trend of the late 1970s and early 1980s described in my article, "Yuan Qiongqiong and the Rage for Eileen Zhang Among Taiwan's *Feminine* Writers."

33. What has often gone unnoticed, however, is the implicit act of gendering behind many Modernist assumptions. For instance, traditionalist lyrical prose was often equated with sentimentalism and femininity, while "western" realist fiction was associated with rationality and masculinity.

34. This conservative mindset became the target of criticism from a small group of left-wing intellectuals whose most vocal spokesperson was Chen Yingzhen. Chen complained that the "consciousness of happiness" was breeding political apathy and an ostrich mentality among Taiwan's middle-class urbanites. This was a major theme of Chen's works in the 1980s, mostly conspicuously *Zhao Nandong* (1987) and "Shanlu" [Mountan path] (1984).

35. By the *chunwenxue* group I refer to mostly prose writers active in the 1950s, such as Zhang Xiuya, Zhong Meiyin, Xu Zhongpei, Su Xuelin, Qijun, and Ai Wen, and fiction writers like Lin Haiyin, Meng Yao, and Fan Lu.

36. The group apparently adopted its sinocentric culturalist ideology from its spiritual mentor, journalist/writer Hu Lancheng, who was the ex-husband of Zhang Ailing, then living in Japan. A collaborator with the Japanese in wartime Shanghai, Hu was exiled to Japan after the war. Partly because of his adoration of Zhang Ailing, Zhu Xining received Hu warmly as a family guest the mid-1970s, when Hu was invited to Taiwan as a visiting lecturer at the Chinese Culture College.

37. Also see Chang, "Chu T'ien-wen and Taiwan's Recent Cultural and Literary Trends."
38. Similar idolization of Japanese culture can be found in the aesthetic rendition of a "Japanese national essence" in Hou Hsiao-hsien's films, *A City of Sadness* and *Puppet Master*.
39. The younger generation's appropriation of traditional Chinese symbols, especially in the music industry, is treated in Shu-mei Shih's article.

5. LOCALIST POSITION AS A PRODUCT OF SOCIAL OPPOSITION

1. Yingzhe Huang's article documents in detail how the resinicization project was carried out in the literary field in the immediate postwar years (1946–50).
2. The list would include such names as Wu Xinrong, Wu Yongfu, Wang Changxiong, Wang Shilang, Huang Deshi, and Zhang Shenqie, among others. A few writers, like Long Yingzong and Zhang Wenhuan, still produced novels written in Japanese (*Hongchen* [Red dust] by Long and *Gundilang* [The man who crawls on the ground] by Zhang), which were later translated into Chinese.
3. Yang Kui and Ye Shitao are the best-known examples.
4. See references in Yingzhe Huang's article (e.g., 161).
5. In particular, the faction that cooperated with Chinese Communist agents. Ye Shitao's 1991 memoir contains a personal account of the chaotic situation (*Yige* ch. 3–6).
6. In the 1970s heyday of the leftist Nativists, these themes were exemplified in fiction by Wang Tuo, Yang Qingchu, and Song Zelai. The dominant leftist faction also included such fine writers as Huang Chunming and Wang Zhenhe, whose artistry suggested Modernist influences. As the decade wore on, however, the Nativists became increasingly dogmatic. By the early 1980s, their literary output had markedly decreased, with the only noteworthy works coming from Chen Yingzhen himself, including the "Washington Tower" story series. Nevertheless, as the first serious challenge to the Nationalist cultural hegemony, the Nativist movement had a tremendous impact on Taiwan's politically subjugated intellectual community, opening it up to alternative ideological paradigms. In the same way, it produced broad effects within the literary field, although it largely failed to popularize its ideological agenda.
7. For an account of the history of the *Newsletter*, see the second volume of Zhong's 1998 memoir (9–46).
8. This went beyond meeting the linguistic requirement. In his memoir, Zhong Zhaozheng notes that manuscripts submitted by staff of the *Newsletter* were frequently rejected for reasons other than language. Anti-Communist writings and works eulogizing the Nationalist ruling regime, which he and his fellow *Newsletter* correspondents refused to write, then dominated the field (*Huiyilu* I 224–225).

9. See, for example, Zhong's account of his activities during the Nativist literary movement in the late 1970s (*Huiyilu I* 211–217).

10. Ye Shitao has received similar honors, including an honorary degree from National Chengkung University. Another Localist writer, Li Qiao, author of the best-known big-stream novel, *Wintry Night*, was appointed to the Advisory Board on National Strategies.

11. Opinions about Zhong are polarized, however. One cites the resistance model currently dominating Localist discourse, retrospectively discovering Zhong's earlier work to be heroically oppositional. More hard-line Taiwanese nationalists, however, point out that Zhong repeatedly played up to the Nationalist regime, suggesting that his token value as a cooperative native Taiwanese writer, rather than any artistic accomplishment, is the major source of his literary fame.

12. The primary source of information is reports in *Zhongshi dianzi bao*, the electronic version of *China Times*.

13. Yu began to publish his early poems in the literary section of *Free China Review* in the mid-1950s, together with such Mainstream mainlander writers as Lin Haiyin. By the late 1950s he was already editor of the poetry pages in *Apollo* and *Literary Review*, two elitist literary forums, and the *Blue Star Poetry Pages*.

14. According to his memoir, Ye's friendship with a Taiwanese Communist was based on their common interest in literature and music. This cost him several years' imprisonment (*Yige* 59–72).

15. Chen is a woman of solid professional credentials, a renowned pianist and music educator who demonstrated her dedication to the Localist cause by cofounding the White Egret Foundation to promote Taiwanese folk culture with her late husband, well-known DPP legislator Lu Xiuyi.

6. FUKAN-BASED LITERARY CULTURE AND MIDDLE-CLASS GENRES

1. The twin volumes *Qishi niandai: lixiang jixu ranshao* [The seventies: Ideals that continue to incense] and *Kuangbiao bashi: jilu yige jiti fasheng de shidai* [The tumultuous eighties: Records from a decade of collective voices], edited by Yang Ze and published by *China Times* Publishing Co. in 1994 and 1999, respectively, provide excellent snapshots of the 1970s and 1980s cultural scene. Contributors to these volumes included some of the most active cultural agents from the period.

2. The Meilidao Incident (sometimes also called the Kaohsiung Incident) was the first landmark event in the history of contemporary Taiwan's oppositional political movement. A demonstration in Kaohsiung on International Human Rights Day in 1979 was suppressed by KMT troops, resulting in the military trial and subsequent imprisonment of fifteen opposition leaders. These leaders and their defending lawyers later were core members of the Democratic Progressive Party, which was founded in 1986 and became the ruling party in 2000.

3. The *fukan* of the two major newspapers began to institute different kinds of annual literary contests in the mid- to late 1970s.

4. This category includes many renowned fiction writers and poets like Su Weizhen, Zhang Dachun, Ping Lu, Yang Ze, Xiang Yang, Chen Yizhi, Chen Yuhang, and Xu Huizhi (Jiang, Zhongming).

5. Writers of this popular genre include Lin Qingxuan, Liu Yong, Ku Ling, Zhang Manjuan, Huang Mingjian, and Wu Danru, to name just a few.

6. Both *China Times* and *United Daily News* started weekly book review sections and offered different kinds of weekly and annual awards beginning in the late 1980s. *Kaijuan zhoubao* [Unrolling the scroll, a weekly], the book review section of the *China Times*, founded in 1988, has been especially influential.

7. For an overview of the relationship between sociopolitical changes and *fukan* in contemporary Taiwan, see Pan Jiaqing's article in Yaxian and Chen.

8. For a discussion of Gao's contribution to the *fukan* phenomenon, see Lin Qiyang's 1993 M.A. thesis, "Wenxue chuanbo."

9. This was particularly true when Jin Hengwei served as the chief editor of *Renjian*.

10. For the development of *fukan* in 1970s and 1980s, see Lin Qiyang's thesis.

11. Many of the significant social movements in contemporary Taiwan began in the late 1970s and continued throughout the 1980s, including the feminist movement, the environmental movement, the aboriginal rights movement, the veterans' appeal to legalize visits to mainland China, and various "*zili jiuji*" or self-help street protests, staged even before the lifting of martial law and the ban on public demonstrations.

12. The political agenda was apparent in the titles of the seminars organized by *Lianfu*, such as one held in 1980s: "Yongbu ximie de juehuo: Guangfu qian Taiwan wenxue zhong de minzu yishi yu kangri jingshen" [Nationalist consciousness and anti-Japanese spirit in literature of Taiwan before the retrocession].

13. The young writers who received this stipend included Jiang Xiaoyun, Xiao Ye, Wu Nianzhen, Li Ang, Li He, Jiang Jiayu, Xiao Sa, Ding Yamin, Zhu Tianwen, and Zhu Tianxin (Jiang, Zhongming 49).

14. This 1997 volume, *Garden of the Gods*, provides excellent sources on the role of *fukan* in molding Taiwan's distinctive literary culture. It contains twenty-six essays by writers, scholars, critics, and editors on the accomplishments of *Lianfu* since it was founded in 1951; a preface by Wang Dingjun; an afterword by Yaxian; and two photo sections. In addition, it has three useful appendices: an essay written by the *United Daily News* editor-in-chief in 1991 in commemoration of the newspaper's fortieth anniversary; a list of works and authors that won the *United Daily News* Annual Literary Awards between 1976 and 1996; and a chronicle of important events sponsored by *Lianfu* between 1951 and 1991. As most of the now middle-aged authors of the essays were

actively involved in *Lianfu*'s activities during its fifteen years of growth, expansion, and transformation, the period between the mid-1970s and late 1980s receives the most attention.

15. The tacit assumption that works under review are being evaluated for their potential significance in "modern Chinese literary history," for instance, ignores the fact that many of the contemporary literary works are more appropriately classified as "popular literature."

16. Just as the popularity of Qiongyao has been renewed several times via different communication channels—print, film, and TV—the Zhang Ailing craze went through several cycles and spread through different Chinese societies and the diaspora.

17. See the discussion in the last part of chapter 3.

18. For instance, in the 1990s, newspapers opened new sections and *fukan* columns on such specialized topics as sports literature, travel literature, children's literature, women's issues, celebrities, etc., to take better advantage of the segregated reading market.

19. It is interesting that Ang Lee was not exposed extensively to Taiwan's dominant literary culture in 1980s. Hence, not only his career development but also the informing spirit of his art, in both its generic and thematic aspects, stand in stark contrast to works by Taiwan new cinema filmmakers.

20. See Chang, "Yuan Qiongqiong."

21. See essays by Zhan Hongzhi, Xiao Ye, Li Zhuotao, Qi Longren, and Wu Nianzhen, collected in chapter 3 of *Taiwan New Cinema* (Jiao 81–124), in particular section 5, "Minguo qishiliu nian Taiwan dianying xuanyan" [1987 Manifesto of Taiwan cinema] (111–118). Two other articles on related topics, by Bai Luo and Li Zhuotao, are included in chapter 18 of the same book (387–389, 390–396).

22. For a general discussion of Taiwan's political fiction in the 1980, see the article by Ying-hsiung Chou in *Modern Chinese Literature*. An earlier draft of this section was presented at the "Conference on Chinese Labor Camp" at UC Irvine in January 2000.

23. The author named his protagonist, Lai Suo, after the hero of a translated novel by Saul Bellow, *He Suo* (*Herzog*).

24. "Conference on Chinese Labor Camp: Theory, Actuality, and Fictional Representation,. sponsored by the Center for Ideas and Society, University of California at Riverside, Riverside, and held on Jan. 15–16, 2000.

25. While I also consider the film conservative, my views are different from the negative criticism launched against *A City of Sadness* by radical groups in Taiwan (the "New Left") in the late 1980s. Deeply enmeshed in local cultural politics, these critics focused more on Taiwan new cinema filmmakers' political identification than on the relationship between ideology and aesthetics.

7. High Culture Aspirations and Transformations
of Mainstream Fiction

1. With a college degree in economics, Zhan often writes literary criticism featuring perspectives different from those of critics trained in the humanities. A visionary intellectual and entrepreneur, Zhan has had a distinguished career including newspaper editing, cultural criticism, film production, publishing company management, and recently, electronic publishing.

2. These include the Modernists Wang Wenxing, Bai Xianyong, and Li Yongping; the Nativists Chen Yingzhen and Wang Zhenhe; and the Localists Li Qiao, Lin Shuangbu, and Dong Fangbai. While some of their works were also published in *fukan*, the gap between their artistic and ideological orientations and *fukan*'s middle-class readership was obvious.

3. This motif recurs frequently, in straightforward terms, in Yuan Qiongqiong's essays collected in *Hongchen xinshi* and *Suiyi*.

4. See Wang Dewei's introduction to *Hua yi qianshen* and a critical essay by Huang Jinshu included in the same volume ("Shenji").

5. Zhu has been the screenwriter (or co-writer) for all of Hou's films since 1983, which include: *The Boys from Fengkuei* (1983), *A Summer at Grandpa's* (1984), *A Year to Live, A Year to Die* (1985), *Dust in the Wind* (1986), *Daughter of the Nile* (1987), *A City of Sadness* (1989), *The Puppet Master* (1993), *Good Men, Good Women* (1995), *Good-bye, South, Good-bye* (1996), and *Flowers of Shanghai* (1998).

6. Chen and his associates produced a pictorial magazine, *Renjian* [Human world] (1985–89), that successfully raised public consciousness of a number of sensitive social issues and nurtured an activist ethos that in many ways anticipated the across-the-board radical turn that occurred in the early post–martial law period.

7. Chiefly *Zhao Nandong* and stories in the *Washington Tower* series.

8. Some of these were adapted from Zhang's fiction, including *Red Rose, White Rose* and *Eighteen Springs*, while others are simply cast in "Zhang Ailing style," like *In the Mood for Love* and Wang Anyi's *Song of Everlasting Sorrow*, the only literary work on the list.

9. "King of Chess" was printed in *Unitas, a literary monthly* in June 1986, with a critical essay by Chen Bingzao, and "King of Children" in the *fukan* of *Independent Evening News*, with an essay by Guo Feng, in August 1986. Both were met with enthusiastic critical reception.

10. The best-known examples included *A City of Sadness* and the novella *To Live* by Yu Hua, on which Zhang Yimou's movie of the same name was based. In the wake of radically changing political regimes, writers in China and Taiwan concurred in celebrating the mundane life of ordinary people, not only as a means of surviving unjust political intrusions but also as an oblique form of resistance.

11. The representativeness of this collection, a project sponsored by the National Institute of Translation and Compilation of the Republic of China, is noteworthy. Though published by Oxford University Press in 1994, it was conceived much earlier, in 1986, and its selection of stories was based on a longer list compiled by Zhan Hongzhi and contributed to by other active scholars in the field.

12. It is necessary to add that not all these writers included in the volume were Mainstream writers; the arch-Nativist Chen Yingzhen is an obvious exception. Furthermore, some of them—Zhang Xiguo (Chang Hsi-kuo), Liu Daren (Liu Ta-jen), Ping Lu (P'ing Lu), and Bao Zhen (Pao Chen)—were expatriate writers at the time (Ping Lu returned to settle in Taiwan in 1993–94). However, as the latter group primarily published in Taiwan, the distinction is sometimes rather vague.

13. This point is nicely captured by David D. Wang's comments, in the book's introduction, on Shu Guozhi's (Shu Kuo-chih) story "Rustic Quandary" (ix–xv).

14. The Chinese words for these terms are: *xiangtu zhuyi* (Nativism), *bentu zhuyi* (Localism), *guixiu wenxue* (boudoir literature), and *xin xiangtu zhuyi* (neo-Nativism).

15. The overthrow of literary schools established by earlier returned scholars (New Criticism, semiotics, myth criticism, etc.) by new returnees mirrored shifting critical paradigms in the U.S. academy, albeit with a brief time lag. In film, for instance, Taiwan new cinema, which had received significant support from returned students like Jiao Xiongping in the early 1980s, suffered a radical critique by a group of intellectuals influenced by the New Left who returned to Taiwan in the mid- to late 1980s. The attacks were voiced in the well-known essay collection, *Xin dianying zhi si* (Mizou and Liang).

16. Following are some well-known examples. In her novel *An ye* [Dark night] (1985), Li Ang incorporates a hypocrite preaching neo-Marxist "false consciousness" into a somewhat trite story of love triangles and extramarital affairs. Devices inspired by magic realism lend a mysterious ambience to Su Wenzhen's *Likai Tongfang* [Leaving Tongfang] (1990). Somewhat more intriguing were stories with better integrated experimental designs. For instance, Zhang Dachun's highly acclaimed 1988 "Jiangjun bei" [General's monument] features a Nationalist general who travels back and forth in time, reviewing his own past and future, and making some cynical remarks on modern Chinese history along the way. Huang Fan's experimentalist piece, "Ruhe celiang shuigou de kuandu" [How to measure the width of a ditch] in *Dushi shenghao* [Urban life] (1986) is also interesting (see Wang Dewei's discussion of this feature, *Zhongsheng* 263–264). Zhang and Huang's stories were similarly read as metacommentaries on the mechanisms with which specific genres of narratives—history, fiction—are created.

17. For a detailed discussion of the "Taiwanese consciousness debate," see Charles Marshall McArthur's dissertation, "'Taiwanese Literature' After the Nativist

Movement: Construction of a Literary Identity Apart from a Chinese Model," especially chapter 2, fourth section.

18. See articles collected in Lin Zhuoshui's *Wajie huaxia diguo* [The disintegrating Chinese empire].

19. In addition to literature, Liu Jihui discusses the same phenomenon in the performing arts, citing examples from stage plays of Wang Qimei and Lai Shengchuan, and the dance theater of Lin Huaimin (*Gu'er* 9–12).

20. In addition to Hou Hsiao-hsien and the screenwriters Wu Nianzhen and Zhu Tianwen, the film also registers input from a small core group that includes Zhan Hongzhi, Jiao Xiongping, Xie Caijun (writer-editor and husband of Zhu Tianxin), and Zhang Dachun, most of whom clearly occupied a Mainstream position in the 1980s.

8. New Developments in the Post–Martial Law Period

1. The Council of Cultural Affairs, or *Wenjianhui*, is a division of the Executive Yuan of the Republic of China and is the main government bureau in charge of distributing state funds to cultural agents.

2. "*Beiqing*," which can be rendered as either "sad condition" or "sorrowful sentiments," is a poetic-sounding term frequently used in the 1990s cultural and political discourses to describe the many grievances Taiwanese people have experienced in the last hundred years. Hou Hsiao-hsien's 1989 award-winning film *A City of Sadness* [Beiqing chengshi], featuring the February 28 Incident, may have contributed to the currency of this term.

3. Viewed in historical context, this development was symptomatic of the broader division between the majority of the country's western/liberal-inclined intellectuals (including some of the newly returned younger scholars) and more radical scholars. This, in turn, mirrors similar divisions at other points in modern Chinese history, most notably the decade following the May Fourth movement, and the new left versus liberal division in the PRC today.

4. Two magazines of different nature, the more mainstream, commercially financed pictorial magazine *Human World* and the small leftist coterie journal *Summer Tide* that began publishing in the 1970s, during the Nativist literary movement, were instrumental in disseminating socialist ideals. The former exerted considerable influence on mainstream intellectual circles, while the latter was mostly read by smaller groups of college students and young intellectuals.

5. See discussions in the last part of chapter 5.

6. As noted in chapter 1, the last decade has also witnessed the institutionalization of Taiwanese literary studies in academia, and the number of scholars and graduate students specializing in the area has quickly multiplied. Whether this development will eventually exert any influence on creative practices in contemporary Taiwan, however, is yet to be seen.

7. For contemporary Taiwanese literature on gay and lesbian themes that appeared in the 1990s, see Part IV of *The Emerging Lesbian*, by Deborah Tze-lan Sang, and *Angelwings*, a collection of queer fiction from Taiwan translated by Fran Martin.

8. The proceedings of the conference were published in the same year (Chen, Yizhi).

9. Take fiction, for example; the ten books selected as "classics" are: *Taibei ren* [Tales of the Taipei characters] by Bai Xianyong, *Luo* [The gong] by Huang Chunming, *Jiangjun zu* [A race of generals] by Chen Yingzhen, *Wo ai hei yanzhu* [I love black eyes] by Qideng Sheng, *Bansheng yuan* [Eighteen springs] by Zhang Ailing, *Family Catastrophe* by Wang Wenxing, *Shafu* [The butcher's wife] by Li Ang, *Jiazhuang yi niuche* [An oxcart for dowry] by Wang Zhenhe, *Orphan of Asia* by Wu Zhuoliu, and *Whirlwind* by Jiang Gui. With the exceptions of Zhang Ailing, Wu Zhuoliu, and Jiang Gui, the majority of the authors are "Modernists"—while Huang Chunming and Wang Zhenhe are often considered representative Nativist writers, largely because of the content of their fiction, they nonetheless received their artistic orientation during the Modernist literary movement.

10. Notably, Localist historian Chen Fangming and Localist/Mainstream writer Li Ang (Jiang, Zhongming, "Zhengzhi zhengque," "Yantaohui").

11. The written protest was led by writer-critic Li Qiao, President of the Taiwanese PEN Association, and signed by seven organizations, including the Taiwanese PEN Association, *Taiwanese Literature, Wenxue Taiwan* [Literary Taiwan], etc. Additional protests came from writers who were not selected. Poet Luo Men, for example, distributed flyers at the conference complaining about unfairness. Paper presenters and participants in discussion at the conference also expressed critical opinions, but mostly in moderate tones.

12. That the protest elicited an apologetic and defensive response from CCA Director Lin Chengzhi bespeaks its political nature. Lin promised to hold second and third selections to make up for those works unfairly left out, a proposal quickly rejected by the protesters.

13. See essays by Peng Ruijin and Yang Cui in the *Taiwan Times*. Yang, in particular, bitterly accused the "repressive state agents and cultural hegemons" of usurping the name and the "rights for interpretation" of Taiwanese literature just when the term "Taiwan" had acquired prestige and become a valuable form of cultural capital.

Anderson, Benedict. *Imagined Communities: Reflections on the Origin and Spread of Nationalism*. London: Verso, 1983.

Appadurai, Arjun. *Modernity at Large: Cultural Dimensions of Globalization*. Minneapolis: University of Minnesota Press, 1996.

Bai, Xianyong. *Niezi* [Crystal boys]. Taipei: Yuanjing chuban gongsi, 1983.

——. *Taibei ren* [Tales of Taipei characters]. Taipei: Chenzhong chuban she, 1971.

Boyang. *Boyang zai Huoshao dao: xie gei nü'er de xin* [Boyang at Huoshao dao: Letters to his daughter]. Taipei: Han yi se yan wenhua gongsi, 1988.

Bourdieu, Pierre. *The Field of Cultural Production: Essays on Art and Literature*. Edited and introduced by Randal Johnson. New York: Columbia University Press, 1993.

——. *Distinction: A Social Critique of the Judgement of Taste*. Trans. Richard Nice. Cambridge: Harvard University Press, 1984.

——. *Outline of a Theory of Practice*. Cambridge: Cambridge University Press, 1977.

Cai, Yuanhuang. "Fulu, Zhang Dachun de tianfang yetan: ping 'Zi manglin yuechu'" [Appendix, the wonder tales by Zhang Dachun: On "Leaping out of the wild jungle"]. In Dachun Zhang, *Sixi you guo* [Sixi worries about the country]. Taipei: Yuanliu chuban gongsi, 1988, 99–102.

Calhoun, Craig, Edward LiPuma, and Moishe Postone, eds. *Bourdieu: Critical Perspectives*. Chicago: University of Chicago Press, 1993.

Chang, Sung-sheng Yvonne. "Foreword." *Exiles at Home: Stories by Ch'en Ying-chen*. Trans. Lucien Miller. Michigan Classics in Chinese Studies. Ann Arbor: Center for Chinese Studies, University of Michigan, 2002, vii–xiii.

——. *Wenxuechangyu de bianqian: dangdai Taiwan xiaoshuo lun* [Changes in the literary field: Contemporary fiction from Taiwan]. Taipei: Lianhe wenxue chuban she, 2001.

——. "Taiwanese New Literature and the Colonial Context: A Historical Survey." In Murray A. Rubinstein, ed., *Taiwan: A History 1600–1994*. Armonk, N.Y.: M. E. Sharpe, 1999, 261–274.

——. "Modernist Literature in Taiwan Revisited—with an Analysis of Wang Wenxing's *Backed Against the Sea, Part II*." *Tamkang Review* 24.2 (Winter 1998): 1–19.

——. "Beyond Cultural and National Identities: Current Re-evaluation of the Kominka Literature from Taiwan's Japanese Period." *Journal of Modern Literature in Chinese* 1.1 (July 1997): 75–107. Reprinted in Rey Chow, ed., *Modern Chinese Literary and Cultural Studies in the Age of Theory: Reimagining a Field*. Durham: Duke University Press, 2000, 99–126.

——. *Modernism and the Nativist Resistance: Contemporary Chinese Fiction from Taiwan*. Durham: Duke University Press, 1993.

——. "Chu T'ien-wen and Taiwan's Recent Cultural and Literary Trends." *Modern Chinese Literature* 6.1–2 (1992): 61–84.

——. "Yuan Qiongqiong and the Rage for Eileen Zhang Among Taiwan's *Feminine* Writers." *Modern Chinese Literature* 4.1–2 (Spring & Fall 1988): 201–23. Reprinted in Tani E. Barlow, ed., *Gender Politics in Modern China*. Durham: Duke University Press, 1993, 215–237.

——. "Xiandai zhuyi yu Taiwan xiandai pai xiaoshuo" [Modernism and the modernist school of fiction in Taiwan]. *Wenyi yanjiu* [Aesthetic studies] 4 (July 1988): 69–80. Reprinted in Wang Xiaoming et al., eds., *Ershi shiji Zhongguo wenxue yanjiu lunwenji* [Anthology of critical essays on twentieth-century Chinese literature], vol. 1. Shanghai: Dongfang chuban zhongxin, 1997, 135–148.

——. "Language, Narrator, and Stream-of-consciousness: The Two Novels of Wang Wen-hsing." *Modern Chinese Literature* 1.1 (1984): 43–55.

Chang, Sung-sheng Yvonne, ed. *Perspectives on Taiwanese Literature*. Spec. issue of *Journal of Modern Literature in Chinese* 4.1 (July 2000). Hong Kong: Centre for Translation and Literature, Lingnan University.

——, ed. "Cong dangqian dui riju shiqi wenxue de xueshu tantao kan 'Taiwan wenxue yanjiu' tizhihua de jige mianxiang" [Perspectives on the institutionalization of Taiwanese literary studies: A review of current scholarship on literature of the Japanese period]. In *Perspectives on Taiwanese Literature*. Spec. issue of *Journal of Modern Literature in Chinese* 4.1 (July 2000). Hong Kong: Centre for Translation and Literature, Lingnan University, 139–155.

Chang, Sung-sheng Yvonne and Michelle Yeh, eds. *Contemporary Chinese Literature: Crossing the Boundaries*. Spec. issue of *Literature East and West* 28 (1995).

Chatterjee, Partha. *Nationalist Thought and the Colonial World: A Derivative Discourse*. 1986; reprint, Minneapolis: University of Minnesota Press, 1993.

Chen, Fangming. "Taiwan wenxueshi fenqi de yige jiantao" [A re-examination of the periodization of Taiwanese literary history]. In *Taiwan wenxue fazhan xianxiang: wush nian lai Taiwan wenxue yantaohui lunwenji* (II). Taipei: Wenjianhui, 1996, 13–34.

Chen, Guangxing, ed. *Wenhua yanjiu zai Taiwan* [Cultural studies in Taiwan]. Taipei: Juliu tushu gongsi, 2000.

Chen, Jiying. *Di cun zhuan* [The legend of Di village]. Taipei: Chongguang wenyi chuban she, 1951.

Chen Kunhou, dir. *Xiao Bi de gushi* [The story of Xiao Bi]. Screenplay by Zhu Tianwen. Taipei: Zhongyang dianying gongsi, 1983.

Chen, Lifen. *Xiandai wenxue yu wenhua xiangxiang: cong Taiwan dao Xianggang* [Modern literature and cultural imagination: From Taiwan to Hong Kong]. Taipei: Shulin chuban she, 2000.

——. "Wei yi xiao de ren qiaocui: xunzhao Taiwan" [For her, he pines away: In search of Taiwan]. In *Xiandai wenxue yu wenhua xiangxiang: cong Taiwan dao Xianggang* [Modern literature and cultural imagination: From Taiwan to Hong Kong]. Taipei: Shulin chuban she, 2000, 195–212.

Chen, Pingyuan. *Chen Pingyuan zixuanji* [Selected works by author]. Guilin: Guangxi Shifan Daxue chuban she, 1997.

——. "Jin bai nian Zhongguo jingying wenhua de shiluo" [The loss of elite culture in China of the last hundred years]. In *Chen Pingyuan zixuanji* [Selected works by author]. Guilin: Guangxi Shifan Daxue chuban she, 1997, 306–319.

Chen, Sen. *Pin hua baojian* [Precious mirror that ranks the beauties]. Taipei: Tianyi chuban she, 1974.

Chen, Sihe. *Chen Sihe zixuanji* [Selected works by author]. Guilin: Guangxi Shifan Daxue chuban she, 1997.

——. "Minjian he xiandai dushi wenhua" [The "folk" and modern urban culture]. In *Chen Sihe zixuanji* [Selected works by author]. Guilin: Guangxi Shifan Daxue chuban she, 1997, 276–307.

——. "Lun zhishi fenzi zhuanxingqi de sanzhong jiazhi quxiang" [Research on the three value choices during the period of model transformation of intellectuals]. In *Chen Sihe zixuanji* [Selected works by author]. Guilin: Guangxi Shifan Daxue chuban she, 1997, 169–181.

Chen, Wanyi. *Yu wusheng chu ting jinglei: Taiwan wenxue lunji* [Listening to thunder at a silent place: Collected essays on Taiwanese literature]. Tainan: Nanshi wenhua, 1996.

Chen, Wenfen. "Taiwan bihui yu wenxue qianbei fabiao qiangjiu shengming, huyu liji quxiao meiyou Taiwan wenxue shi yishi de 'Taiwan wenxue jingdian'" [The Taiwanese PEN Association and leading figures in the literary field delivered a manifesto, proposing to immediately abolish the "Taiwanese literary classics" that do not embody a sense of Taiwanese literary history]. *Zhongguo shibao* [China times] 20 Mar. 1999:11.

Chen, Xue. *E mo de nü'er* [Daughter of the devil]. Taipei: Lianhe wenxue chuban she, 1999.

——. *E nü shu* [Writings about perverse women]. Taipei: Huangguan wenhua chuban gongsi, 1995.

Chen, Yingzhen. "Jiyue de qingchun: lun Lü Heruo de xiaoshuo 'Niuche' he 'Baofengyu de gushi'" [Passionate youth: On Lü Heruo's stories "Oxcart" and "A Story of the Storm"]. In *Lü Heruo zuopin yanjiu: Taiwan diyi caizi* [Studies of the works of Lü Heruo: Taiwan's most talented man of letters]. Taipei: Lianhe wenxue chuban she, 1997, 296–313.

——. *Zhao Nandong* [Zhao Nandong]. Published by author (Chen Yongshan). Taipei: Renjian chuban she, 1987 (distributor).

——. *Chen Yingzhen zuopinji* [Collected works of Chen Yingzhen]. 15 vols. Taipei: Renjian chuban she, 1988.

——. "Xiangtu wenxue de mangdian" [The blind spots of Nativist literature]. *Taiwan wenyi* [Taiwanese literature] 2 (1977): 107–112.

Chen, Yingzhen, et al. *Lü Heruo zuopin yanjiu: Taiwan diyi caizi* [Studies of the works of Lu Heruo: Taiwan's most talented man of letters]. Taipei: Lianhe wenxue chuban she, 1997.

Chen, Yizhi, ed. *Taiwan wenxue jingdian yantaohui lunwenji* [Collection of essays on Taiwanese literary classics]. Taipei: Lianjing chuban she, 1999.

——. "Xu er: guanyu 'Taiwan wenxue jingdian'" [Preface II: About "Taiwanese literary classics"]. In *Taiwan wenxue jingdian yantaohui lunwenji* [Collection of essays on Taiwanese literary classics]. Taipei: Lianjing chuban she, 1999, 4–8.

Cheng, Yingshu. *Gongzhu cheye weimian* [The princess didn't sleep all night]. Taipei: Lianhe wenxue chuban she, 1994.

Chou, Ying-hsiung. "Imaginary Homeland: Postwar Taiwan in Contemporary Political Fiction." *Modern Chinese Literature* 6.1–2 (1992): 23–38.

Chow, Rey, ed. *Modern Chinese Literary and Cultural Studies in the Age of Theory: Reimagining a Field*. Durham: Duke University Press, 2000. The bulk of this book was originally published in *Boundary 2* 25.3 (1998).

——. *Woman and Chinese Modernity: The Politics of Reading Between West and East*. Minneapolis: University of Minnesota Press, 1991.

Chu, T'ien-wen (Zhu Tianwen). *Notes of a Desolate Man*. Trans. Howard Goldblatt and Sylvia Li-chun Lin. New York: Columbia University Press, 1999.

Chun, Allen. "Fuck Chineseness: On the Ambiguities of Ethnicity as Culture as Identity." *Boundary 2* 23.2 (1996): 1–11.

——. "From Nationalism to Nationalizing: Cultural Imagination and State Formation in Postwar Taiwan." *Australian Journal of Chinese Affairs* 31 (1994): 49–69.

Dai, Guohui (Tai, Kokuki). *Taiwan jie yu Zhongguo jie* [Taiwan complex and China complex]. Taipei: Yuanliu chuban gongsi, 1994.

Dai, Tian. "Quan bei Gang Tai wenhua nong yun le" [They've all lost their heads over the culture of Hong Kong and Taiwan]. In "Wang Shuo vs. Jin Yong." Special section. *Mingbao yuekan* [Ming pao monthly] 408 (Dec. 1999): 43–44.

Debord, Guy. *Society of the Spectacle*. Detroit: Black & Red, 1983.

Deng, Peiyun. *Baling niandai Taiwan xuesheng yundong shi* [A history of student movements in Taiwan in the 1980s]. Taipei: Qianwei chuban she, 1993.

Dirlik, Arif and Xudong Zhang, eds. *Postmodernism and China*. Spec. issue of *Boundary 2* 24.3 (Fall 1997).

Dongfang, Bai. *Lang tao sha* [Waves lap the sand]. Irvine, Calif.: Taiwan chuban she; Taipei: Qianwei chuban she, 1990.

Duye. "Jiduanpian fengyun" [The whirlwind of mini-short stories]. In Yaxian, ed., *Zhongshen de huayuan: Lianfu de lishi jiyi* [Garden of the gods: Historical memories of Lianfu]. Taipei: Lianjing chuban she, 1997, 55–60.

Fairbank, John K. *The Great Chinese Revolution: 1800–1985*. New York: Harper & Row, 1986.

Fan, Mingru. *Zhong li xun ta: Taiwan nüxing xiaoshuo zonglun* [Searching for her in the crowd: On Taiwanese women's fiction]. Taipei: Maitian chuban gongsi, 2002.

Fan, Mingru and Baochai Jiang, eds. *Daoyu wen sheng: Taiwan nüxing xiaoshuo duben* [Anthology of Taiwanese women's fiction]. Taipei: Juliu tushu gongsi, 2000.

Fan, Yun, ed. *Xinshengdai de ziwo zhuixun* [The search for self by the new generation]. Taipei: Qianwei chuban she, 1993.

Faurot, Jeannette L., ed. *Chinese Fiction from Taiwan: Critical Perspectives*. Bloomington: Indiana University Press, 1980.

Gold, Thomas. *State and Society in the Taiwan Miracle*. Armonk, N.Y.: M. E. Sharpe, 1986.

Goldman, Merle. *Literary Dissent in Communist China*. Cambridge: Harvard University Press, 1967.

Gunn, Edward M. *Unwelcome Muse: Chinese Literature in Shanghai and Beijing, 1937–1945*. New York: Columbia University Press, 1980.

Han, Bangqing. *Haishang hua liezhuan* [Biographies of the flowers of the sea]. In *Haishang hua kai: Guoyu Haishang hua liezhuan* [Flowers of the sea blooming: Mandarin version of the Biographies of the flowers of the sea], annotated and translated by Zhang Ailing. Taipei: Huangguan wenhua chuban gongsi, 1992.

Hao, Yuxiang. *Xi* [Bathing]. Taipei: Lianhe wenxue chuban she, 1998.

Harrell, Stevan and Huang Chun-chieh, eds. *Cultural Change in Postwar Taiwan*. Boulder: Westview Press, 1994.

He, Chunrui. *Haoshuang nüren: nüxing zhuyi yu xing jiefang* [Untrammeled woman: Feminism and sexual liberation]. Taipei: Huangguan wenxue chuban gongsi, 1994.

Hockx, Michel, ed. *The Literary Field of Twentieth-Century China*. Honolulu: University of Hawai'i, 1999.

Hohendahl, Peter Uwe. *Building a National Literature: The Case of Germany, 1830–1870*. Trans. Renate Baron Franciscono. Ithaca and London: Cornell University Press, 1989.

———. *The Institution of Criticism*. Ithaca and London: Cornell University Press, 1982.

Hou, Hsiao-hsien, dir. *Fengkuei lai de ren* [The boys from Fengkuei]. Screenplay by Zhu Tianwen. Taipei: Wannianqing youxian gongsi, 1983.

———. *Dongdong de jiaqi* [A summer at grandpa's]. Screenplay by Zhu Tianwen. Taipei: Wanbaolu youxian gongsi, 1984.

———. *Tongnian wangshi* [A year to live, a year to die]. Screenplay by Zhu Tianwen. Taipei: Zhongyang dianying gongsi, 1985.

———. *Lianlian fengchen* [Dust in the wind]. Screenplay by Zhu Tianwen. Taipei: Zhongyang dianying gongsi, 1986.

———. *Niluo he nü'er* [Daughter of the Nile]. Screenplay by Zhu Tianwen. Taipei: Xuefu youxian gongsi, 1987.

———. *Beiqing chengshi* [A city of sadness]. Screenplay by Zhu Tianwen. Taipei: Niandai guoji gufen youxian gongsi, 1989.

———. *Ximeng rensheng* [The puppet master]. Screenplay by Zhu Tianwen. Taipei: Niandai guoji gufen youxian gongsi, 1993.

———. *Hao nan hao nü* [Good men, good women]. Screenplay by Zhu Tianwen. Taipei: Hou Hsiao-hsien dianyingshe youxian gongsi, 1995.

———. *Zaijian, nanguo, zaijian* [Good-bye, south, good-bye]. Screenplay by Zhu Tianwen. Taipei: Hou Hsiao-hsien dianyingshe youxian gongsi, 1996.

———. *Haishang hua* [Flowers of Shanghai]. Screenplay by Zhu Tianwen. Taipei: Hou Hsiao-hsien yingxiang zhizuo youxian gongsi, 1998.

Hsia, C. T. *History of Modern Chinese Fiction*. New Haven: Yale University Press, 1961.

Hu, Lancheng. *Jinsheng jinshi* [This life, this world]. Taipei: Yuanjing chuban gongsi, 1976.

———. *Shanhe suiyue* [Mountains, rivers, and years of one's life]. Taipei: Yuanjing chuban gongsi, 1975.

Huang, Fan. *Huang Fan xiaoshuo jingxuanji* [Best short stories of Huang Fan]. Taipei: Lianhe wenxue chuban she, 1998.

———. *Lai suo* [Lai Suo]. Taipei: Shibao wenhua chuban gongsi, 1980.

Huang, Jianye, et al., eds. *Hou Hsiao-hsien* [Hou Hsiao-hsien]. Taipei: Chinese Taipei Film Archive, 2000.

Huang, Jinshu. *Ma Hua wenxue yu Zhongguo xing* [Malaysian-Chinese literature and Chineseness]. Taipei: Yuanzun wenhua, 1998.

———. "Shenji zhi wu: (hou) sishi hui? (hou) xiandai qishilu?" [Dance of an immortal fairy: The (later-appended) forty chapters of the *Dream of the Red Chamber*? Or a (post)modern apocalyptic story?] In Tianwen Zhu, *Hua yi qianshen* [Flower remembers her previous lives]. Taipei: Maitian chuban gongsi, 1996, 265–312.

Huang, Wuzhong. "Baodao diaoling shengsheng tan: yi Lianfu *Baodao ji*" [Sighing over the withering of the precious swords: Remembering the *Precious*

Swords Collection of Lianfu]. In Yaxian, ed., *Zhongshen de huayuan: Lianfu de lishi jiyi* [Garden of the gods: Historical memories of Lianfu]. Taipei: Lianjing chuban she, 1997, 37–42.

Huang, Yingzhe. "'Taiwan wenhua xiejinhui' yanjiu (1946.6–1950.12): lun zhanhou Taiwan wenhua tizhi de jianli" [A study of the "Association of Taiwanese cultural promotion" (1946.6–1950.12): On the establishment of the literary institution in postwar Taiwan]. In Jiongming Zheng, *Yuelang qianxing de yi dai: Ye Shitao ji qi tong shidai zuojia wenxue guoji xueshu yantaohui lunwenji* [A generation that marches forward against the tide: Proceedings of the International Conference on Ye Shitao and his contemporary writers]. Gaoxiong: Chunhui chuban she, 2002, 155–188.

——. "Zhanhou chuqi Taiwan de wenhua chongbian (1945–1947): Taiwan ren 'nuhua' le ma?" [The cultural reconstruction in early postwar Taiwan (1945–1947): Had Taiwanese been "transformed into slaves"?]. In *Taiwan bunka sai kouchiku no Hikari to Kage: 1945–1947* [The cultural reconstruction in Taiwan during the early postwar period: 1945–1947]. Tokorozawa, Japan: Soutousha, 1999, 172–192.

Hutcheon, Linda. *A Poetics of Postmodernism: History, Theory, Fiction.* New York: Routledge, 1988.

——. *The Politics of Postmodernism.* London and New York: Routledge, 1989.

Hutchinson, John. *The Dynamics of Cultural Nationalism: The Gaelic Revival and the Creation of the Irish Nation State.* London: Allen & Unwin, 1987.

——. *Modern Nationalism.* London: Fontana Press, 1994.

Jameson, Frederic. "Remapping Taipei." In Nick Browne, Paul G. Pickowicz, Vivian Sobchack, and Esther Yau, eds., *New Chinese Cinemas: Forms, Identities, Politics.* Cambridge, England, and New York: Cambridge University Press, 1994, 117–150.

Ji, Dawei. *Ganguan shijie* [Queer senses: A story cycle of sexualities]. Taipei: Tansuo chuban gongsi, 2000.

——. *Lianwu pi* [Fetish: Stories]. Taipei: Shibao wenhua chuban gongsi, 1998.

——. *Mo* [Membrane]. Taipei: Lianjing chuban shiye gongsi, 1996.

——, ed. *Ku'er kuanghuan jie: Taiwan dangdai queer wenxue duben* [Queer carnival: A reader of the queer literature in Taiwan]. Taipei: Yuanzun wenhua qiye gongsi, 1997.

——, ed. *Ku'er qishi lu: Taiwan dangdai queer lunshu duben* [Queer archipelago: A reader of the queer discourses in Taiwan]. Taipei: Yuanzun wenhua qiye gongsi, 1997.

Jian, Zhujun. "'Taiwan wenxue jingdian' juexuan huiyi jishi: Taiwan wenxue di yi fen shudan" [Meeting report of the final selection of "Taiwanese literary classics": The first book list of Taiwanese literature]. *Lianhe bao* [United daily news] 3–5 Feb. 1999:37.

Jiang, Gui. *Jiang Gui zixuanji* [Selected works by author]. Taipei: Liming wenhua shiye gongsi, 1980.

——. *Wuwei ji* [Collection of nontransgressive writings]. Taipei: Youshi wenyi she, 1974.

——. *Xuanfeng* [Whirlwind]. Taipei: Minghua shuju, 1959.

Jiang, Xiaoyun. *Sui yuan: duanpian xiaoshuoji* [Following the predestined fate: A short story collection]. Taipei: Huangguan chuban she, 1977.

Jiang, Zide, ed. *Zhimindi jingyan yu Taiwan wenxue: diyijie Taixing Taiwan wenxue xueshu yantaohui lunwenji* [Colonial experience and Taiwanese literature: Proceedings of the First Taixing Scholarly Conference on Taiwanese Literature]. Taipei: Yuanlui chuban gongsi, 2000.

Jiang, Zhongming. "Yantaohui bimu, jingdian hai zai xingcheng zhong" [The conference has concluded; the canon is still being formed]. *Lianhe bao* [United daily news] 22 Mar. 1999:14.

——. "Zhengzhi zhengque fei jianli Taiwan wenxue shi biaozhun" ["Political correctness" is not a criterion for establishing Taiwanese literary history]. *Lianhe bao* [United daily news] 22 Mar. 1999:14.

——. "Liuzhu yi chuan xinghui: Wang Tiwu xiansheng zizhu nianqing zuojia de gushi" [Storing a boatful of starlight: The story about Mr. Wang Tiwu's assistance of young writers]. In Yaxian, ed., *Zhongshen de huayuan: Lianfu de lishi jiyi* [Garden of the gods: Historical memories of Lianfu]. Taipei: Lianjing chuban she, 1997, 47–54.

Jiao, Xiongping. *Taiwan xindianying* [Taiwan new cinema]. Taipei: Shibao wenhua chuban gongsi, 1988.

"Jin Yong he Wang Shuo teji" [Special collection on Jin Yong and Wang Shuo]. http://www.shuku.net:8080/novels/zatan/jywstq/jwtq.html.

Jiqi zhanjing, ed. *Taiwan de xin fandui yundong* [New oppositional movements in Taiwan]. Taipei: Tangshan chuban she, 1991.

Kinkley, Jeffrey C. "The New Chinese Literature: The Mainland and Beyond." *Choice: Current Reviews of Academic Books* 31.8 (April 1994): 1249–1265.

Kuo, Jason C. *Art and Cultural Politics in Postwar Taiwan*. Bethesda, Md.: CDL Press, 2000.

Lai, Suling. "Zhang Ailing suan bu suan Taiwan zuojia? Qi Bangyuan 'erdu piaoliu lundian" tigong sikao kongjian" [Does Zhang Ailing count as a Taiwanese writer? Qi Bangyuan's theory of "double-exile" provides food for thought]. *Minsheng bao* [People's life daily] 20 Mar. 1999:10.

Lan, Bozhou. *Huang mache zhi ge* [Song of the canopied chariot]. Taipei: Shibao wenhua chuban gongsi, 1989.

Lau, Joseph Shiu-ming. "Celestials and Commoners: Exiles in Pai Hsien-yung's Stories." *Monumenta Serica* 36 (1984–85): 409–423.

——, ed. *Chinese Stories from Taiwan: 1960–1970*. New York: Columbia University Press, 1976.

——. "The Concepts of Time and Reality in Modern Chinese Fiction." *Tamkang Review* 4.1 (1973): 25–40.

——. "'Crowded Hours' Revisited: The Evocation of the Past in Taipei Jen." *Journal of Asian Studies* 35.1 (1975): 31–47.

——. "Death in the Void: Three Tales of Spiritual Atrophy in Ch'en Ying-chen's Post-Incarceration Fiction." *Modern Chinese Literature* 2.1 (Spring 1986): 21–28.

——. "'How Much Truth Can a Blade of Grass Carry?': Ch'en Ying-chen and the Emergence of Native Taiwan Writers." *Journal of Asian Studies* 32.4 (1973): 623–638.

——. "Obsession with Taiwan: The Fiction of Chang Hsi-kuo." In Jeanette L. Faurot, ed., *Chinese Fiction from Taiwan: Critical Perspectives*. Bloomington: Indiana University Press, 1980, 148–165.

——. "Shinian lai de Taiwan xiaoshuo: 1965–75—qianlun Wang Wenxing de Jiabian" [Taiwan fiction during the last ten years: 1965–75—with a commentary on Wang Wenxing's *Family Catastrophe*], *Zhongwai wenxue* [Zhongwai literary monthly] 4.12 (May 1976): 4–16.

——. "The Tropics Mythopoetized: The Extraterritorial Writing of Li Yung-p'ing in the Context of the Hsiang-t'u Movement." *Tamkang Review* 12.1 (Fall 1981): 1–26.

——, ed. *The Unbroken Chain: An Anthology of Taiwan Fiction Since 1926*. Bloomington: Indiana University Press, 1983.

Laughlin, Charles A. "The Battlefield of Cultural Production: Chinese Literary Mobilization During the War Years." *Journal of Modern Literature in Chinese* 2.1 (July 1998): 83–103.

Lee, Leo Ou-fan. *The Romantic Generation of Modern Chinese Writers*. Cambridge: Harvard University Press, 1973.

Li, An (Ang Lee), dir. *Tui shou* [Pushing hands]. Central Motion Pictures Corporation/Good Machine & Ang Lee Productions. 1992.

——. *Xiyan* [The wedding banquet]. Central Motion Pictures Corporation/Good Machine, The Samuel Goldwyn Company. 1993.

——. *Yin shi nan nu* [Eat drink man woman]. Central Motion Pictures/Ang Lee/Good Machine, The Samuel Goldwyn Company. 1994.

——. *Wohu canglong* [Crouching tiger, hidden dragon]. Sony Classics/Columbia Pictures/Good Machine/Edko Films/Zoom Hunt, Sony. 2000.

Li, Ang. *Zizhuan no xiaoshuo* [Fiction: An autobiography]. Taipei: Huangguan wenhua chuban gongsi, 2000.

——. *Beigang xianglu renren cha: dai zhencao dai de mogui* [Everyone puts their incense sticks in the Pei-kang incense burner: The devil with a chastity belt]. Taipei: Maitian chuban gongsi, 1997.

——. "Dai zhencao dai de mogui" [The devil with a chastity belt]. In *Beigang xianglu renren cha: dai zhencao dai de mogui* [Everyone puts their incense sticks in the Pei-kang incense burner: The devil with a chastity belt]. Taipei: Maitian chuban gongsi, 1997, 49–82.

——. *Mi yuan* [Lost garden]. Published by author. Taipei: Maoteng famai gongsi, 1991 (distributor).

——. *An ye* [Dark nights]. Taipei: Shibao wenhua chuban gongsi, 1985.

——. *Sha fu: Lucheng gushi* [Butcher's wife: Stories of Lucheng]. Taipei: Lianhe bao she, 1984.

Li, Qiao. *Han ye* [Wintry night]. Taipei: Yuanjing chuban gongsi, 1980.

Li, Rongchun. *Huai mu: Li Rongchun zuopinji* [Remembering my mother: Collected works by Li Rongchun]. Taichung: Chenxing, 1997.

——. *Zuguo yu tongbao* [Motherland and compatriots]. Taipei: The author, 1956.

Li Rongchun zhuanji [Special issue on Li Rongchun]. *I-Lan wenxian zazhi* [I-lan journal of history] 31 (Jan. 1998).

Li, Ruiteng. "Lianfu de yundong xingge" [The campaign spirit of Lianfu]. In Yaxian, ed., *Zhongshen de huayuan: Lianfu de lishi jiyi* [Garden of the gods: Historical memories of Lianfu]. Taipei: Lianjing chuban she, 1997, 61–68.

Li, Yongping. *Zhu Ling manyou xianjing* [Zhu Ling in the wonderland]. Taipei: Lianhe wenxue chuban she, 1998.

——. *Hai dong qing: Taibei de yize yuyan* [East ocean green: A parable of Taipei]. Taipei: Lianhe wenxue chuban she, 1992.

Li, Yuanzhen, ed. *Hongde fazi: Taiwan xiandai nüxing shixuan* [Anthology of modern Taiwanese women's poetry]. Taipei: Nushu wenhua shiye gongsi, 2000.

Liao, Xianhao. *Ai yu jiegou: dangdai Taiwan wenxue pinglun yu wenhua guancha* [Love and deconstruction: Literary criticism and cultural observations on contemporary Taiwan]. Taipei: Lianhe wenxue chuban she, 1995.

Liao, Qingxiu. *Enchou xielei ji* [Good will and revenge: A record of blood and tears]. Taipei: The author, 1957.

Liao, Binghui (Ping-hui Liao). "Taiwan wenxue zhong de sizhong xiandai xing: yi *Beihai de ren* xiaji wei li" [Four modes of modernity and narrative identity in Taiwan literature: Using part II of *Back Against the Sea* as an example]. *Zhongwai wenxue* [Chung-wai literary monthly] 30.6 (Nov. 2001): 75–92.

——. *Linglei xiandai qing* [On alternative modernities]. Taipei: Yunchen chuban-she, 2001.

——. "Rewriting Taiwanese National History: The February 28 Incident as Spectacle." *Public Culture* 5 (1993): 281–296.

Lin, Fangmei. *Jiedu Qiongyao aiqing wangguo* [Deciphering the romantic kingdom of Qiongyao]. Taipei: Shibao wenhua chuban gongsi, 1994.

——. "Yasu zhi fen yu xiangzheng xing quanli douzheng: you wenxue shengchan yu xiaofei jiegou de gaibian tan zhishi fenzi de dingwei" [An institutional perspective on the changing relationship between serious and popular literature:

Cultural distinction, symbolic power struggle, and intellectuals' new positions]. *Taiwan shehui yanjiu jikan* [Taiwan: A radical quarterly in social studies] 16 (March 1994): 55–78.

Lin, Haiyin. *Jianying hua wentan* [Reminiscences of the *wentan* through clippings of images]. Taipei: Chunwenxue chuban she, 1984.

——. *Yunchuang yedu* [Night reading at a rue window]. Taipei: Chunwenxue chuban she, 1982.

——. "Liushui shi nian jian—zhubian Lianfu zayi" [Ten years like flowing water—remembering my life as the Lianfu editor]. In *Yunchuang yedu* [Night reading at a rue window]. Taipei: Chunwenxue chuban she, 1982, 273–309.

——. "Xiaoshuojia yingyou guangda de tongqing" [Fiction writers should possess a broad sense of compassion]. In *Xia Ji'an xiansheng jinianji* [Essays in remembrance of Mr. Xia Ji'an]. Hong Kong: Xiandai chuban she, 1978, 22–23. Originally published in *Wenxing* [Literary star] 90 (March 1965).

Lin, Mei-chun. "Chen Lauds Local Artists." Editorial. *Taipei Times* 5 Aug. 2000:1.

Lin, Qiyang. "'Fu' kan 'da' ye: Taiwan baozhi fukan de wenxue chuanbo moshi fenxi" [The grand *fukan* project: An analysis of the modes of literary dissemination in *fukan* of the Taiwanese newspapers]. In Yaxian, and Yizhi Chen, eds., *Shijie zhongwen baozhi fukanxue zonglun* [On studies of the *fukan* in Chinese newspapers of the world]. Taipei: Wenjianhui, 1997, 117–135.

——. "Wenxue chuanbo yu shehui bianqian zhi guanlianxing yanjiu: yi qishi niandai Taiwan baozhi fukan de meijie yunzuo wei li" [A case study of the relationship between literary media and social change: The intermediary function of *fukan* in 1970s Taiwanese newspapers]. M.A. thesis, Graduate Program in Journalism, Chinese Culture University, 1993.

Lin, Shuyang. *Cong Er-er-ba dao wuling niandai baise kongbu* [From February 28 to the White Terror of the 1950s]. Taipei: Shibao wenhua chuban gongsi, 1992.

Lin, Zhuoshui, et al. *Wajie de Huaxia diguo* [The disintegrating Chinese empire]. Monterey Park, Calif.: Taiwan chuban she, 1985.

Link, Perry. *The Uses of Literature: Life in the Socialist Chinese Literary System*. Princeton: Princeton University Press, 2000.

——. *Mandarin Ducks and Butterflies: Popular Fiction in Early Twentieth-Century Chinese Cities*. Berkeley: University of California Press, 1981.

Liu, Kexiang. "Yige shuli de huiyi: quanyu 'Disanlei jiechu' zhuanji de zhizuo" [An alienated memory: Concerning the production of the column "third encounter"]. In Yaxian, ed., *Zhongshen de huayuan: Lianfu de lishi jiyi* [Garden of the gods: Historical memories of Lianfu]. Taipei: Lianjing chuban she, 1997, 69–75.

Liu, Jihui. *Gu'er, nüshen, fumianshuxie: Wenhua fuhao de zhengzhuang shi yuedu* [Orphan, goddess, and the writing of the negative: The performance of our symptoms]. Taipei: Lixu chuban she, 2000.

Lu, Feiyi. *Taiwan dianying: zhengzhi, jingji, meixue, 1949–1994* [Taiwan cinema: Politics, economics, and aesthetics, 1949–1994]. Taipei: Yuanliu chuban gongsi, 1998.

Lu, Yujia. "Cong 'Dushu,' 'Zhi de paihangbang,' dao 'Dushu ren.'" [From "reading," "quality rating," to "the reader"]. In Yaxian, ed., *Zhongshen de huayuan: Lianfu de lishi jiyi* [Garden of the gods: Historical memories of Lianfu]. Taipei: Lianjing chuban she, 1997, 83–92.

Lü, Xiulian (Annette Lü). *Zhe sange nü ren* [These three women]. Taipei: Zili wanbao she, 1985.

Lü, Zhenghui. *Wenxue jingdian yu wenhua rentong* [The literary canon and cultural identification]. Taipei: Jiuge chuban she, 1995.

——. "Fenlie de xiangtu, xufu de wenhua: bashi niandai de Taiwan wenxue" [Divided homeland, superfluous culture: Taiwanese literature of the 1980s]. In *Zhanhou Taiwan wenxue jingyan* [Literary records of postwar Taiwan]. Taipei: Xindi wenxue chuban she, 1992, 129–135.

——. *Zhanhou Taiwan wenxue jingyan* [Literary records of postwar Taiwan]. Taipei: Xindi wenxue chuban she, 1992.

Luo, Yijun. *Yueqiu xingshi* [Clan names from the moon]. Taipei: Lianhe wenxue chuban she, 2000

Lupke, Christopher. "Xia Ji'an's (T. A. Hsia) Critical Bridge to Modernism in Taiwan." *Journal of Modern Literature in Chinese* 4.1 (July 2000): 35–63.

Martin, Fran, ed. *Angelwings: Contemporary Queer Fiction from Taiwan*. Trans. Fran Martin. Honolulu: University of Hawai'i Press, 2003.

Martin, Helmut. "The History of Taiwanese Literature." *Chinese Studies* 14.1 (June 1996): 1–51.

McArthur, Charles Marshall. "'Taiwanese Literature' After the Nativist Movement: Construction of a Literary Identity Apart from a Chinese Model." Ph.D. diss., Asian Studies Department, University of Texas at Austin, 1999.

Mei, Jialing, ed. *Xingbie lunshu yu Taiwan xiaoshuo* [Gender discourse and Taiwan fiction]. Taipei: Maitian chuban gongsi, 2000.

——. "Wuling niandai guojia lunshu/wenyi chuangzuo zhong de 'jiaguo xiangxiang': yi Chen Jiying fangong xiaoshuo wei li de tantao" ["National imagination" in national discourse/creative writing of the 1950s: Chen Jiying's anti-Communist fiction, a case study]. Conference paper. "Wenyi lilun yu tongsu wenhua: silingliuling niandai guoji yantaohui" [International conference on literary theories and popular culture: 1940s to 1960s]. Academia Sinica, Taipei, Jan. 2–3, 1998.

Mizou, and Xinhua Liang, eds. *Xindianying zhi si: cong Yiqie wei mingtian dao Beiqing chengshi* [Death of the new cinema: From *Everything for the Sake of Tomorrow* to *A City of Sadness*]. Taipei: Tangshan chuban she, 1991.

Ouyang, Zi. *Bashe shanshui lishi jian: shang du Wenhua ku lu* [Trudging through mountains, streams, and history: Reading *A Bitter Journey of Chinese Culture*] Taipei: Erya chuban she, 1998.

Pan, Jiaqing. "Fukan neirong chuantong yu xinwen lilun de jieshi nengli" [The content of *fukan* and the interpretive power of journalistic theory]. In Yaxian, and Yizhi Chen, eds., *Shijie zhongwen baozhi fukanxue zonglun* [On studies of the *fukan* in Chinese newspapers of the world]. Taipei: Wenjianhui, 1997, 87–113.

Pan, Renmu. *Lianyi biaomei* [My cousin Lianyi]. 1952; reprint, Taipei: Chunwenxue chuban gongsi, 1985.

Peng, Ge. *Butan renxing, he you wenxue* [Without human nature, how can we have literature?]. Taipei: Lianhebao she, 1978.

——. *Luoyue* [Setting moon]. Taipei: Ziyou Zhongguo she, 1956.

Peng, Ruijin. "Shemo jingdian? Shei de wenxue?" [What classics? Whose literature?]. Editorial. *Taiwan shibao* [Taiwan times] 22 Mar. 1999:11.

——. *Taiwan xinwenxue yundong sishi nian* [Forty years of the new Taiwanese literature movement]. Taipei: Zili wanbao, 1991.

Perng, Ching-hsi, and Chiu-kuei Wang, eds. *Death in a Cornfield, and Other Stories from Contemporary Taiwan*. Hong Kong: Oxford University Press, 1994.

Ping, Lu. *Ningzhi wenquan* [Jadelike skin in hot springs]. Taipei: Lianhe wenxue chuban she, 2000.

——. *Xing dao tianya: Sun Zhongshan yu Song Qingling de geming yu aiqing gushi* [A journey to the end of the world: A tale of revolution and romance about Sun Yat-sen and Song Qingling]. Taipei: Lianhe wenxue chuban she, 1995.

——. *Yumi tian zhi si* [Death in a cornfield]. Taipei: Lianhe bao she, 1985.

Postone, Moishe, Edward LiPuma, and Craig Calhoun. "Introduction: Bourdieu and Social Theory." In Craig Calhoun, Edward LiPuma, and Moishe Postone, eds., *Pierre Bourdieu: Critical Perspectives*. Chicago: University of Chicago Press, 1993, 1–13.

Pye, Lucien. "How China's Nationalism Was Shanghaied." In Jonathan Unger, ed., *Chinese Nationalism*. Armonk, N.Y.: M. E. Sharpe, 1996, 86–112.

Qin, Xianci. "Wusi shiqi de 'Xuedeng' yu 'Chenbao fukan'" ["Lamp of knowledge" and "*Fukan* of the *Morning News*" of the May Fourth era]. In Yaxian, and Yizhi Chen, eds., *Shijie zhongwen baozhi fukanxue zonglun* [On studies of the *fukan* in Chinese newspapers of the world]. Taipei: Wenjianhui, 1997, 1–27.

Qiu, Guifen, ed. "Daolun" [Introduction]. *Riju yi lai Taiwan nü zuojia xiaoshuo xuandu* [Anthology of Taiwanese women's fiction since the Japanese period]. 2 vols. Taipei: Nüshu wenhua gongsi, 2001, 3–51.

——. *"(Bu)tongguo nüren" guazao: fangtan dangdai Taiwan nü zuojia* [Interviews with Taiwan women writers]. Taipei: Yuanzun wenhua qiye gongsi, 1998.

——. *Zhong jie Taiwan nüren: houzhimin nüxing guandian de Taiwan yuedu* [Reading Taiwan/woman: A postcolonial perspective]. Taipei: Yuanzun wenhua qiye gongsi, 1997.

Qiu, Miaojin. *Mengmate yishu* [Posthumous writings from Mengmate]. Taipei: Lianhe wenxue chuban she, 1996.

——. *E yu shou ji* [Notes on crocodiles]. Taipei: Shibao wenhua chuban gongsi, 1994.

Rigger, Shelley. *Politics in Taiwan: Voting for Democracy*. London and New York: Routledge, 1999.

Rubinstein, Murray A., ed. *Taiwan: A History 1600–1994*. Armonk, N.Y.: M. E. Sharpe, 1999.

——. *The Other Taiwan: 1945 to the Present*. Armonk, N.Y.: M. E. Sharpe, 1994.

Sang, Tze-lan Deborah. *The Emerging Lesbian: Female Same-Sex Desire in Modern China*. Chicago: University of Chicago Press, 2002.

Shi, Ming. *Taiwanren sibainian shi: Hanwen ban* [A four-hundred-year history of the Taiwanese: The Hanwen version]. San Jose, Calif.: Paradise Culture Associates, 1980.

Shi, Mingzheng. *Shi Mingzheng ji* [Selected short stories by Shi Mingzheng]. Ed. Ruiming Lin. Taipei: Qianwei chuban she, 1993.

——. "He niao zhe" [The urine drinker]. In *Shi Mingzheng ji* [Selected short stories by Shi Mingzheng]. Ed. Ruiming Lin. Taipei: Qianwei chuban she, 1993, 115–131.

——. "Ke si zhe" [The death seeker]. In *Shi Mingzheng ji* [Selected short stories by Shi Mingzheng]. Ed. Ruiming Lin. Taipei: Qianwei chuban she, 1993, 169–178.

Shi, Minhui, ed. *Taiwan yishi lunzhan xuanji: Taiwan jie yu Zhongguo jie de zong jiesuan* [A collection of essays on the Taiwanese consciousness debate: Final confrontation between the China complex and the Taiwan complex]. Taipei: Qianwei chuban she, 1988.

Shi, Shu. "Shou yu ti: riju shidai Taiwan xiaoshuo zhong tuifei yishi de qiyuan" [Head and body: The rise of decadence in Taiwanese fiction of the Japanese period]. In Yingzhen Chen, ed., *Lü Heruo zuopin yanjiu: Taiwan diyi caizi* [Studies of works of Lü Heruo: Taiwan's most talented man of letters]. Taipei: Lianhe wenxue chuban she, 1997, 205–223.

——. "Shuzhai, chengshi yu xiangcun: riju shidai de zuoyi wenxue yundong ji xiaoshuo zhong de zuoyi zhishi fenzi" [Studio, city, and village: The leftist literary movement and leftist intellectuals in fiction of the Japanese period]. *Wenxue Taiwan* [Literary Taiwan] 15 (Summer 1995): 68–102.

Shi, Shuqing. *Xianggang sanbuqu* [The Hong Kong trilogy]. 3 vols. Taipei: Hongfan shudian, 1993, 1995, 1997.

Shih, Shu-mei. "The Trope of 'Mainland China' in Taiwan's Media." *Positions* 3.1 (1995): 149–183.

Song, Zelai. *Feixu Taiwan* [The wasteland that is Taiwan]. Taipei: Qianwei chuban she, 1985.

Smith, Anthony D. "Towards a Global Culture?" In Mike Featherstone, ed., *Global Culture: Nationalism, Globalization, and Modernity*. Spec. issue of *Theory, Culture and Society*. (7). London, Newbury Park, and New Delhi: Sage Publications, 1990.

Su, Weizhen. *Chenmo zhi dao* [An island of silence]. Taipei: Shibao wenhua chuban gongsi, 1994.

——. *Likai Tongfang* [Leaving Tongfang]. Taipei: Lianjing chuban she, 1990.

Taiwaner, A. "Pseudo Taiwanese: Isle Margin Editorials." Trans. S. Yvonne Chang and Marshall McArthur. *Positions* 4.1 (Spring 1996): 145–171.

Tang, Xiaobing. "On the Concept of Taiwan Literature." *Modern China* 25.4 (1999): 379–422.

Transnational China Project. Baker Institute, Rice University. http://www.ruf.rice .edu/~tnchina/.

Unger, Jonathan, ed. *Chinese Nationalism*. Armonk, N.Y.: M. E. Sharpe, 1996.

Vecchoine, Judith, writer, director, and producer. *Tug of War: The Story of Taiwan*. WGBH Educational Foundation. South Burlington, Vt.: WGBH Boston Video, 1998.

Wachman, Alan M. *Taiwan: National Identity and Democratization*. Armonk, N.Y.: M. E. Sharpe, 1994.

Wang, Anyi. "Jiachang" [Like what is in everyday life]. *Mingbao yuekan* [Ming pao monthly] 34.6 (June 1999): 45.

——. *Chang hen ge* [Song of everlasting sorrow]. Taipei: Maitian chuban Gongsi, 1996.

Wang, Ban. *The Sublime Figure of History: Aesthetics and Politics in Twentieth-Century China*. Stanford: Stanford University Press, c1997.

Wang, David Der-wei (Wang Dewei). "The Monster That Is History: Taowu xianping, Taowu Cuibian, JinTaowu zhuan." In *The Monster That Is History*. Berkeley: University of California Press, forthcoming.

——. "Cangtai huangye di, rimu duo xuanfeng: lun Jiang Gui Xuanfeng" [Dark green mosses, yellow leaves covering the ground: At dusk, whirlwinds abound]. In Yizhi Chen, ed., *Taiwan wenxue jingdian yantaohui lunwenji* [Collection of essays on Taiwanese literary classics]. Taipei: Lianjing chuban she, 1999, 23–34.

——. *Ruhe xiandai, zenyang wenxue?: shijiu, ershi shiji Zhongwen xiaoshuo xinlun* [Making of the modern, the making of a literature: New perspectives on nineteenth- and twentieth-century Chinese fiction]. Taipei: Maitian chuban gongsi, 1998.

——. *Fin-de-siècle Splendor: Repressed Modernities of Late Qing Fiction, 1849–1911*. Stanford: Stanford University Press, 1997.

——. "Yizhong shiqu de wenxue?: fangong xiaoshuo xinlun" [A bygone literature?: New perspectives on anti-Communist fiction]. In *Ruhe xiandai, zenyang wenxue?: shijiu, ershi shiji Zhongwen xiaoshuo xinlun* [Making of the modern, the making of a literature: New perspectives on nineteenth- and twentieth-century Chinese fiction]. Taipei: Maitian chuban gongsi, 1998, 141–158.

——. "Xulun, cong 'Kuangren riji' dao *Huangren shouji*: lun Zhu Tianwen, jian ji Hu Lancheng yu Zhang Ailing" [Introduction, from "A Madman's Diary" to *Notes of a Desolate Man*: On Zhu Tianwen, and also Hu Lancheng and Zhang Ailing]. In Tianwen Zhu, *Hua yi qianshen* [Flower remembers her previous lives]. Taipei: Maitian chuban gongsi, 1996, 7–23.

——. "Introduction." In Ching-hsi Perng and Chiu-kuei Wang, eds., *Death in a Cornfield, and Other Stories from Contemporary Taiwan*. Hong Kong: Oxford University Press, 1994, iv–xv.

——. *Xiao shuo Zhongguo: wan Qing dao dangdai de Zhongwen xiaoshuo* [Narrating China: Chinese fiction from the late Qing to the contemporary era]. Taipei: Maitian chuban gongsi, 1993.

——. *Zhongsheng xuanhua: sanling yu baling niandai de Zhongguo xiaoshuo* [Heteroglossia: Chinese fiction of the 1930s and 1980s]. Taipei: Yuanliu chuban gongsi, 1988.

Wang, Dingjun. *Suiyuan pomi* [Following your destiny, seeing through the myth]. Taipei: Erya chuban she, 1997.

——. *Numu shaonian* [Young man with a furious stare]. Taipei: The author, 1995.

——. *Zuotian de yun* [Clouds of yesterday]. Taipei: The author, 1992.

——. *Zuo xinfang xuanwo* [Whirlpool of the left atrium]. Taipei: Erya chuban she, 1988.

——. *Danshen wendu* [The bachelor's body temperature]. Taipei: Erya chuban she, 1988. Reprint of *Danshenhan de tiwen*.

——. *Zixu* [Preface by the author]. In *Danshen wendu* [The bachelor's body temperature]. Taipei: Erya chuban she, 1988, 1–7.

——. *Qingren yan* [Lover's eyes]. Taipei: Dalin chuban she, 1977.

——. *Sui liuli* [Shattered crystals]. Taipei: Jiuge chuban she, 1978.

——. *Kaifang de rensheng* [An open-minded life]. Taipei: Erya chuban she, 1976.

——. *Danshenhan de tiwen* [A bachelor's body temperature]. Taipei: Dalin shudian, 1970.

——. "Tu" [Soil]. In *Danshenhan de tiwen* [A bachelor's body temperature]. Taipei: Dalin shudian, 1970, 1–35.

Wang, Jing. *High Culture Fever: Politics, Aesthetics, and Ideology in Deng's China*. Berkeley: University of California Press, 1996.

Wang, Meng, et al. "Informal Roundtable Discussion by Three Authors: Wang Meng, Liu Sola, Zha Jianying." Trans. Marshall McArthur. Translational China Project: Analysis and Commentary. Baker Institute, Rice University, March 10, 1998. http://www.ruf.rice.edu/~tnchina/.

Wang, Shuo. "Wo kan Jin Yong" [My view on Jin Yong]. *Mingbao yuekan* [Ming pao monthly] 408 (Dec. 1999): 38–41.

"Wang Shuo vs. Jin Yong." Special section. *Mingbao yue kan* [Ming pao monthly] 408 (Dec. 1999): 35–52.

Wang, Tuo. "Jinshui shen" [Aunt Jinshui]. In *Jinshui shen* [Aunt Jinshui]. Taipei: Xiangcao shan chuban gongsi, 1976, 189–256.

Wang Wenxing. *Beihai de ren (shang; xia)* [Backed against the sea, parts I & II]. Taipei: Hungfan shudian, 1981, 1999.

———. *Jiabian* [Family catastrophe]. Taipei: Huanyu chuban she, 1973.

Wang, Zhenhe. *Meigui, meigui, wo ai ni* [Rose, rose, I love you]. Taipei: Yuanjing chuban gongsi, 1984.

Williams, Raymond. *Marxism and Literature.* Oxford: Oxford University Press, 1977.

Winckler, Edwin A. "Cultural Policy on Postwar Taiwan." In Stevan Harrell and Huang Chun-chieh, eds., *Cultural Change in Postwar Taiwan.* Boulder: Westview Press, 1994, 22–46.

Wu, Jiwen. *Shijimo shaonian'ai duben* [Pamphlet on the love of young boys in the fin-de-siècle]. Taipei: Shibao wenhua chuban gongsi, 1996.

Wu, Zhuoliu. *Taiwan lianqiao* [Taiwanese forsythia]. Trans. Zhong Zhaozheng. Irvine, Calif.: Taiwan chuban she, 1987.

———. *Wuhuaguo* [The fig tree]. Irvine, Calif.: Taiwan chuban she, 1984. Originally serialized in *Taiwan wenyi* [Taiwanese literature] 19–21 (1968).

———. *Wu Zhuoliu zuopinji* [Collected works of Wu Zhuoliu]. Ed. Liangze Zhang. 6 vols. Taipei: Yuanxing chuban she, 1977.

———. *Yaxiya de gu'er* [Orphan of Asia]. Trans. Fu Rongen. Taipei: Nanhua chuban she, 1962.

Wuhe. *Gui'er yu Ayao* [Queer and Ayao]. Taipei: Maitian chuban gongsi, 2000.

———. *Yu sheng* [Remains of life]. Taipei: Maitian chuban gongsi, 2000.

Xia, Ji'an (Tsi-an Hsia). "Appendix: Taiwan." In C. T. Hsia, *History of Modern Chinese Fiction.* New Haven: Yale University Press, 1961, 509–529.

———. "Ping Luoyue jian lun xiandai xiaoshuo" [A critique of *Setting Moon* and a discussion of modern fiction]. *Wenxue zashi* [Literary review] 1.2 (Oct. 1956).

Xiao, Aqin. "Guomindang zhengquan de wenhua yu daode lunshu: zhishi shehuixue de fenxi" [The cultural and moral discourses of the Nationalist regime: An analysis of the sociology of knowledge]. M.A. thesis, Department of Sociology, National Taiwan University, 1991.

Xiao, Baixing. "Lai zi bi an de 'xin' sheng: zhanhou chuqi 'shengli gongxueyuan (shengli Chengda)' jianzhu sheji de lunshu xinggou (1940 zhong–1960 chu)" [New voice coming from the other shore: Discursive formation of the architecture design in the Provincial College of Engineering (Provincial Cheng Kung University) (mid-1940s–early 1960s)]. Conference paper. "Taiwan shehui yanjiu yijiujiuba pipan de xinshengdai lunwen yantaohui" [1998 conference of the new critical generation, organized by *Taiwan: A Radical Quarterly in Social Studies*], National Taiwan University, Taipei, June 20–21, 1998.

Xiao, Lihong. *Qianjiang you shui qianjiang yue* [A thousand moons on a thousand rivers]. Taipei: Lianhe bao she, 1981.

Xu, Ben. *Disenchanted Democracy: Chinese Cultural Criticism After 1989.* Ann Arbor: University of Michigan Press, 1999.

Xu, Junya. "Niaokan Rizhi shiqi Taiwan baozhi fukan: yi *Taiwan xinmin bao* xitong wei fenxi changyu" [Overview of the *fukan* in Taiwanese newspapers of the Japanese period: An examination of the *Taiwan New Citizen* journalistic family.] In Yaxian, and Yizhi Chen, eds., *Shijie zhongwen baozhi fukanxue zonglun* [On studies of the *fukan* in Chinese newspapers of the world]. Taipei: Wenjianhui, 1997, 28–67.

Xu, Xinliang. *Xinxing minzu* [An emergent nation]. Taipei: Yuanliu chuban gongsi, 1995.

Yang, Cui. "Yang Qi jujue chengwei bei pingxuan de keti" [Yang Qi refuses to become an object of the selection]. Editorial. *Taiwan shibao* [Taiwan times], 22 Mar. 1999:11.

Yang, Ze. *Qishi niandai: lixiang jixu ranshao* [The seventies: Ideals that continue to incense]. Taipei: Shibao wenhua chuban gongsi, 1994.

———. *Kuangbiao bashi: jilu yige jiti fasheng de shidai* [The tumultuous eighties: Records from a decade of collective voices]. Taipei: Shibao wenhua chuban gongsi, 1999.

Yang, Zhao. "Sishi nian Taiwan dazong wenxue xiao shi" [A minor history of Taiwanese popular literature in the last forty years]. In *Wenxue, shehui yu lishi xiang xiang: zhanhou wenxue shi sanlun* [Literary, social, and historical imagination: Random remarks on the postwar literary history]. Taipei: Lianhe wenxue chuban she, 1995, 25–69.

———. *An xiang mi ye* [Dark alley in a misty night]. Taipei: Lianhe wenxue chuban she, 1994.

Yao, Jiawen. *Taiwan qi se ji* [The seven-colored account of Taiwan]. Taipei: Zili wanbao, 1991.

Yaxian, ed. *Zhongshen de huayuan: Lianfu de lishi jiyi* [Garden of the gods: Historical memories of Lianfu]. Taipei: Lianjing chuban she, 1997.

Yaxian, and Yizhi Chen, eds. *Shijie zhongwen baozhi fukanxue zonglun* [On studies of the *fukan* in Chinese newspapers of the world]. Taipei: Wenjianhui, 1997.

Ye Shitao. *Yige Taiwan laoxiu zuojia de wuling niandai* [The fifties as remembered by an old and useless Taiwanese writer]. Taipei: Qianwei chuban she, 1991.

———. *Taiwan wenxue shigang* [An outline of the history of Taiwanese literature]. Gaoxiong: Wenxuejie zazhi she, 1987.

———. "Cong xiangtu wenxue dao Sanmin zhuyi wenxue: fang Ye Shitao xiansheng tan Taiwan wenxue de lishi" [From nativist literature to literature of the Three Principles of the People: An interview with Mr. Ye Shitao on the history of Taiwanese literature]. In *Wenxue huiyilu* [Recollections on literature]. Taipei: Yuanjing chuban gongsi, 1983.

——. *Taiwan xiangtu zuojia lunji* [Essays on Taiwanese nativist writers]. Taipei: Yuanjing chuban she, 1979.

——. "Taiwan xiangtu wenxue shi daolun" [An introduction to the history of Taiwanese nativist literature]. *Xiachao* [Summer tide] 4 (May 1977). Rpt. in Yu, Tiancong, *Xiangtu wenxue taolunji* [A collection of discussions on nativist literature]. Taipei: Yuanliu chuban gonsi, 1978, 69–92.

Yee, Angelina C. "Re-writing the Colonial Self: Yang Kui's Resistant Texts and National Identity." *Chinese Literature: Essays, Articles, Reviews* 17 (Dec. 1995): 111–132.

Yeh, Michelle. "Bianyuan, qianwei, chaoxianshi: dui Taiwan wuliushi niandai xiandai zhuyi de fansi" [Periphery, avant-garde, surrealism: Introspection on modernism of the 1950s and 1960s in Taiwan]. In *Taiwan xiandai shi shi lun* [Collected articles on the history of modern poetry in Taiwan]. Taipei: Wenxun chuban she, 1996.

Yip, June. "Constructing a Nation: Taiwanese History and the Films of Hou Hsiao-hsien." In Sheldon Hsiao-peng Lu, ed., *Transnational Chinese Cinema: Identity, Nationhood, Gender*. Honolulu: University of Hawai'i Press, 139–168.

Ying, Fenghuang. "Reassessing Taiwan's Literary Field of the 1950s." Ph.D. diss., Asian Studies Department, University of Texas at Austin, 2000.

——, ed. *Jiang Gui de xiaoshuo: xu bian* [The fiction of Jiang Gui: A sequel]. Taipei: Jiuge chuban she, 1987.

Yu, Guangzhong. *Shou ye ren: Zhong Ying duizhao shiji* [The night watchman: A bilingual selection of poems]. Trans. Yu Guangzhong. Taipei: Jiuge chuban she, 1992.

——. "Wangchuan" [River of forgetfulness]. In *Zai lengzhan de niandai* [In time of cold war]. 1969; reprint, Taipei: Chunwenxue chuban she, 1984, 92–94.

——. "Lang laile" [The wolf is here]. *Lianhe bao fukan* [Literary supplement of the united daily news] [Taipei] 20 Aug. 1977. Rpt. in Yu, Tiancong, *Xiangtu wenxue taolun ji* [A collection of discussions on nativist literature]. Taipei: Yuanliu chuban gonsi, 1978, 264–267.

——. *Qingqing bianchou* [Homesick border blues]. Taipei: Chunwenxue chuban she, 1977.

——. "Lun Zhu Ziqing de sanwen" [On the prose of Zhu Ziqing]. In *Qingqing bianchou* [Homesick border blues]. Taipei: Chunwenxue chuban she, 1977, 13–37.

——. "Shanhe suiyue hua yuqiao: ping Hu Lancheng xinchu de jiushu" [Mountain, river, and years of one's lifetime: On the newly published old book by Hu Lancheng." In *Qingqing bianchou* [Homesick border blues]. Taipei: Chunwenxue chuban she, 1977, 261–267.

——. *Tingting na lengyu* [Listen to the cold rain]. Taipei: Chunwenxue chuban she, 1974.

——. "Tingting na lengyu" [Listen to the cold rain]. In *Tingting na lengyu* [Listen to the cold rain]. Taipei: Chunwenxue chuban she, 1974, 31–38.

——. *Fen he ren* [Cremation of crane]. Taipei: Chunwenxue chuban she, 1972.

——. "Women xuyao jiben shu" [We need several books]. In *Fen he ren* [Cremation of crane]. Taipei: Chunwenxue chuban she, 1972, 89–103.

——. *Wang xiang de mushen* [Look homeward, Satyr]. Taipei: Chunwenxue chuban she, 1968.

——. *Xiaoyao you* [The untrammeled traveler]. Taipei: Dalin chuban she, 1965.

——. "Xia Wusi de banqi" [Lower the May Fourth banner]. In *Xiaoyao you* [The untrammeled traveler]. Taipei: Dalin chuban she, 1965, 1–4.

——. "Jiandiao sanwen de bianzi" [Cut off the pigtails of our prose]. In *Xiaoyao you* [The untrammeled traveler]. Taipei: Dalin chuban she, 1965, 27–38.

——. "Feng, ya, chun" [Phoenix, crow, and quail]. In *Xiaoyao you* [The untrammeled traveler]. Taipei: Dalin chuban she, 1965, 47–61.

——. "Guiyu" [Ghost rain]. In *Xiaoyao you* [The untrammeled traveler]. Taipei: Dalin chuban she, 1965, 133–144.

——. "Shadan ye" [Shakespearean birthday eve]. In *Xiaoyao you* [The untrammeled traveler]. Taipei: Dalin chuban she, 1965, 145–152.

——. "Xiaoyao you" [The untrammeled traveler]. In *Xiaoyao you* [The untrammeled traveler]. Taipei: Dalin chuban she, 1965, 153–160.

——. "Jiuzhang chuang" [Nine beds]. In *Xiaoyao you* [The untrammeled traveler]. Taipei: Dalin chuban she, 1965, 171–178.

——. "Siyue, zai guzhanchang" [April, at an ancient battlefield]. In *Xiaoyao you* [The untrammeled traveler]. Taipei: Dalin chuban she, 1965, 179–186.

——. "Houji" [Afterword]. In *Xiaoyao you* [The untrammeled traveler]. Taipei: Dalin chuban she, 1965, 207–209.

——. "Houji" [Afterword]. In *Lian de lianxiang* [Associations of the lotus]. Taipei: Dalin chuban she, 1964. 159–161.

——. *Zhang shang yu* [Rain on the cactus]. Taipei: Dalin chuban she, 1964.

——. *Zuoshou de miusi* [Left-handed muse]. Taipei: Dalin chuban she, 1963.

Yu, Qiuyu. *Wenhua ku lu* [A bitter journey of Chinese culture]. Taipei: Erya chuban she, 1992.

Yu, Tiancong. *Xiangtu wenxue taolunji* [A collection of discussions on nativist literature]. Taipei: Yuanliu chuban gonsi, 1978.

Yuan, Qiongqiong. *Kongbu shidai* [The age of horror]. Taipei: Shibao wenhua chuban gongsi, 1998.

——. *Jinsheng yuan* [Affinities of this life]. Taipei: Lianhe wenxue chuban she, 1988.

——. *Yuan Qiongqiong jiduanpian* [Mini-short stories by Yuan Qiongqiong]. Taipei: Erya chuban she, 1988.

——. *Cangsang* [The mulberry sea]. Taipei: Hongfan shudian, 1985.

——. *Suiyi* [Following one's own will]. Taipei: Hongfan shudian, 1983.

——. *Hongchen xinshi* [Intimate thoughts in the red dust]. Taipei: Erya chuban she, 1981.

——. *Ziji de Tiankong* [A space of one's own]. Taipei: Hongfan shudian, 1981.

——. "Ziji de tiankong" [A space of one's own]. In *Ziji de Tiankong* [A space of one's own]. Taipei: Hongfan shudian, 1981, 133–151.

Zeng, Jianmin. *Neixie'nian women zai Taiwan . . .* [In those years, we were in Taiwan]. Taipei: Renjian chubanshe, 2001.

Zha, Jianying. "China's Popular Culture in the 1990s." In William A. Joseph, ed., *China Briefing: The Contradictions of Change*. Armonk, N.Y.: M. E. Sharpe, 1997, 109–150.

——. *China Pop: How Soap Operas, Tabloids, and Bestsellers Are Transforming a Culture*. New York: New Press, 1995.

Zhan, Hongzhi. "Xu, jizhong yuyan jianyu: du Zhang Dachun de xiaoshuo jinzuo" [Introduction, several kinds of prison of language: On recent fiction by Zhang Dachun]. In Dachun Zhang, *Sixi you guo* [Sixi worries about the country]. Taipei: Yuanliu chuban gongsi, 1988, 5–10 .

——. *Liangzhong wenxue xinling* [Two types of literary gestalts]. Taipei: Huangguan chuban she, 1986.

——. "Fulu 2—Taiwan ren de Taiwan yishi" [Appendix 2: The Taiwanese consciousness of the Taiwanese people]. In *Liangzhong wenxue xinling* [Two types of literary gestalts]. Taipei: Huangguan chuban she, 1986, 72–78. Originally published in *Meizhou Zhongguo shibao* [China times, U.S. edition], 24 Dec. 1982.

——. "Liangzhong wenxue xinling" [Two types of literary gestalts]. In *Liangzhong wenxue xinling* [Two types of literary gestalts]. Taipei: Huangguan chuban she, 1986, 43–60. Originally published in *Shuping shumu* [Book review and bibliography] 93 (1980).

Zhang, Ailing. "Tongyan wuji" [Innocent words of the children]. In *Zhang Ailing sanwen quanbian* [Complete collection of essays by Zhang Ailing]. Hangzhou: Zhejiang wenyi chuban she, 1992, 95–105.

——. *Yang ge* [Rice-sprout song]. Taipei: Huangguan zashi she, 1968.

Zhang, Dachun. *Jile Dongjing* [Tokyo paradise]. Unfinished. Completed parts serialized in *Xin xinwen* [The journalist], Taipei, 2002.

——. *Wulin waishi* [Unofficial history of the knights-errant]. Unfinished. Completed parts serialized in the literary supplement of *Lianhe bao* [United daily news], Taipei, 2000.

——. *Chengbang baoli tuan* [Gang of the city state]. 4 vols. Taipei: Shibao wenhua chuban gongsi, 1999–2000.

——. *Benshi* [Pseudo-knowledge]. Taipei: Lianhe wenxue chuban she, 1998.

——. "Hou wang an kao: Sun Wukong kaogu tanyuan shijian" [An investigation of the case of monkey king: Textual research on the original source of the tale of Sun Wukong]. In *Benshi* [Pseudo-knowledge]. Taipei: Lianhe wenxue chuban she, 1998, 180–201. Originally printed in *Zhongshi wanbao* [China times evening news], 2 Feb. 1992.

——. "'Hou wang' shi zangwu?: xiang Zhang Dachun zhiyi 'hou wang' wenti" [Is "monkey king" stolen goods?: Questions for Zhang Dachun with regard to "monkey king"]. (Under pseudonym Huaishang Ke.) In *Benshi* [Pseudo-knowledge]. Taipei: Lianhe wenxue chuban she, 1998, 202–206. Originally printed in *Lianhe wenxue* [Unitas, a literary monthly] 123.

——. "Benlai dou shi wo, he chu re hou mao?: jingda Huaishang Ke guanyu 'hou wang' zhi zhiyi" [They were all originally written by me, whence all this confusion?: A respectful reply to Mr. Huaishang Ke regarding questions about "monkey king"]. In *Benshi* [Pseudo-knowledge]. Taipei: Lianhe wenxue chuban she, 1998, 207–212. Originally printed in *Lianhe wenxue* [Unitas, a literary monthly] 123.

——. *Xiaoshuo bailei* [On genres of fiction]. Taipei: Lianhe wenxue chuban she, 1998.

——. *Sahuang de xintu* [Disciple of the liar]. Taipei: Lianhe wenxue chuban she, 1996.

——. *Ye haizi* [Wild kids]. Taipei: Lianhe wenxue chuban she, 1996.

——. *Wo meimei* [My kid sister]. Taipei: Taipei: Lianhe wenxue chuban she, 1993.

——. *Shaonian Datouchun de shenghuo zhouji* [The weekly journals of Big Head Chun]. Taipei: Lianhe wenxue chuban she, 1992.

——. *Meiren xiexin gei shangxiao* [No one wrote the letter to Colonel]. Taipei: Lianhe wenxue chuban she, 1994.

——. *Da shuohuang jia* [The big liar]. Taipei: Yuanliu chuban gongsi, 1989.

——. "Jiangjun bei" [General's monument]. In *Sixi you guo* [Sixi worries about the country]. Taipei: Yuanliu chuban gongsi, 1988, 11–31.

——. *Sixi you guo* [Sixi worries about the country]. Taipei: Yuanliu chuban gongsi, 1988.

Zhang, Liangze, ed. *Wu Zhuoliu zuopinji* [Collected works by Wu Zhuoliu]. 6 vols. Taipei: Yuanxing chuban she, 1977.

Zhang, Xiaofeng. *Xiaofeng zixuanji* [Selected works by author]. Taipei: Liming wenhua shiye gongsi, 1979.

——. "Chouxiang shi" [Rock of homesickness]. In *Xiaofeng zixuanji* [Selected works by author]. Taipei: Liming wenhua shiye gongsi, 1979, 50–54.

——. "Shiyue de yangguang" [Sunshine in October]. In *Xiaofeng zixuanji* [Selected works by author]. Taipei: Liming wenhua shiye gongsi, 1979, 61–66.

——. "Hei sha" [Black armband]. In *Xiaofeng zixuanji* [Selected works by author]. Taipei: Liming wenhua shiye gongsi, 1979, 72–77.

——. "Dichuan, I" [The water-spring beneath the earth, part I]. In *Xiaofeng zixuanji* [Selected works by author]. Taipei: Liming wenhua shiye gongsi, 1979, 91–100.

——. "Buxia hongtan zhi hou" [After stepping down the red wedding rug]. In *Xiaofeng zixuanji* [Selected works by author]. Taipei: Liming wenhua shiye gongsi, 1979, 103–109.

——. *Ditan de nayiduan* [The other side of the red rug]. Taipei: Wenxing chuban she, 1966.

——. *Geini, Yingying* [To you, Yingying]. Taipei: Xianggang jidujiao wenyi chuban she, 1968.

Zhang, Xudong. *Chinese Modernism in the Era of Reforms: Cultural Fever, Avant-garde Fiction, and the New Chinese Cinema*. Durham: Duke University Press, 1997.

Zhang Yi, dir. *Wo zheyang guo le yisheng* [Kuei-mei, a woman]. Adapted from Xiao Sa, "Xiafei zhi jia" [House of Joffre]. Taipei: Zhongyang dianying gongsi, 1985.

Zhang, Yingtai. *Xizang airen* [Romance in Tibet]. Taipei: Jiuge chuban she, 2000.

Zhang, Zhaowei. *Shei zai neibian chang ziji de ge* [Who're out there singing their own songs]. Taipei: Shibao wenhua chuban gongsi, 1994.

Zheng, Jiongming. *Yuelang qianxing de yi dai: Ye Shitao ji qi tong shidai zuojia wenxue guoji xueshu yantaohui lunwenji* [A generation that marches forward against the tide: Proceedings of the International Conference on Ye Shitao and his contemporary writers]. Gaoxiong: Chunhui chuban she, 2002.

Zheng, Meili. "Women and the Media." Paper presented at International Symposium on Chinese Women in the Millennium, Kuala Lumpur, May 26–27, 2001.

Zheng, Mingli. "Dangdai Taiwan wenyi zhengce de fazhan, yingxiang yu jiantao" [An examination of the development and influence of cultural policy in contemporary Taiwan]. In *Dangdai Taiwan zhengzhi wenxue lun* [Politics and contemporary Taiwanese literature]. Taipei: Shibao wenhua chuban gongsi, 1994, 11–71.

Zhong, Acheng. *Bian di fengliu* [A land for life, a land for love]. Taipei: Maitian chuban gongsi, 2001.

——. "Qingtang guashui bushi yu" [Watery soup, and no fish]. *Zhongguo shibao fukan* [China times, literary supplement], 11–13 Aug. 1994:24.

——. *Qi wang shu wang haizi wang* [King of chess, king of trees, and king of children]. Taipei: Xindi wenxue chuban she, 1996.

Zhong, Lihe. *Yu* [Rian]. Taipei: Xuesheng chuban she, 1961.

——. *Lishan nongchang* [A farm on Li Mountain]. Taipei: Xuesheng chuban she, 1961.

Zhong, Zhaozheng. *Zhong Zhaozheng huiyilu* [Memoirs of Zhong Zhaozheng]. 2 vols. Taipei: Qianwei chuban she, 1998.

——. "Ye suan zuji: *Wenyou tongxun* zhengshi fabiao zhuiyan" [Our footprints: Words delivered on the publication of *Newsletter for Literary Friends*]. *Wenxuejie* [Literary world] 5 (Spring 1983): 118–123.

——. *Taiwanren sanbuqu* [Trilogy of the Taiwanese]. 3 vols. Yuanjing chuban gongsi, 1980.

——. *Zhuoliu sanbuqu* [Trilogy of the turbid stream]. 3 vols. Taipei: Yuanjing chuban she, 1979.

——. *Zhong Zhaozheng zixuanji* [Selected works by author]. Yonghe, Taipei: Liming wenhua shiye gongsi, 1979.

Zhong, Zhaozheng, and Dongfang Bai. *Taiwan wenxue liangdi shu* [Correspondences between two places on Taiwanese literature]. Ed. Zhang Liangze. Taipei: Qianwei chuban she, 1993.

Zhongshi dianzi bao [Electronic news of *China Times*]. "Difang xinwen" [Local news]; "Yiwen chuban" [Publications on culture and arts]. 29 June 2000, 2 July 2000. http://news.chinatimes.com/.

Zhou, Fenling. *Yanyi: Zhang Ailing yu Zhongguo wenxue* [Astounding beauty: Eileen Zhang and Chinese literature]. Taipei: Yuanzun wenhua, 1999.

Zhu, Tianwen. *Hua yi qianshen* [Flower remembers her previous lives]. Taipei: Maitian chuban gongsi, 1996.

——. *Huangren shouji* [Notes of a desolate man]. Taipei: Shibao wenhua chuban gongsi, 1994.

——. *Shijimo de huali* [Fin-de-siècle splendor]. Taipei: Yuanliu chuban gongsi, 1990.

——. *Yanxia zhi du: Zhu Tianwen zuopin* [Capital inferno: Works of Zhu Tianwen]. Taipei: Shibao wenhua chuban gongsi, 1987 (Yuanliu chuban gongsi, 1989).

Zhu, Tianxin. *Manyouzhe* [The wanderer]. Taipei: Lianhe wenxue chuban she, 2000.

——. *Gudu* [Ancient capital]. Taipei: Maitian chuban gongsi, 1997.

——. *Xiang wo juancun de xiongdi men* [In remembrance of my brothers from the military compound]. Taipei: Maitian chuban gongsi, 1992.

——. *Wo jide . . .* [I remember . . .]. Taipei: Yuanliu chuban gongsi, 1989.

——. "Congqian congqian you ge Pudao Tailang [Once upon a time, there was a Ura shima ta roo]. In *Xiang wo juancun de xiongdi men* [In remembrance of my brothers from the military compound]. Taipei: Maitian chuban gongsi, 1992, 101–139.

Zhu, Xining. *Weiyan pian* [Chapters of minced words]. Taipei: Sansan shufang, 1981.